Better Homes and Gardens®

skinny
dinners

200 Calorie-Smart Recipes Your Family Will Love

Copyright © 2014 by Meredith Corporation, Des Moines, IA.

All rights reserved.

For information about permission to reproduce selections from this book, write to Permissions, Houghton Mifflin Harcourt Publishing Company, 215 Park Avenue South, New York, New York 10003.

Houghton Mifflin Harcourt
Boston New York 2014

www.hmhco.com

Library of Congress Cataloging-in-Publication Data
Skinny Dinners: 200 calorie-smart recipes your family will love / Better Homes and Gardens®.
    pages cm
  Includes index.
  ISBN 978-0-544-33669-8 (pbk); ISBN 978-0-544-33443-4 (ebk)
1. Reducing diets—Recipes. 2. Low-calorie diet—Recipes. 3. Menus. I. Better Homes and Gardens Books (Firm) II. Better homes and gardens. III. Title: Better Homes and Gardens skinny dinners.
  RM222.2.S564 2014
  641.5'635—dc23
                              2014026304

Printed in the United States of America

DOW 10 9 8 7 6 5 4 3 2 1

4500513594

Meredith Corporation

Editor: Jan Miller

Project Editor: Tricia Bergman, Waterbury Publications, Inc.

Contributing Editor: Lisa Kingsley, Waterbury Publications, Inc.

Contributing Writer: Kristi Thomas, R.D.

Contributing Copy Editor: Terri Fredrickson

Contributing Proofreader: Peg Smith

Recipe Development: Jane Burnett, Carla Christian

Recipe Testing: Better Homes and Gardens® Test Kitchen

Houghton Mifflin Harcourt

Publisher: Natalie Chapman

Editorial Director: Cindy Kitchel

Executive Editor: Anne Ficklen

Executive Editor: Linda Ingroia

Managing Editor: Marina Padakis Lowry

Director of Production: Tom Hyland

Design Director: Ken Carlson, Waterbury Publications, Inc.

Associate Design Director: Doug Samuelson, Waterbury Publications, Inc.

Production Assistant: Mindy Samuelson, Waterbury Publications, Inc.

Our seal assures you that every recipe in *Better Homes and Gardens® Skinny Dinners* has been tested in the Better Homes and Gardens® Test Kitchen. This means that each recipe is practical and reliable and meets our high standards of taste appeal. We guarantee your satisfaction with this book for as long as you own it.

Cover photo: Veggie-Tofu Pita Pizza, page 63

contents

the skinny on skinny

Whether you're looking to lose weight, get fit, or simply want to eat more healthfully, changing your diet in a way that is achievable without deprivation is the key to long-term success. *Skinny Dinners* provides the information you need and the recipes you want to feel great, lose weight, and keep it off for good.

lose weight for the right reasons

Before you embark on a weight-loss plan, take inventory of your ability to carry out your goals. Are you stressed out? Are you changing jobs, relationships, or relocating? Being in the right frame of mind can affect whether you are successful in losing weight or not. Additionally, it is best to lose weight for yourself and your health—not for your spouse, your mother, or your friends. It is also not wise to starve yourself to lose weight at lightning speed for an event. Not only is this unhealthy, the weight loss most likely won't last. When you do decide the time is right, did you know:

Preventing weight gain or reversing recent weight gain can improve your health?

Health can improve with a relatively minor weight reduction (5 to 10 percent of body weight)?

Adopting a healthy lifestyle by eating better and moving more has positive health implications even when you don't lose any weight at all?

common sense dieting

Many trendy fad diets encourage you to avoid whole categories of foods. By doing so, you run the risk of missing necessary nutrients needed to stay healthy. For a healthy eating plan, the Dietary Guidelines for Americans suggest:

1. Consume less sodium, saturated and trans fats, added sugars, and refined grains.
2. Enjoy your food, but eat less.
3. Avoid oversized portions.
4 Make half your plate fruits and vegetables.
5. Switch to fat-free or low-fat (1%) milk.
6. Compare sodium in foods like soup, bread, and frozen meals—and choose the foods with lower numbers.
7. Drink water instead of sugary drinks. For additional information, see www.choosemyplate.gov.

Rather than thinking about eating "good food" or "bad food," focus on eating a variety of nutrient rich foods. That means focusing on fresh foods rather than packaged or fast foods. The least amount of processing the food has undergone, the better. What is better for you: A powdered soup from a package or a homemade soup with fresh veggies and lean meat? The choice is obvious.

Bruce Ames, PhD, professor of biochemistry and molecular biology at the University of California in Berkeley believes that a deficiency of micronutrients due to eating a low-quality diet can lead to obesity. He hypothesizes that a person who is starved of critical nutrients will keep eating in order to obtain these missing nutrients. This deficiency diminishes the feeling of being satisfied after eating.

Excessive hunger is a big reason why some diets don't work. A study reported in *Nutrition Journal* showed that increasing the nutrient quality of the diets of 768 participants dramatically reduced hunger—even when the prescribed diet was substantially lower in calories. The higher-quality diet decreased food cravings and overeating behaviors, even when meals were occasionally skipped. Nearly 80 percent of the respondents reported that their experience of hunger dropped since beginning a high-nutrient-density diet. The study concluded that a high-quality diet provides benefits for long-term health as well as weight loss.

calorie counting: to count or not to count?

For busy people, keeping track of calories isn't easy. In one study, a group of Harvard scientists illustrated that eating a healthy diet is not just about counting calories. The study showed that people who ate certain healthful foods, such as yogurt and nuts, tended to gain less weight or even lost weight, while those who often ate foods such as french fries and sugary drinks tended to gain weight. It is true that what you eat is as important as how much you eat. The conclusion: Don't count calories; make calories count.

get your plate in shape

Keeping healthy food top of mind, therefore, is key to any successful weight-loss plan. The Academy of Nutrition and Dietetics offers these tips when choosing foods to lose weight and to be healthy.

Make half of your plate fruits and vegetables. Choose reduced-sodium or no-salt-added canned vegetables. Add fruit to meals and snacks. Buy fresh fruits or fruits that are dried, frozen, or canned in water or 100 percent juice. Fresh, frozen, or canned fruits and vegetables are all viable choices.

Make at least half your grains whole. Choose 100 percent whole grain breads, cereals, crackers, pasta, and brown rice.

Switch to fat-free or low-fat milk. Fat-free and low-fat milk have the same amount of calcium and other essential nutrients as whole milk, but less fat and calories. Note: If you are lactose intolerant, try lactose-free milk or a calcium-fortified soy beverage.

Vary your protein choices. Eat a variety of foods from the protein food group each week, such as seafood, nuts, and dried beans or legumes, as well as lean meat, poultry, and eggs. Twice a week make seafood the protein on your plate and keep meat and poultry portions small and lean (see "Serving Sizes and Portions," page 10).

Cut back on sodium. Add spices or herbs to season food without adding salt, which can increase blood pressure and cause fluid retention.

Reduce empty calories from solid fats and added sugars. Drink water instead of sugary drinks and choose 100 percent fruit juice instead of fruit-flavor drinks. Opt for fruit for dessert and choose sugary desserts less often.

Reduce solid fat intake. Make major sources of saturated fats such as desserts, pizza, cheese, sausages, and hot dogs occasional treats. Buy lean cuts of meat or poultry and fat-free or low-fat milk, yogurt, and cheese. Also, switch from solid fats to vegetable oils when preparing food.

FOOD GROUP BREAKDOWN
The recommended number of servings for adults and the amount of food that counts as a serving.

FRUIT
Amount You Need Each Day
1½ to 2 cups or equivalent

VEGETABLES
Amount You Need Each Day
2½ to 3 cups or equivalent

DAIRY
Amount You Need Each Day
3 cups or equivalent

PROTEIN
Number of Servings You Need Each Day
5 to 6 ounces or equivalent

FATS AND OILS
Fats and oils are not a food group, however they provide essential nutrients. Adults can allow 5 to 6 teaspoons fats and oils in a healthy diet per day. Many people are able to consume enough fat in the foods they eat, but if you don't, adding foods with healthy fats can benefit your health.

boost your nutrients while dieting

With the goal of eating more nutrient-dense foods, when slashing calories you must be more diligent in choosing what you eat. The following nutrients should be considered when cutting calories:

Carbohydrates Low-carb diets top the list of popular diets. In reality, the type of carbs to limit should be soft drinks, candy, and other foods with added sugars. Focus more on choosing whole and fortified grains (6 to 7 servings per day, at least half of them fiber-rich whole grains). Additionally, eat fruit (2 cups) and vegetables (2½ cups) every day. Cutting categories of foods from your diet is not the best way to lose weight because you cut out valuable nutrients.

Protein Don't be tempted to ditch protein foods in order to lose weight. Protein foods help you build muscle, which is important in helping you look leaner. Protein helps keep you satisfied over the long run, especially when eaten at breakfast. Yogurt, a high-protein smoothie, or hard-boiled eggs are good breakfast choices. Low-fat dairy foods, lean meats, poultry, seafood, nuts, and dried beans and legumes (a total of 6 ounces per day) should be part of your meals.

Fat Eating a diet high in fat translates to higher calories. But when it comes to fat, it is a matter of balance. To a certain extent, fat is needed in a diet. Purchase leaner meats, such as ground turkey breast instead of ground turkey or ground round or sirloin instead of ground chuck. Reduce sneaky hidden fats in dairy foods by switching from whole milk to low-fat milk. Use unsaturated oils, such as olive oil, in cooking.

Vitamin B12 Vitamin B12 is a vitamin only found in foods of animal origin. Strict vegans who eat no animal products or vegetarians who eat only eggs and milk may need to supplement their diet by eating fortified cereals or by taking a B12 (cobalamin) supplement. Low levels of this vitamin are often found in people over the age of 50. It is also common in conditions such as digestive problems and anemia, causing fatigue, weakness, memory loss, and problems with the nervous system.

Calcium Foods rich in this mineral help keep your heart and muscles strong and may help prevent high blood pressure and colon cancer. It has also been shown to help reduce body fat. Low-fat milk, cheeses, and yogurt, of course, have calcium, but so do tofu, leafy vegetables, and calcium-fortified juices.

Iron Cut your iron intake and you could develop iron-deficiency anemia, which will make you feel tired and sluggish. Without energy, who wants to cook healthy meals? Include good sources of iron in your meal plans, such as lean red meat, iron-fortified cereals, poultry, fish, dried beans, and leafy green vegetables.

Fiber Adequate fiber helps food move efficiently through your digestive tract. It also helps prevent heart disease, diabetes, digestive problems, constipation, hemorrhoids, and weight gain. A diet high in fiber is generally lower in calories and helps make you feel full faster. Whole grains, dried beans, fruits, and vegetables provide fiber. The daily requirement is 25 grams for women and 38 grams for men. After age 50, your daily fiber needs drops to 21 grams for women and 30 grams for men.

NUTRITION LABELS
The "Nutrition Facts Panel," which is usually found on the side or back of the package.

SERVING SIZE
Serving sizes are noted in household measures. There will also be a weight listed with the serving size.

SERVINGS PER CONTAINER
The information is for one serving. Be aware—some packages contain more than one serving in the package.

NUTRIENTS PER SERVING
The values for the amount of calories, total fat, saturated fat, trans fat, cholesterol, sodium, total carbohydrate, dietary fiber, sugars, and protein found in one serving of the product. The % Daily Value is the percentage of the daily recommended level of that nutrient found in one serving, based on a 2,000-calorie-per-day diet.

VITAMINS AND MINERALS
Levels for vitamin A, vitamin C, calcium, and iron listed as percentages of the recommended levels that you should aim to consume in a day. Other vitamins and minerals may also be included.

serving sizes and portions

When reading food labels or the Nutrition Facts for the nutrients the food provides, a serving size is also listed. Many times these serving amounts are too much, especially if you are watching your calorie intake. Here are several ways to determine food portions or serving sizes visually when you don't have a measuring cup or spoons handy.

- 3 ounces of meat = a deck of cards or palm of hand
- 1½ ounces of cheese = four stacked dice
- 1 cup of pasta = a baseball
- 1 cup of vegetables or fruit = a loose fist
- ½ cup of vegetables or fruit = a tennis ball or tight fist
- 1 tablespoon = the length of a thumb
- 1 teaspoon of margarine or butter = one dice

To avoid eating large portions, use a small plate, bowl, and drinking glass. It is smart to limit eating out when you can. Eating at home more often will help you control what is going into your food. Choose lower-calorie menu options when you do eat out. Look for menu items that include vegetables, fruits, and/or whole grains, and foods that are steamed, broiled, grilled, or baked.

One great way to keep track of what and how much you eat is to take a picture of your meals with your smartphone. This helps keep you honest! Or keep a log of what you eat to keep track of how much you eat. Most importantly, when you sit down to eat, be mindful of your meals and savor every bite.

strategies from weight-loss winners

According to the Academy of Nutrition and Dietetics, a study in 2012 found four key behaviors that separated people who have kept weight off and those who haven't. Here is what the maintainers do:

1. Weigh away. You've often heard to throw the scale away, but maintainers regularly weigh themselves. Weigh yourself in the morning, take note of increases or decreases, and gauge your food intake accordingly.

2. Stay on track. Successful maintainers continue with their newfound behaviors, such as eating breakfast, journaling to keep track of food intake or exercise, and good portion control.

3. Be a planner. Plan your meals, schedule your exercise, and have healthy foods on hand for snacks and meals. Planning helps ensure success.

4. Be kind to yourself. Use positive self-talk as a way to encourage yourself on your journey. A journal with positive thoughts is a popular way to give yourself a boost that you need. Also, celebrate your successes with a meaningful token: A movie, a new piece of jewelry, or a luxurious body lotion.

healthy substitutions

Choose wisely when selecting snack foods or making meal decisions. Here's a list to help you save calories, while boosting nutrition.

Instead of this:	Eat this:
Bagel	Whole wheat English muffin
Burger from ground chuck	Burger from ground sirloin
Candy bar	Dark chocolate covered almonds
Crackers and cheese	Popcorn (air popped) sprinkled with grated Parmesan
Cream cheese	Hummus
Doughnut	Whole wheat toast with low-sugar jam
Peanut butter cup	1 or 2 squares of dark chocolate with a smear of natural peanut butter
Pork sausage	Turkey sausage
Potato chips	Veggie chips (with beet or sweet potato)
Ranch-style salad dressing	Italian or vinaigrette salad dressing
Salad croutons	Shelled pumpkin seeds
Soda	Seltzer water with slices of lemon, lime, and/or orange
Spaghetti	Spaghetti squash
Strawberry ice cream	Strawberries with light whipped cream (canned)
Tortilla chips	Mini whole wheat pretzels
Chicken salad sandwich	Turkey (sliced) sandwich

you are not alone

Look for ways to enlist help on your journey. It goes without saying that exercise should be part of any goal for good health. Ask a buddy to go walking with you or to an exercise class. If you are new to physical activity, start slow. Do what you can for at least 10 minutes at a time and gradually increase your time. You should strive for 30 minutes per day.

For additional help, seek out cookbooks, such as *Skinny Dinners, Skinny Slow Cooker,* or books from trusted sources to assist you in reaching your goals of weight loss and healthy living. By choosing delicious recipes that meet all of your nutritional needs (which means including foods from all food groups), you can create a plan that will grow with your long-term health goals—while you grow thinner. Bon appétit and to your health!

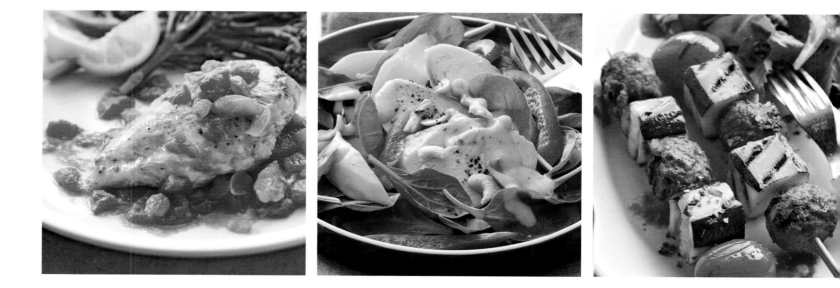

CHAPTER 1

5 ingredients

Count on one hand the number of ingredients (plus a few staples)
you need to make a delicious, satisfying dinner.

This warming weeknight stew gets a kick-start from a brightly colored frozen vegetable blend that comes in a low-fat garlic-herb sauce.

green chile pork stew

START TO FINISH: 30 minutes

1 **pound natural pork tenderloin**
   Salt and ground black pepper
1 **tablespoon olive oil**
3 **7-ounce packages frozen yellow carrots, spinach and white bean medley in garlic-herb sauce*, thawed**
1 **4.5-ounce can diced green chiles**
1 **teaspoon ground cumin**
   Fresh cilantro
   Lime wedges (optional)

1. Cut pork into ¾-inch pieces; sprinkle lightly with salt and pepper. In Dutch oven heat olive oil over medium-high heat. Add pork; cook 4 to 5 minutes or until browned. Stir in two of the packages of the thawed vegetables, chiles, and cumin.

2. In a blender, combine remaining thawed vegetables and 1 cup water. Process until smooth. Add pureed vegetables to Dutch oven. Bring to a simmer. Cook, covered, over medium heat about 15 minutes or until pork is cooked through, stirring occasionally. Ladle into soup bowls. Top with cilantro and, if desired, a squeeze of lime juice. **Makes 4 servings.**

PER SERVING: 297 cal., 11 g fat (2 g sat. fat), 74 mg chol., 823 mg sodium, 21 g carb., 7 g fiber, 30 g pro.

*tip: If you can't find the frozen vegetable blend, in a medium bowl stir together one 15-ounce can navy beans, rinsed and drained; 1 cup frozen sliced carrots, thawed, ½ of a 10-ounce package frozen chopped spinach, thawed and well-drained, and ¼ cup Italian vinaigrette salad dressing. Stir 2 cups of the mixture into the pork with the chiles and cumin and blend the remaining 1 cup with the water. Continue as above.

make it a meal

Toasted country-style bread
Mixed greens salad
Sliced mango

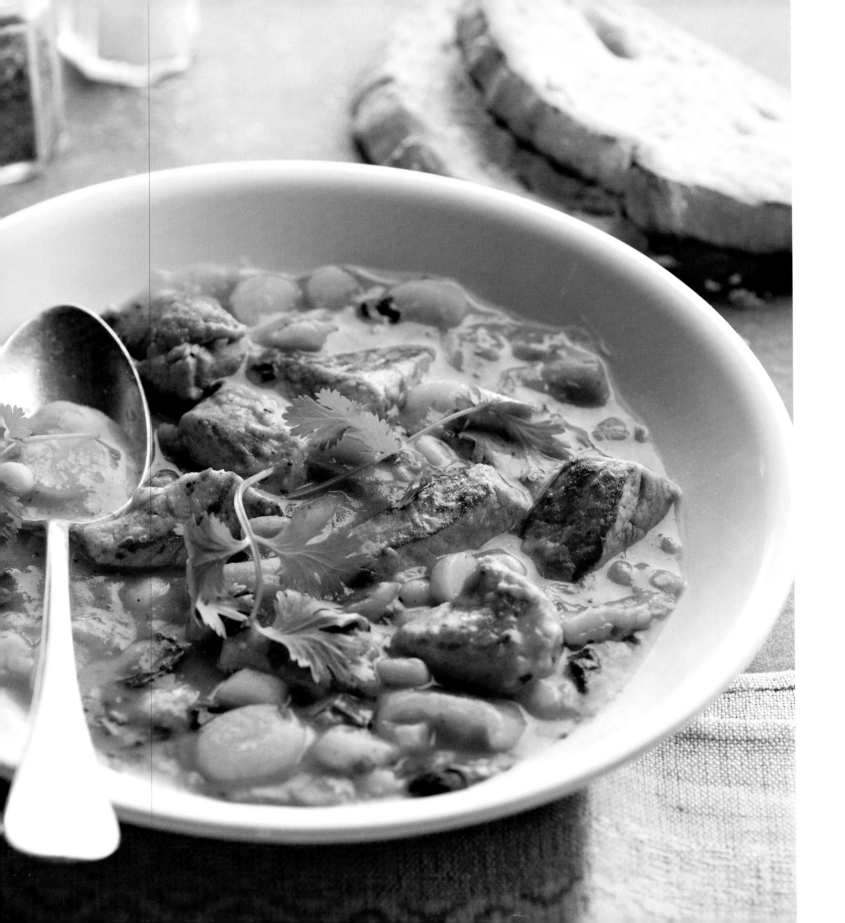

Even the heartiest appetites will be satisfied by these generously sized stuffed chops that come in at under 400 calories per serving.

mediterranean orzo stuffed pork chops

PREP: 20 minutes   **COOK:** 4 minutes   **BAKE:** 15 minutes at 375°F

¼   cup dried whole wheat orzo
½   cup chopped dried tomatoes (not oil-packed)
1   to 2 tablespoons chopped pitted kalamata olives
2   tablespoons crumbled feta cheese
¾   teaspoon salt
¼   teaspoon ground black pepper
4   8- to 10-ounce boneless pork loin chops
4   teaspoons olive oil

1. Preheat oven to 375°F. Line a 15×10×1-inch baking pan with foil; set aside. Cook orzo according to package directions; drain. In a medium bowl combine the cooked orzo, tomatoes, olives, cheese, ¼ teaspoon of the salt, and ⅛ teaspoon of the pepper.

2. Trim fat from chops. Make a pocket in each chop by cutting horizontally from the fat side almost to the opposite side. Divide stuffing among pockets in chops. If necessary, secure the openings with wooden toothpicks. Sprinkle chops with remaining salt and pepper.

3. In an extra-large skillet cook chops in hot oil for 4 minutes or until browned, turning once halfway through cooking. Transfer to the prepared baking pan. Bake, uncovered, for 15 minutes or until juices run clear and chops and stuffing registers 145°F on a meat thermometer. **Makes 4 servings.**

PER SERVING: 393 cal., 14 g fat (4 g sat. fat), 160 mg chol., 634 mg sodium, 12 g carb., 3 g fiber, 53 g pro.

[**make it a meal**

Green beans
Cherry tomato-herb salad
Raspberry sorbet]

A small portion of deeply flavorful and buttery-textured ribeye feels luxurious. White beans provide fiber and an additional protein boost—and a bit of Tuscan flair.

pan-fried garlic steak

START TO FINISH: 30 minutes

4	**4- to 5-ounce beef ribeye steaks (Delmonico)**
	Olive oil
	Salt
	Ground black pepper
6	**cloves garlic, peeled and thinly sliced**
2	**tablespoons butter**
1	**15- to 19-ounce can cannellini beans (white kidney beans), rinsed and drained**
¼	**cup snipped fresh Italian parsley**
	Snipped fresh Italian parsley (optional)

1. Trim fat from steaks. Lightly drizzle steaks with oil; sprinkle with salt and pepper.

2. Heat a very large heavy skillet over medium-high heat. Add steaks to skillet; reduce heat to medium. Cook steaks for 3 to 4 minutes per side (145°F for medium-rare or 160°F for medium). Remove steaks from skillet; cover and keep warm. Add garlic to pan. Cook and stir about 1 minute or until softened; remove garlic from pan.

3. Add butter to skillet. Add beans to hot butter; heat through. Stir in the ¼ cup parsley; cook for 1 minute more. Top steaks with garlic and serve with beans. If desired, sprinkle with additional parsley. **Makes 4 servings.**

PER SERVING: 326 cal., 15 g fat (7 g sat. fat), 72 mg chol., 325 mg sodium, 16 g carb., 5 g fiber, 29 g pro.

make it a meal

Summer Corn and Tomatoes, recipe page 258
Kale salad
Low-fat brownie bites

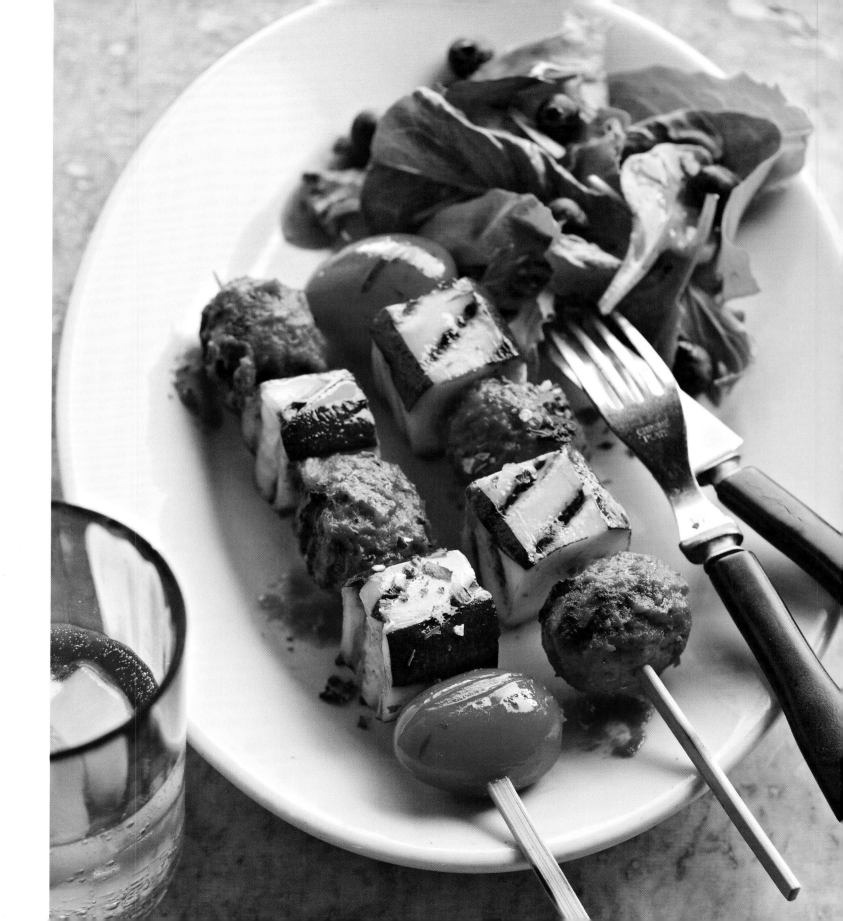

A quick, thick tomato sauce made from tomato paste clings to and coats the meatballs as these colorful, low-carb kabobs are grilled or broiled.

italian meatball, zucchini, and tomato kabobs

PREP: 20 minutes   **GRILL:** 8 minutes

½ **of a 6-ounce can tomato paste with Italian seasoning (⅓ cup)**
¼ **cup water**
½ **teaspoon Italian seasoning, crushed**
16 **1-inch refrigerated or frozen Italian-style meatballs, thawed**
2 **small zucchini**
8 **large cherry tomatoes**
Nonstick cooking spray

1. Preheat indoor electric grill or broiler. In a medium bowl combine tomato paste, the water, and Italian seasoning to make a thick sauce. Add meatballs to sauce and stir to coat; set aside.

2. Using a vegetable peeler, cut four strips from zucchini. Cut zucchini in 1-inch cubes.

3. On metal or bamboo skewers*, alternately thread meatballs and zucchini; thread a tomato on each end. Lightly coat kabobs with nonstick cooking spray. Grill or broil kabobs 3 to 4 inches from heat 4 to 5 minutes on each side or until meatballs are heated through and vegetables are crisp-tender. Brush remaining sauce on kabobs during last 2 minutes of cooking. **Makes 4 servings.**

PER SERVING: 222 cal., 15 g fat (7 g sat. fat), 43 mg chol., 623 mg sodium, 12 g carb., 3 g fiber, 10 g pro.

*tip: Soak bamboo skewers in water 30 minutes before using to prevent the skewers from burning.

[make it a meal
Multigrain rice pilaf
Baby lettuces and blueberries salad
Sparkling water with mint]

Pounding the chicken breasts to a thin, even thickness helps them cook more evenly—and more quickly. Quick cooking means the chicken stays juicy—and you get in and out of the kitchen fast.

lemony chicken and green beans

START TO FINISH: 20 minutes

4   **skinless, boneless chicken breast halves (about 1¼ pounds total)**
1   **tablespoon Dijon-style mustard**
¼   **teaspoon salt**
¼   **teaspoon ground black pepper**
¼   **cup seasoned fine dry bread crumbs**
2   **tablespoons olive oil**
8   **ounces fresh green beans, trimmed**
2   **lemons, 1 sliced and 1 juiced**
1   **tablespoon capers, rinsed and drained (optional)**
    Lemon wedges (optional)

1. Place each chicken breast half between two pieces of plastic wrap. Using the flat side of a meat mallet, pound each chicken breast half lightly until an even thickness. Remove plastic wrap. Brush chicken with mustard; sprinkle evenly with salt and pepper. Sprinkle bread crumbs evenly over all sides of chicken to coat.

2. In an extra-large skillet heat half of the oil over medium heat. Add chicken; cook about 8 minutes or until chicken is done (170°F), turning once halfway through cooking. Transfer to four dinner plates; keep warm. Add the remaining oil to skillet. Cook green beans in hot oil about 4 minutes or until crisp-tender, scraping up browned bits. Add the lemon slices, lemon juice, and capers (if using) to skillet. Cook and stir for 1 minute. Serve beans with chicken. If desired, serve with lemon wedges. **Makes 4 servings.**

PER SERVING: 278 cal., 11 g fat (2 g sat. fat), 91 mg chol., 599 mg sodium, 12 g carb., 3 g fiber, 32 g pro.

make it a meal

Mashed sweet potatoes
Barley with pecans and dried cherries
Frozen grapes

To save time, look in the produce section of your supermarket for fresh whole pineapples that are already cored, prepared and ready to eat.

sweet and spicy pineapple chicken kabobs

PREP: 25 minutes   **GRILL:** 20 minutes

1	**pound skinless, boneless chicken breast halves, cut into 1½-inch pieces**
½	**of a small pineapple, cut into 1½-inch cubes (about 2½ cups)**
2	**red sweet peppers, cut into 1½-inch pieces**
1	**large red onion, cut into 1½-inch wedges**
¼	**teaspoon salt**
¼	**teaspoon ground black pepper**
¼	**cup Asian sweet red chili sauce**

1. On metal or bamboo skewers (see tip, page 19), alternately thread chicken, pineapple, sweet peppers, and onion, leaving ¼ inch between pieces. Sprinkle with salt and pepper.

2. For a charcoal grill, arrange medium-hot coals around a drip pan. Test for medium heat above pan. Place chicken kabobs on the grill rack over drip pan. Cover and grill for 20 minutes or until chicken is no longer pink, turning once halfway through grilling and brushing with the chili sauce during the last 5 minutes of grilling. (For a gas grill, preheat grill. Reduce heat to medium. Adjust for indirect cooking. Grill as above.) **Makes 4 servings.**

PER SERVING: 255 cal., 3 g fat (1 g sat. fat), 72 mg chol., 406 mg sodium, 27 g carb., 4 g fiber, 26 g pro.

make it a meal

Jasmine rice
Sauteed spinach with garlic and lemon
Coconut macaroons

Sweetness and acidity are great flavor stand-ins for fat in calorie-conscious dishes such as this one. Here, tomato provides the acidity and dried apricots and golden raisins kick in a bit of natural sweetness.

tomato-apricot chicken

PREP: 25 minutes

4	skinless, boneless chicken breasts
	Salt
	Ground black pepper
1	tablespoon olive oil
1	clove garlic, sliced
1	28-ounce can diced tomatoes, undrained
½	cup snipped dried apricots
⅓	cup golden raisins

1. Season chicken with salt and pepper. In an extra-large skillet cook chicken in hot oil for 8 minutes or until browned, turning once halfway through cooking. Add garlic; cook and stir for 1 minute more.

2. Add tomatoes, apricots, and raisins; bring to boiling. Reduce heat and simmer, covered, for 3 to 5 minutes or until chicken is no longer pink (170°F). Uncover and cook until sauce reaches desired consistency. Season to taste with additional salt and pepper. **Makes 4 servings.**

PER SERVING: 314 cal., 5 g fat (1 g sat. fat), 82 mg chol., 636 mg sodium, 34 g carb., 6 g fiber, 36 g pro.

make it a meal

Cauliflower rice
Pan-roasted broccoli rabe with lemon wedges
Frozen Greek yogurt

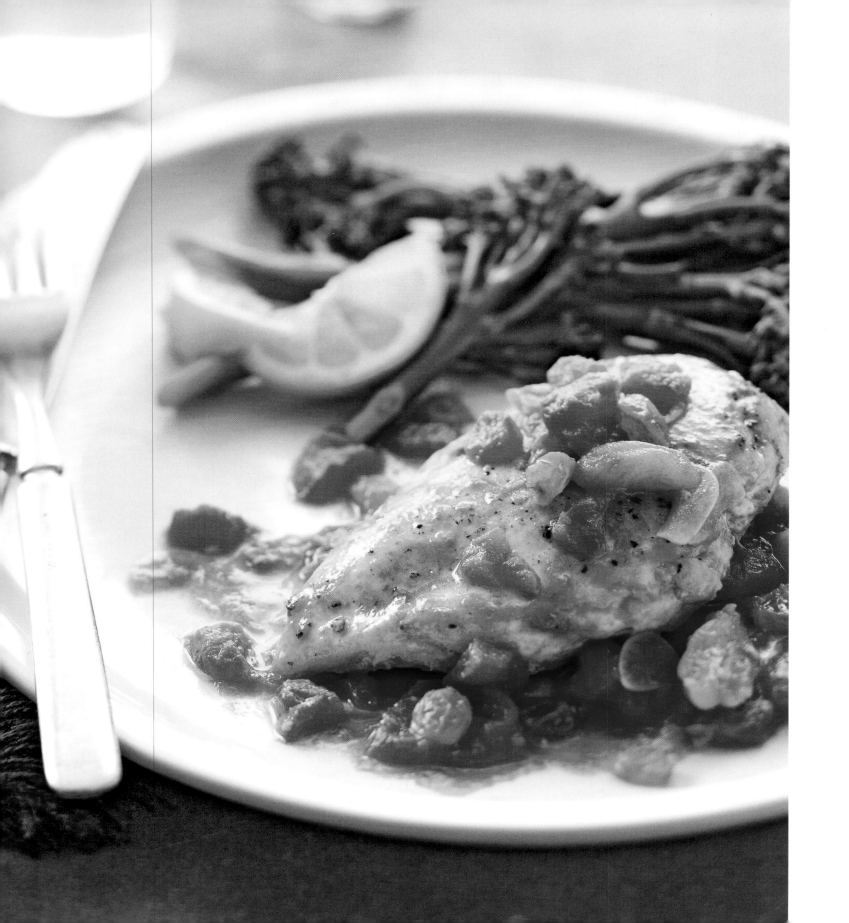

Caramelizing the onions—cooking them slowly over low heat in heart-healthy olive oil—intensifies their natural sweetness and gives them a buttery texture.

open-faced french onion chicken sandwich

PREP: 25 minutes   **COOK:** 16 minutes   **GRILL:** 18 minutes

1	tablespoon olive oil
4	cups sliced onions (4 large)
½	teaspoon salt
¼	teaspoon ground black pepper
1	pound skinless, boneless chicken breast halves
	Nonstick cooking spray
4	slices French bread bias cut about 1 inch thick
½	cup shredded Gruyère cheese (2 ounces)
	Snipped fresh Italian parsley (optional)

1. In a large skillet heat oil over medium-low heat. Add onions, ¼ teaspoon of the salt and ⅛ teaspoon of the pepper. Cook, covered, for 13 to 15 minutes or until onions are tender, stirring occasionally. Uncover; cook and stir over medium-high heat for 3 to 5 minutes or until golden. Remove from heat; set aside.

2. Season chicken with remaining salt and pepper. For a charcoal or gas grill, place chicken on the greased rack of a grill directly over medium heat. Cover and grill for 15 to 18 minutes or until no longer pink (170°F), turning once halfway through grilling. Remove chicken; keep warm. Lightly coat bread with cooking spray. Place bread on the grill. Cover and grill for 1 to 2 minutes or until lightly toasted on one side only. Slice chicken into ½-inch-thick slices.

3. Top toasted side of bread with chicken slices, caramelized onions, and cheese. Return to grill. Cover and grill for 2 minutes or until cheese is melted and sandwiches are heated through. If desired, sprinkle with parsley. **Makes 4 servings.**

PER SERVING: 406 cal., 12 g fat (4 g sat. fat), 88 mg chol., 668 mg sodium, 39 g carb., 4 g fiber, 35 g pro.

make it a meal

Sweet potato fries
Broccolini
Honeydew melon slices

Watching your calories and your budget is a balancing game. Heirloom tomatoes are a little more expensive than standard tomatoes, but the flavor, color, and juiciness they bring to a dish is worth it.

crispy seared salmon with tomato cucumber salad

CHILL: 30 minutes   **PREP:** 20 minutes   **COOK:** 6 minutes

4   **medium fresh heirloom tomatoes (purple, red, green, and/or yellow), cut into wedges (4 cups)**
3   **cups sliced cucumber**
2   **tablespoons rice wine vinegar**
1   **tablespoon sugar**
½   **teaspoon salt**
½   **teaspoon ground black pepper**
4   **6-ounce fresh skinless salmon fillets**
1   **tablespoon olive oil**
    Lemon wedges (optional)

1. For the tomato-cucumber salad, in a medium bowl stir together tomatoes, cucumber, vinegar, sugar, ¼ teaspoon of the salt, and ¼ teaspoon of the pepper. Cover and chill for at least 30 minutes.

2. Rinse fish; pat dry with paper towels. Measure thickness of fillets. Season fish with remaining salt and pepper. In a large nonstick skillet cook salmon in hot oil over medium-high heat for 3 to 5 minutes per ½-inch thickness or until salmon flakes easily when tested with a fork, carefully turning once halfway through cooking. Serve salmon over the tomato-cucumber salad. If desired, serve with lemon wedges. **Makes 4 servings.**

PER SERVING: 328 cal., 15 g fat (2 g sat. fat), 94 mg chol., 391 mg sodium, 14 g carb., 3 g fiber, 36 g pro.

make it a meal

Quinoa with goat cheese and black olives
Endive salad
Watermelon wedges

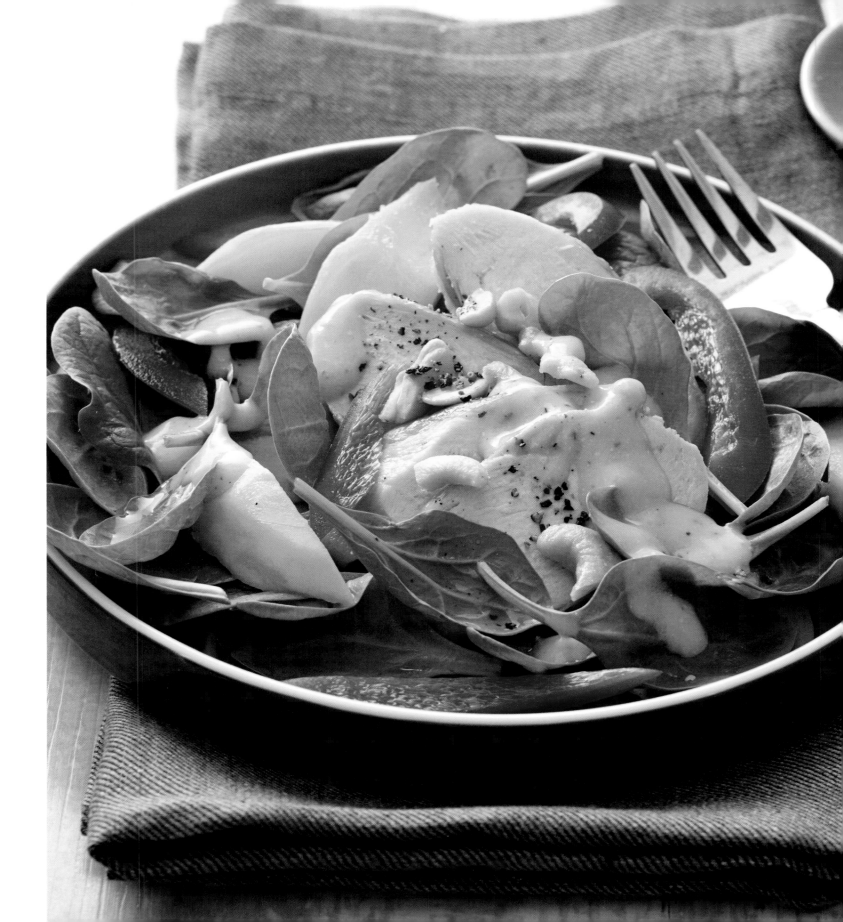

Ripe mango gives the dressing for this eye-catching salad fabulously intense flavor and a creamy texture. Just a tablespoon each of cashews and olive oil give it richness and a dose of healthy fats.

spinach chicken salad with mango dressing

START TO FINISH: 20 minutes

1	large ripe mango, halved, seeded, peeled, and cut into ¾-inch pieces
4	tablespoons coarsely chopped cashews
1	tablespoon olive oil
1	tablespoon water
¼	teaspoon salt
¼	teaspoon ground black pepper
1	5-ounce package fresh baby spinach
1	medium red sweet pepper, seeded and sliced
12	ounces cooked skinless, boneless chicken breast, sliced

1. For dressing, in a food processor or blender combine one-fourth of the mango, 1 tablespoon of the cashews, the olive oil, the water, salt, and black pepper. Cover and process or blend until smooth.

2. Arrange spinach leaves on four serving plates. Top with sweet pepper, chicken, and the remaining mango. Drizzle with the dressing. Sprinkle with the remaining cashews. **Makes 4 servings.**

PER SERVING: 234 cal., 10 g fat (2 g sat. fat), 54 mg chol., 255 mg sodium, 16 g carb., 3 g fiber, 21 g pro.

tip: Challenge yourself before every meal to include at least 2 veggies and/or fruits. You won't have as much room for less healthy stuff.

[**make it a meal**

Multiseed crackers
Hummus
Ginger cookies]

Toasting the couscous gives it a deliciously nutty flavor and helps the tiny pasta pearls keep from clumping as they cook.

shrimp, mango, and couscous skillet

START TO FINISH: 35 minutes

1	cup Israeli (large pearl) couscous
4	teaspoons olive oil
1¼	cups water
1½	pounds medium shrimp, peeled and deveined
¼	cup bottled mango-chipotle salad dressing
¼	teaspoon salt
¼	teaspoon ground black pepper
1½	cups chopped mango
½	cup crumbled queso fresco

1. In a medium saucepan toast couscous in 2 teaspoons hot oil over medium-high heat for 3 to 4 minutes or until lightly brown. Add the water and simmer, covered, for 8 to 10 minutes, or until pasta is tender. Set aside.

2. In an extra-large nonstick skillet cook shrimp in remaining 2 teaspoons hot oil for 3 minutes or until shrimp are opaque. Stir in the cooked couscous, dressing, salt, and pepper. Cook and stir for 2 to 3 minutes more or until heated through. Stir in mango. Sprinkle with queso fresco. **Makes 4 servings.**

PER SERVING: 413 cal., 13 g fat (3 g sat. fat), 208 mg chol., 632 mg sodium, 42 g carb., 3 g fiber, 32 g pro.

make it a meal

Carrot-beet slaw
Strawberry-tangerine salad
Vanilla Tres Leches Cake, recipe page 268

Light Alfredo sauce makes a creamy and indulgent-tasting base for this mushroom and broccolini pizza. If you like, you can substitute broccoli rabe (also called rapini) for the broccolini.

wild mushroom and broccolini pizza

PREP: 20 minutes   **BAKE:** 10 minutes at 450°F

1½ cups 1-inch pieces Broccolini
1   tablespoon olive oil
8   ounces fresh sliced assorted mushrooms (such as shiitake, button, or cremini)
1   12-inch whole wheat thin-crust pizza shell (such as Boboli)
½   cup bottled light Alfredo sauce
¾   cup shredded part-skim mozzarella cheese
    Pinch ground black pepper

1. Preheat oven to 450°F. Bring a large pot of lightly salted water to boiling. Add Broccolini; cook for 4 minutes. Drain; set aside.

2. In an extra-large nonstick skillet heat olive oil over medium-high heat. Add mushrooms. Cook for 5 minutes, stirring occasionally, or until mushrooms are tender and lightly browned. Drain off liquid.

3. Place the pizza shell on a large baking sheet. Spread Alfredo sauce on pizza shell. Top with cooked mushrooms, reserved Broccolini, and the mozzarella. Bake for 10 to 12 minutes or until cheese is melted, and crust is golden brown. Sprinkle with pepper. **Makes 4 servings.**

PER SERVING: 332 cal., 14 g fat (6 g sat. fat), 21 mg chol., 737 mg sodium, 40 g carb., 7 g fiber, 17 g pro.

make it a meal

Jicama sticks with low-fat dressing
Baby greens salad with chopped dates
Fresh raspberries

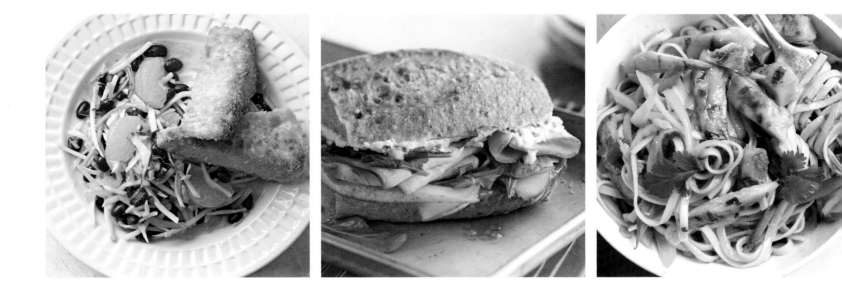

dinner in 30 minutes

Eating in is your best bet for eating healthfully.
These fast-to-fix meals make it easy.

Seasoning blends pack powerful flavor in one fell swoop. Greek seasoning, for instance, can be a melange of onion, garlic, mint, oregano, lemon, black pepper and sea salt—and you only have to measure once.

greek seasoned pork with lemon couscous

START TO FINISH: 20 minutes

4	teaspoons olive oil
1½	cups coarsely chopped, unpeeled eggplant
½	cup chopped red onion (1 medium)
4	4½-inch-thick boneless pork loin chops
1	teaspoon Greek seasoning
1¼	cups reduced-sodium chicken broth
¼	cup oil-packed dried tomatoes, drained and chopped
¾	cup whole wheat couscous
1	teaspoon finely shredded lemon peel
1	tablespoon lemon juice
½	teaspoon bottled minced roasted garlic
¼	teaspoon salt
1	cup coarsely chopped fresh spinach

1. In a large saucepan heat 2 teaspoons of the oil over medium heat. Add eggplant and red onion; cook about 5 minutes or until vegetables are tender, stirring occasionally.

2. Meanwhile, trim fat from chops. Sprinkle chops with Greek seasoning. In a large skillet heat the remaining 2 teaspoons oil over medium-high heat. Add chops; reduce heat to medium. Cook for 5 to 6 minutes or until done (145°F), turning once halfway through cooking. Remove from heat; let stand for 3 minutes.

3. Add broth and dried tomatoes to eggplant mixture. Bring to boiling. Stir in couscous, lemon peel, lemon juice, roasted garlic, and salt; remove from heat. Let stand, covered, for 5 minutes. Stir in spinach. Divide couscous among four serving plates. Top with chops. **Makes 4 servings.**

PER SERVING: 299 cal., 8 g fat (2 g sat. fat), 40 mg chol., 562 mg sodium, 34 g carb., 7 g fiber, 26 g pro.

make it a meal

Sliced tomatoes with light Greek vinaigrette
Cauliflower-broccoli salad
Hot or iced tea

cook smart *You don't have to avoid carbs to lose weight, but choose foods that are also packed with good carbs, such as whole grains, fruits, and vegetables.*

● GLUTEN FREE

Loosely tent the green beans and zucchini with aluminum foil to keep them warm while you cook the pork medallions.

cornmeal-crusted pork with sauteed vegetables

START TO FINISH: 30 minutes

12	ounces fresh green beans
2	zucchini and/or yellow summer squash, thinly bias sliced
2	tablespoons olive oil
⅓	cup yellow cornmeal
½	teaspoon salt
½	teaspoon ground black pepper
1	egg, lightly beaten
1	tablespoon water
1	pound natural pork tenderloin, cut into ½-inch-thick slices
2	tablespoons snipped fresh oregano (optional)
	Fresh oregano sprigs (optional)

1. In a covered very large skillet cook green beans and zucchini in 1 tablespoon of the hot oil over medium-high heat for 8 to 10 minutes or until crisp-tender, stirring occasionally. Remove vegetables from skillet; keep warm.

2. Meanwhile, in a shallow dish combine cornmeal, salt, and pepper. In another shallow dish combine egg and the water. Dip pork in egg mixture and then in cornmeal mixture, turning to coat all sides.

3. Add the remaining 1 tablespoon oil to the hot skillet. Add pork slices; cook over medium-high heat for 4 to 6 minutes or until slightly pink in centers, turning once halfway through cooking time. Serve pork with vegetables. If desired, sprinkle pork and vegetables with the snipped oregano and garnish with oregano sprigs. **Makes 4 servings.**

PER SERVING: 288 cal., 9 g fat (2 g sat. fat), 120 mg chol., 381 mg sodium, 22 g carb., 4 g fiber, 29 g pro.

make it a meal

Broiled mushrooms with thyme and balsamic vinegar
Roasted red potatoes
Sauteed apples with cinnamon

Delicate pancakes flavored with green onions are a Chinese specialty, but here—served with pork kabobs and a peanut sauce for dipping—they take on a Thai twist.

pork kabobs with onion cakes and peanut sauce

START TO FINISH: 30 minutes

1 pound natural pork tenderloin, cut into ½-inch slices

3 teaspoons reduced-sodium soy sauce

2 teaspoons Thai seasoning

1 bunch green onions, chopped (7 or 8)

½ cup all-purpose flour

½ teaspoon baking powder

½ cup water

1 egg, lightly beaten

2 teaspoons vegetable oil

¼ cup peanut butter

1 tablespoon honey

⅓ cup water

1 carrot, shredded
   Fresh cilantro and lime wedges (optional)

1. Preheat broiler. Thread pork onto eight skewers (see tip, page 19); brush with 1 teaspoon of the soy sauce and sprinkle with 1 teaspoon of the Thai seasoning. Broil 3 to 4 inches from the heat for 8 minutes, turning once halfway through cooking.

2. For onion cakes, combine onions, flour, baking powder, the ½ cup water, egg, and the remaining Thai seasoning. In an extra-large skillet heat oil over medium-high. Spread batter in skillet; cook for 10 to 12 minutes, turning once. Cut into wedges.

3. For sauce, in a microwave-safe bowl combine peanut butter, honey, the remaining soy sauce, and the ⅓ cup water. Cook on 100-percent-power (high) for 30 seconds. Whisk; cook for 15 seconds more. Serve kabobs with cakes, sauce, and shredded carrot. If desired, serve with cilantro and lime wedges. **Makes 4 servings.**

PER SERVING: 346 cal., 14 g fat (3 g sat. fat), 127 mg chol., 515 mg sodium, 23 g carb., 3 g fiber, 32 g pro.

[make it a meal

Spiced almonds
Broccoli slaw
Soba noodles with cilantro]

cook smart *Slow down and enjoy your meals—their taste, smell, and texture—so you are more aware of how much you eat and realize when you're full.*

Removing the soft centers of the baguette slices cuts down on carbs a bit—and helps these generously stuffed sandwiches eat more neatly.

hot ham and pear melts

PREP: 15 minutes   **BAKE:** 10 minutes at 350°F

1   **10- to 12-ounce whole grain baguette**
2   **tablespoons lower-sugar apricot preserves**
2   **cups arugula or fresh spinach**
1   **medium pear, quartered, cored, and thinly sliced**
6   **ounces thinly sliced lower-sodium cooked ham**
1   **4-ounce package goat cheese (chèvre), softened**
1   **teaspoon snipped fresh chives**
    Nonstick cooking spray

1. Preheat oven to 350°F. Cut baguette crosswise into four portions. Split each portion in half horizontally. Scoop out the soft centers of tops and bottoms of baguette portions, leaving about a ½-inch shell. (Save soft bread centers for another use.)

2. Spread preserves on cut sides of bottom halves of baguette portions. Top with half of the arugula, the pear slices, ham, and the remaining arugula. In a small bowl stir together goat cheese and chives; spread on cut sides of the top halves of the baguette portions. Place over arugula, cheese sides down. Lightly coat tops and bottoms of sandwiches with cooking spray.

3. Place sandwiches in a shallow baking pan. Cover with foil. Bake for 10 to 15 minutes or until heated through. Serve warm. **Makes 4 servings.**

PER SERVING: 300 cal., 10 g fat (5 g sat. fat), 32 mg chol., 647 mg sodium, 36 g carb., 3 g fiber, 16 g pro.

[make it a meal

Cauliflower salad
Baked sweet potato wedges
Mixed berry tart]

Sweet potatoes are one of the most nutrient-dense vegetables in the produce section. They're loaded with vitamin A, which supports a healthy immune system and eye health.

personal ham and sweet potato pizzas

START TO FINISH: 25 minutes

2   **small sweet potatoes (about 7 ounces each)**

2   **tablespoons orange juice**

4   **whole wheat thin sandwich rolls, such as Arnold Sandwich Thins, split and toasted**

1   **cup packed fresh baby spinach**

1   **cup shaved cooked ham (2 ounces), cut into strips**

½   **cup dried cranberries**

1   **cup shredded farmer or mozzarella cheese (4 ounces)**

1. Preheat broiler. Scrub sweet potatoes; pat dry with paper towels. Prick potatoes with a fork. Place on a microwave-safe plate. Microwave on 100-percent-power (high) for 6 minutes or until tender, rearranging once. Cool slightly. Cut potatoes in half and scoop pulp into a medium bowl; add orange juice. Mash with a potato masher or fork until smooth.

2. Spread sandwich rolls with mashed sweet potato mixture. Top with spinach, ham, and cranberries; sprinkle with cheese. Broil 4 to 5 inches from the heat about 3 minutes or until cheese is melted and starts to brown. **Makes 4 servings.**

PER SERVING: 317 cal., 7 g fat (3 g sat. fat), 27 mg chol., 647 mg sodium, 52 g carb., 8 g fiber, 17 g pro.

tip: Not an eggs or cereal person? Think about making this easy dinner recipe for breakfast. Eating a morning meal is linked to a healthy weight and more weight loss when trying to lose.

[make it a meal

Walnuts with dried cranberries
Blackened asparagus
Fresh pear slices

]

These Vietnamese-style sandwiches are built all at once on a single baguette, then cut into portions—which makes them fast to make in addition to being intensely flavorful.

banh mi vietnamese sandwiches

PREP: 25 minutes **COOK:** 4 minutes

12	ounces natural pork tenderloin
2	tablespoons Asian sweet chili sauce
1	tablespoon reduced-sodium soy sauce
1	small cucumber, seeded and cut in thin strips
1	small red sweet pepper, cut in thin strips
1	medium carrot, shredded
¼	cup green onion, chopped
¼	cup bottled low-fat sesame ginger salad dressing
1	tablespoon lime juice
1	10-ounce loaf whole grain baguette-style French bread, split horizontally
¼	cup fresh cilantro leaves
1	fresh jalapeño pepper, seeded and thinly sliced (see tip, page 62)

1. Trim fat from meat. Cut meat crosswise into ½-inch slices. Press each piece with the palm of your hand to make an even thickness. In a small bowl combine Asian sweet chili sauce and soy sauce. Brush sauce mixture onto pork slices. In a greased grill pan or extra-large skillet cook meat over medium-high heat for 4 to 6 minutes or until slightly pink in center and juices run clear, turning once.

2. In a large bowl combine cucumber, sweet pepper, carrot, green onion, salad dressing, and lime juice.

3. Place meat slices on the bottom half of the baguette. Top with vegetable mixture, cilantro leaves, jalapeño slices, and top half of baguette. Cut into portions to serve. **Makes 6 servings.**

PER SERVING: 220 cal., 4 g fat (0 g sat. fat), 37 mg chol., 481 mg sodium, 26 g carb., 6 g fiber, 19 g pro.

make it a meal

Baked sweet potato chips
Fennel slaw
Lemon cookie bites

It's important to let the filled and toasted loaf stand for 5 minutes before serving so that the gooey, delicious filling doesn't squish out when you cut it into sandwiches.

goat cheese and prosciutto panini

PREP: 15 minutes   **COOK:** 4 minutes   **STAND:** 5 minutes

1   12-ounce loaf whole grain Italian bread
    Nonstick cooking spray
2   ounces goat cheese (chèvre), crumbled
½   cup fresh basil leaves
2   medium tomatoes, sliced
2   ounces thinly sliced prosciutto
2   cups arugula leaves
1   tablespoon balsamic vinegar (optional)

1. Cut the bread in half lengthwise. Hollow out top and bottom halves of bread, leaving a ½-inch-thick shell. Reserve removed bread for another use. (There should be about 4 ounces of bread removed.)

2. Lightly coat outsides of the bread halves with cooking spray. Sprinkle goat cheese over the cut side of the bread bottom. Top evenly with the basil, tomatoes, prosciutto, and arugula. If desired, drizzle with balsamic vinegar. Cover with loaf top.

3. Coat a large nonstick skillet with cooking spray; preheat over medium heat. Place loaf in skillet. Place another skillet on top of the loaf, pressing gently to flatten loaf slightly. Cook for 2½ minutes on one side; turn and cook for 2 to 2½ minutes more or until bread is beginning to brown.

4. Remove from skillet. Let stand on cutting board for 5 minutes. Use a serrated knife to slice loaf into four equal sandwiches. **Makes 4 servings.**

PER SERVING: 253 cal., 10 g fat (3 g sat. fat), 11 mg chol., 606 mg sodium, 30 g carb., 5 g fiber, 13 g pro.

[make it a meal]

Baked tortilla chips
Asparagus salad
Grilled peach halves sprinkled with paprika

cook smart *Double check nutrition facts labels and food ingredient lists for the presence of trans fats found in many processed foods. Products stating "0 grams trans fats" can contain up to 0.5 g of trans fat per serving.*

Powdered peanut butter is made by pressing the oil out of roasted peanuts. It has to be mixed with water before being used, but it has 85 percent fewer fat calories than regular peanut butter.

beef and vegetables in peanut sauce

START TO FINISH: 20 minutes

½ cup cold water
3 tablespoons powdered peanut butter, such as PB2 brand
1 tablespoon reduced-sodium teriyaki sauce
1 tablespoon cider vinegar
2 teaspoons honey
¼ teaspoon ground ginger
¼ teaspoon crushed red pepper
Nonstick cooking spray
6 ounces boneless beef sirloin, cut into thin bite-size strips
1 clove garlic, minced
1 cup fresh snow pea pods, trimmed
½ cup purchased shredded carrots
½ of an 8.8-ounce pouch cooked brown rice (1 cup)

1. For peanut sauce, in a small saucepan stir together the cold water and peanut butter powder until powder dissolves. Stir in teriyaki sauce, vinegar, honey, ginger, and crushed red pepper. Bring to boiling, stirring occasionally. Boil gently, uncovered, for 1 to 2 minutes or until thickened; set aside.

2. Coat an unheated large nonstick skillet with cooking spray; heat over medium-high heat. Add beef and garlic to hot skillet. Cook and stir for 2 minutes. Add pea pods and carrots; cook and stir about 2 minutes more or until vegetables are crisp-tender. Heat brown rice according to package directions.

3. Add the peanut sauce, stirring to coat; if necessary, heat through. Serve beef and vegetable mixture over the rice.
Makes 2 servings.

PER SERVING: 353 cal., 12 g fat (4 g sat. fat), 34 mg chol., 345 mg sodium, 36 g carb., 3 g fiber, 26 g pro.

make it a meal

Spicy tofu spring rolls
Hot and sour soup
Melon-infused water

Dark leafy greens such as Swiss chard are nutritional powerhouses. They're rich in vitamins, minerals, disease-fighting phytochemicals, and calcium—which can help reduce the risk of osteoporosis.

swiss chard and turkey sausage over polenta

START TO FINISH: 30 minutes

4	**ounces light smoked turkey sausage, very thinly sliced**
½	**cup chopped onion (1 medium)**
2	**cloves garlic, minced**
2	**teaspoons olive oil**
1½	**pounds green or red Swiss chard, rinsed, trimmed, and cut into 2-inch-thick slices**
¼	**teaspoon crushed red pepper**
¼	**teaspoon salt**
3	**cups water**
1	**cup cornmeal**
1	**cup cold water**
¼	**cup fat-free milk**
1	**ounce Parmesan cheese, shaved (optional)**

1. In a very large skillet cook sausage, onion, and garlic in hot oil for 2 to 3 minutes or just until sausage is browned and onion is softened. Stir in half of the Swiss chard, the crushed red pepper, and ⅛ teaspoon of the salt. Cook, covered, for 2 minutes. Stir in the remaining Swiss chard. Cook, covered, for 5 minutes more, stirring often.

2. Meanwhile, for polenta, in a large saucepan bring the 3 cups water to boiling. In a medium bowl combine cornmeal and the remaining ⅛ teaspoon salt; stir in the 1 cup cold water. Slowly add cornmeal mixture to boiling water in saucepan, stirring constantly. Cook and stir until mixture returns to boiling. Cook, uncovered, over low heat about 5 minutes or until thick, stirring occasionally. Stir in milk.

3. Serve Swiss chard mixture over polenta. If desired, sprinkle with Parmesan cheese. **Makes 4 servings.**

PER SERVING: 247 cal., 6 g fat (1 g sat. fat), 22 mg chol., 786 mg sodium, 39 g carb., 4 g fiber, 11 g pro.

[**make it a meal**

Roasted mushroom soup
Honey-Bourbon Carrots, recipe page 245
Decaf coffee or tea]

cook smart *Canned beans are convenient compared to soaking and boiling the dry versions, and just as healthy—except for their salt content. Draining and rinsing canned beans reduces their sodium content by about 40 percent.*

A little bit of brown sugar and ground coffee mixed into a traditional jerk seasoning gives this dish an additional layer of flavor and a pleasing crust when grilled.

jerk chicken with avocado-orange salsa

PREP: 15 minutes   **GRILL:** 12 minutes

½	cup uncooked long grain white or brown rice
½	teaspoon cumin seeds (optional)
1	cup canned black beans, rinsed and drained
½	cup snipped fresh cilantro
	Salt
	Ground black pepper
4	teaspoons packed brown sugar
2	teaspoons ground coffee
1½	teaspoons garlic powder
1½	teaspoons dried thyme, crushed
1½	teaspoons ground allspice
1½	teaspoons paprika
½	teaspoon cayenne pepper
8	skinless, boneless chicken thighs
1	avocado, seeded, peeled, and chopped
1	cup canned mandarin orange sections, drained
¼	cup finely chopped red onion
3	tablespoons lime juice
1	teaspoon olive oil

1. Cook rice according to package directions, adding cumin seeds (if desired) to cooking liquid. Remove from heat. Fluff rice with a fork. Stir in beans and cilantro. Season to taste with salt and black pepper; keep warm.

2. In a small bowl stir together brown sugar, ground coffee, garlic powder, thyme, allspice, paprika, and cayenne pepper. Sprinkle mixture evenly over chicken; rub in with your fingers. Sprinkle with additional salt.

3. For a charcoal or gas grill, grill chicken on the rack of a covered grill directly over medium heat for 12 to 15 minutes or until no longer pink (180°F), turning once halfway through grilling.

4. For salsa, in a small bowl stir together avocado, mandarin oranges, onion, lime juice, and oil. Season to taste with additional salt and black pepper.

5. Serve chicken on rice mixture. Spoon salsa over chicken. **Makes 4 servings.**

PER SERVING: 409 cal., 12 g fat (2 g sat. fat), 115 mg chol., 616 mg sodium, 45 g carb., 7 g fiber, 33 g pro.

[make it a meal

Cabbage slaw with radishes
Grilled green beans
Sliced strawberries with mint]

If you don't have any cooked chicken breast sitting in the fridge, use the breast from a supermarket rotisserie chicken—just be sure to remove the skin before chopping the meat.

red pepper-basil raviolettis

START TO FINISH: 25 minutes

1   9-ounce package refrigerated cheese mini ravioli
1   medium red sweet pepper, chopped
1   cup chopped cooked skinless chicken breast
¾   cup chopped fresh basil
1   tablespoon extra virgin olive oil
¼   to ½ teaspoon coarsely ground black pepper
¼   teaspoon salt
2   tablespoons grated Parmesan cheese

1. Cook pasta according to package directions omitting any salt or fat and adding the chopped red sweet pepper the last 1 minute of cooking time.

2. Place the cooked chicken in a colander. Reserve 2 tablespoons of the pasta cooking water; set aside. Drain pasta over the chicken in colander, gently shaking off excess water. Place the pasta mixture on a serving platter or in serving bowls and sprinkle with the reserved pasta water, basil, and olive oil; toss gently. Sprinkle with the pepper and salt and top with the Parmesan cheese. **Makes 5 servings.**

PER SERVING: 310 cal., 12 g fat (5 g sat. fat), 68 mg chol., 545 mg sodium, 30 g carb., 3 g fiber, 21 g pro.

make it a meal

Caramelized Balsamic Onions, recipe page 255
Crusty multigrain bread
Frozen low-fat yogurt

Give fresh citrus a squeeze whenever it is suggested in a recipe. Fresh lime or lemon adds bright, fresh flavor to foods without adding salt or a single calorie or fat gram.

red beans and rice with chicken

START TO FINISH: 20 minutes

10	ounces skinless, boneless chicken breast, cut into 1-inch pieces
¼	teaspoon salt
¼	teaspoon ground black pepper
1	tablespoon olive oil
¾	cup coarsely chopped green sweet pepper (1 medium)
½	cup chopped onion (1 medium)
2	cloves garlic, minced
1	15-ounce can no-salt-added red beans, rinsed and drained
1	1-cup container ready-to-serve cooked brown rice
¼	cup reduced-sodium chicken broth
½	teaspoon ground cumin
¼	teaspoon cayenne pepper
	Lime wedges
	Cayenne pepper (optional)

1. Sprinkle chicken with the salt and black pepper. In a large skillet heat oil over medium-high heat. Add chicken, sweet pepper, onion, and garlic; cook and stir for 8 to 10 minutes or until chicken is no longer pink and vegetables are tender.

2. Stir beans, rice, broth, cumin, and the ¼ teaspoon cayenne pepper into chicken mixture in skillet. Heat through. Serve with lime wedges. If desired, sprinkle with additional cayenne pepper. **Makes 4 servings.**

PER SERVING: 272 cal., 5 g fat (1 g sat. fat), 41 mg chol., 311 mg sodium, 30 g carb., 10 g fiber, 25 g pro.

[
make it a meal
Lowfat corn bread
Sliced avocado with lime and paprika
Fresh pineapple
]

A quick mango mayo gives these sandwiches a pop of spicy-sweet flavor. Mango chutney comes in both mild and hot varieties—choose the one that suits your taste best.

orange-soy chicken sandwiches

START TO FINISH: 30 minutes

½	teaspoon finely shredded orange peel
⅓	cup orange juice
1	tablespoon low-sodium soy sauce
1	clove garlic, minced
1	teaspoon snipped fresh thyme
½	teaspoon paprika
¼	teaspoon ground black pepper
¼	teaspoon crushed red pepper
2	8-ounce skinless, boneless chicken breast halves
2	teaspoons olive oil
1	tablespoon mango chutney
3	tablespoons light mayonnaise
4	multigrain sandwich thins, toasted
2	cups loosely packed watercress

1. In a small bowl stir together orange peel, orange juice, soy sauce, garlic, thyme, paprika, black pepper, and crushed red pepper; set aside.

2. Cut each chicken breast half crosswise in half. Place each piece between two pieces or plastic wrap. Using the flat side of a meat mallet, pound the chicken lightly to about ¼ inch thick. Remove plastic wrap.

3. In a very large nonstick skillet heat the oil over medium-high heat. Cook chicken in hot oil for 4 minutes, turning once. Carefully add orange juice mixture to skillet. Simmer for 3 minutes or until liquid reduces to a glaze, turning to coat chicken.

4. Place chutney in a small bowl; snip any large pieces of fruit. Stir in mayonnaise. To assemble sandwiches, spread mayonnaise mixture on cut sides of toasted sandwich thins. For each sandwich, place ½ cup of the watercress and a chicken portion on bottom half of sandwich thin. Add sandwich thin top, spread side down. **Makes 4 servings.**

PER SERVING: 272 cal., 9 g fat (1 g sat. fat), 51 mg chol., 564 mg sodium, 30 g carb., 5 g fiber, 21 g pro.

make it a meal

Lowfat spinach dip and sweet pepper slices
Baked vegetable chips
Sparkling water with lemon

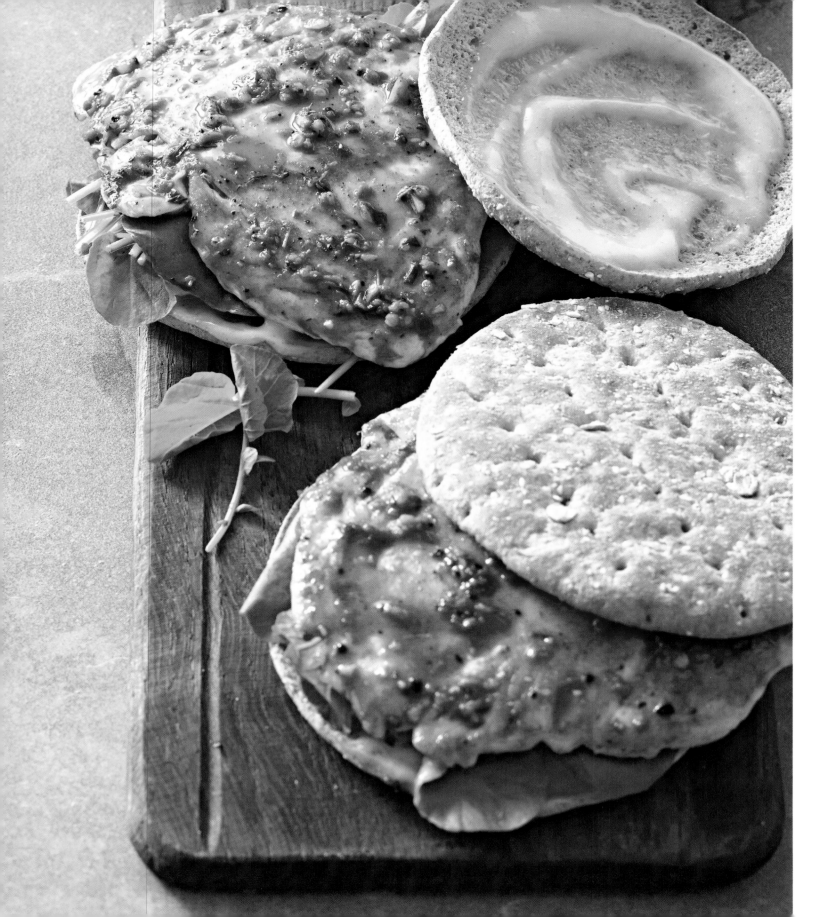

If you can't find small (4- to 5-ounce) boneless, skinless chicken breasts, buy two larger breasts—they most often are found weighing 8 to 10 ounces—and cut each one in half horizontally before cooking.

herbed chicken, orzo, and zucchini

START TO FINISH: 20 minutes

1 cup dried orzo pasta (rosamarina)
4 small skinless, boneless chicken breast halves (1 to 1¼ pounds total)
1 teaspoon dried basil, crushed
3 tablespoons olive oil
2 medium zucchini, sliced
2 tablespoons red wine vinegar
1 tablespoon snipped fresh dill
Lemon wedges (optional)
Fresh dill sprigs (optional)

1. Prepare orzo according to package directions; drain. Return to hot saucepan. Cover and keep warm.

2. Meanwhile, sprinkle chicken with basil. In a large skillet heat 1 tablespoon of the oil over medium heat. Add chicken; cook about 12 minutes or until no longer pink (170°F), turning once halfway through cooking. Remove chicken from skillet. Add zucchini to skillet; cook and stir about 3 minutes or until crisp-tender.

3. In a medium bowl whisk together vinegar, the remaining 2 tablespoons oil, and the snipped dill. Add to orzo; toss to coat.

4. Serve chicken with orzo and zucchini. If desired, garnish with lemon wedges and dill sprigs. **Makes 4 servings.**

PER SERVING: 390 cal., 12 g fat (2 g sat. fat), 66 mg chol., 233 mg sodium, 35 g carb., 3 g fiber, 33 g pro.

make it a meal

Veggies with roasted pepper hummus
Sauteed Swiss chard
Plum halves

A small amount of brown rice noodles gets bulked up with lean protein (chicken) and lots of sweet pepper strips in this slimmed-down version of an Asian favorite.

sesame chicken and noodles

START TO FINISH: 20 minutes

⅓ cup rice vinegar
⅓ cup thinly sliced green onions
2 tablespoons honey
1 tablespoon reduced-sodium soy sauce
1 tablespoon grated fresh ginger
2 teaspoons Asian garlic-chili sauce
2 6-ounce packages refrigerated grilled chicken breast strips
1 12-ounce package brown rice noodles
3 tablespoons toasted sesame oil
2 medium yellow, red, and/or orange sweet peppers, cut in bite-size strips
Snipped fresh cilantro

1. In medium bowl stir together vinegar, green onions, honey, soy sauce, ginger, and garlic-chili sauce. Add chicken; stir to combine.

2. Meanwhile, cook noodles according to package directions. Drain and return to saucepan. Drizzle with oil and toss to coat. Add chicken mixture and toss to combine.

3. Transfer to bowls. Top each with pepper strips and cilantro.
Makes 6 servings.

PER SERVING: 391 cal., 11 g fat (2 g sat. fat), 37 mg chol., 718 mg sodium, 51 g carb., 4 g fiber, 21 g pro.

make it a meal

Seasoned almonds
Peas with lemon zest
Sliced nectarines dusted with cinnamon

cook smart *Eat fish twice a week—especially those high in omega-3 fatty acids, which play an important role in brain function and inflammation prevention.*

Ancho chile powder—the dried and ground incarnation of poblano chiles—infuses these fresh salmon sandwiches with its rich, fruity, sweet, and slightly spicy flavor.

coffee-rubbed salmon sandwiches

PREP: 20 minutes   **COOK:** 5 minutes

¼   cup light sour cream
1   tablespoon snipped fresh parsley
2   teaspoons cider vinegar
1   teaspoon prepared horseradish
1   teaspoon instant espresso coffee powder
1   teaspoon dried ancho chile powder
½   teaspoon packed brown sugar
¼   teaspoon dry mustard
¼   teaspoon ground cumin
⅛   teaspoon cayenne pepper
1   pound skinless salmon fillets
2   teaspoons olive oil
4   whole wheat hamburger buns, toasted
2   cups baby salad greens
8   thin red onion rings

1. In a small bowl stir together sour cream, parsley, vinegar, and horseradish. Set aside.

2. In another small bowl stir together espresso powder, chile powder, brown sugar, mustard, cumin, and cayenne pepper. Cut salmon into four equal pieces. Sprinkle evenly with spice mixture; rub mixture into salmon with your fingers.

3. In a large nonstick skillet heat oil over medium heat. Cook salmon in hot oil for 5 to 7 minutes or until fish begins to flake when tested with a fork.

4. Top bottom halves of toasted buns with salad greens, salmon pieces, and onion rings. Spoon sauce over salmon and onion rings. Add top halves of buns. **Makes 4 servings.**

PER SERVING: 363 cal., 12 g fat (2 g sat. fat), 67 mg chol., 347 mg sodium, 33 g carb., 4 g fiber, 29 g pro.

[make it a meal

Dilled cucumbers
Baked sweet potato fries
Feta stuffed dates]

If you make these tacos with tilapia, look for U.S. farm-raised tilapia. It has better texture and flavor than tilapia that comes from other parts of the world, including China and Central and South America.

fish tacos with jalapeño slaw

PREP: 20 minutes   **GRILL:** 4 minutes

1   **pound fresh or frozen skinless cod, tilapia, or other fish fillets, about ½ inch thick**
1   **recipe Jalapeño Slaw**
½   **teaspoon ground cumin**
¼   **teaspoon ground ancho chile pepper or cayenne pepper**
    Dash salt
4   **8-inch whole grain flour tortillas**
    Peach or mango salsa (optional)
    Lime wedges (optional)

1. Thaw fish, if frozen. Rinse fish; pat dry with paper towels. Set aside. Prepare Jalapeño Slaw; cover and chill.

2. In a small bowl combine cumin, ground ancho chile pepper, and salt; sprinkle evenly over one side of each fish fillet.

3. Stack tortillas and wrap in heavy foil. For a charcoal grill, place fish and tortilla stack on the greased grill rack directly over medium coals. Grill, uncovered, for 4 to 6 minutes or until fish flakes easily when tested with a fork and tortillas are heated through, turning fish and tortilla stack once. (For a gas grill, preheat grill. Reduce heat to medium. Place fish and tortilla stack on greased grill rack over heat. Cover and grill as above.)

4. To serve, cut fish into four serving-size pieces. Divide Jalapeño Slaw among tortillas and top with fish. If desired, serve with salsa and lime wedges. **Makes 4 servings.**

jalapeño slaw: In a medium bowl combine 2½ cups coleslaw mix, ¼ cup halved and thinly sliced red onion, and 1 small fresh jalapeño pepper (see tip, page 62). In a small bowl whisk together 2 tablespoons lime juice, 2 tablespoons orange juice, 2 tablespoons olive oil, ½ teaspoon ground cumin, and a dash of salt. Pour over cabbage mixture and toss to coat.

PER SERVING: 304 cal., 11 g fat (2 g sat. fat), 48 mg chol., 467 mg sodium, 20 g carb., 11 g fiber, 29 g pro.

[make it a meal

Smashed avocados
Fresh pineapple
Melon agua fresca]

If your fennel bulbs have fresh-looking fronds, snip and sprinkle them on each serving along with the parsley and lemon peel.

farfalle with tuna, lemon, and fennel

START TO FINISH: 30 minutes

6 ounces dried whole grain farfalle
(bow-tie) pasta

1 5-ounce can solid white tuna
(packed in oil)
Olive oil (optional)

1 cup thinly sliced fennel
(1 medium bulb)

2 cloves garlic, minced

½ teaspoon crushed red pepper

¼ teaspoon salt

2 14.5-ounce cans no-salt-added
diced tomatoes, undrained

2 tablespoons snipped fresh Italian
parsley

1 teaspoon finely shredded lemon
peel

1. Cook pasta according to package directions, omitting salt; drain. Return pasta to pan; cover and keep warm.

2. Meanwhile, drain tuna, reserving oil. If necessary, add enough olive oil to measure 3 tablespoons total. Flake tuna; set aside. In a medium saucepan heat the 3 tablespoons oil over medium heat. Add fennel; cook for 3 minutes, stirring occasionally. Add garlic, crushed red pepper, and salt; cook and stir about 1 minute or just until garlic is golden.

3. Stir in tomatoes. Bring to boiling; reduce heat. Simmer, uncovered, for 5 to 6 minutes or until mixture starts to thicken. Stir in tuna; simmer, uncovered, about 1 minute more or until tuna is heated through.

4. Pour tuna mixture over pasta; stir gently to combine. Sprinkle each serving with parsley and lemon peel. **Makes 4 servings.**

PER SERVING: 356 cal., 14 g fat (2 g sat. fat), 11 mg chol., 380 mg sodium, 43 g carb., 9 g fiber, 17 g pro.

make it a meal

Grilled romaine hearts with creamy low-fat dressing
Roasted cauliflower with cumin seeds
Sliced mango

Be quick about cooking baby bok choy. It can go from perfectly crisp-tender to overdone in a flash. Watch it carefully so the stalk stays slightly crisp and the dark leafy green is just barely wilted.

sauteed baby bok choy and shiitake with shrimp

START TO FINISH: 25 minutes

1	pound fresh or frozen large shrimp in shells
1	tablespoon toasted sesame oil
1½	cups sliced shiitake mushrooms
2	cloves garlic, minced
4	cups halved, trimmed baby bok choy (about 1 pound)
2	cups fresh snow pea pods, trimmed
1	tablespoon oyster sauce
2	teaspoons reduced-sodium soy sauce
¼	teaspoon ground black pepper
1	tablespoon sesame seeds, toasted (see tip, page 64)

1. Thaw shrimp, if frozen. Peel and devein shrimp, leaving tails intact. Rinse shrimp; pat dry with paper towels.

2. In a very large skillet heat sesame oil over medium-high heat. Add shrimp, mushrooms, and garlic; cook and stir for 4 to 6 minutes or just until shrimp are opaque. Carefully add baby bok choy; cook for 2 minutes more. Add pea pods, oyster sauce, soy sauce, and black pepper to skillet; cook and stir for 1 minute more. Divide among four serving plates or bowls. Sprinkle with sesame seeds. **Makes 4 servings.**

PER SERVING: 221 cal., 7 g fat (1 g sat. fat), 172 mg chol., 415 mg sodium, 15 g carb., 3 g fiber, 27 g pro.

make it a meal

Kale chips
Seared cantaloupe sprinkled with smoked paprika
Hot orange tea

cook smart *Make your evening meal the last calories of the day. Lean on the earlier hours for eating most of your calories. People who do tend to weigh less.*

Whether you leave the tails on the shrimp is up to you. Intact tails are pretty, but the shrimp are easier to eat if they're cut off before cooking.

shrimp and winter greens with pasta

START TO FINISH: 25 minutes

6	ounces dried multigrain or whole grain rotini or penne pasta
12	ounces fresh or frozen peeled and deveined shrimp, with tails intact if desired
4	cloves garlic, thinly sliced
1	tablespoon olive oil
½	teaspoon ground black pepper
4	cups coarsely chopped fresh kale and/or Swiss chard
1	14.5-ounce can no-salt-added diced tomatoes with basil, garlic, and oregano, undrained
1	8-ounce can no-salt-added tomato sauce
⅓	cup pitted kalamata olives, halved
¼	cup shredded Parmesan cheese (1 ounce)

1. Cook pasta according to package directions; drain.

2. Meanwhile, thaw shrimp, if frozen. Rinse shrimp; pat dry with paper towels. In an extra-large nonstick skillet cook shrimp and garlic in hot oil over medium-high heat for 3 to 4 minutes or until shrimp are opaque, stirring occasionally. If shrimp or garlic browns too quickly, reduce heat to medium. Remove from heat. Sprinkle shrimp and garlic with ¼ teaspoon of the pepper; toss to coat. Remove shrimp and garlic from skillet.

3. Add kale to the same skillet. Cook and stir for 3 to 4 minutes or just until tender. Stir in tomatoes, tomato sauce, olives, the remaining ¼ teaspoon pepper, pasta, and shrimp mixture. Cook and stir for 2 to 3 minutes or until heated through.

4. Divide shrimp mixture among serving plates. Sprinkle with cheese. **Makes 4 servings.**

PER SERVING: 377 cal., 9 g fat (1 g sat. fat), 112 mg chol., 771 mg sodium, 53 g carb., 15 g fiber, 23 g pro.

[make it a meal]

Edamame with sweet peppers
Whole wheat baguette
Apricots drizzled with honey

A tiny bit of butter—only 2 teaspoons—is used to sear the scallops and add flavor to this lightened-up Alfredo sauce. Be sure to get the scallops as dry as possible before cooking to get a nice, browned crust.

scallop and asparagus alfredo

START TO FINISH: 30 minutes

8 ounces fresh or frozen sea scallops
2 ounces dried whole wheat penne pasta
1 pound fresh asparagus spears, cut into 1-inch pieces (2 cups)
2 teaspoons butter
2 cloves garlic, minced
1 5-ounce can evaporated fat-free milk
2 tablespoons reduced-fat cream cheese (Neufchâtel)
2 tablespoons finely shredded Parmesan cheese
1 tablespoon lemon juice
¼ teaspoon lemon-pepper seasoning
Snipped fresh Italian parsley (optional)

1. Thaw scallops, if frozen. Rinse scallops; pat dry with paper towels. Set aside. Cook pasta according to package directions, adding asparagus for the last 3 minutes of cooking time. Drain and keep warm.

2. In a large skillet melt butter over medium-high heat. Add scallops and garlic. Cook for 4 to 5 minutes or until scallops are golden brown, turning once. Remove scallops from skillet; cover and keep warm.

3. Whisk evaporated milk into the drippings in the skillet. Reduce heat to medium-low. Add cream cheese, Parmesan cheese, lemon juice, and lemon-pepper seasoning. Cook and stir until heated through and cheeses are melted.

4. Add cooked pasta and asparagus to the skillet; toss to coat. Divide pasta mixture between two dinner plates. Top with the cooked scallops. If desired, garnish with parsley. **Makes 2 servings.**

PER SERVING: 398 cal., 11 g fat (6 g sat. fat), 66 mg chol., 530 mg sodium, 40 g carb., 3 g fiber, 36 g pro.

make it a meal

Oranges sections drizzled with citrus vinaigrette
Shiitake and Bok Choy, recipe page 261
Lemon tea

cook smart *Enlist social media to make you more accountable on your weight-loss journey. Post victories, healthy meal or snack ideas—even photos. You may end up with a virtual support group or even a weight-loss club.*

The appeal of this dish lies in its contrasts. Warm wedges of creamy, coconut-and-panko-crusted tofu are served on a cool, crisp slaw flavored with mandarin oranges, coconut milk and crushed red pepper.

coconut-crusted tofu with black bean slaw

PREP: 15 minutes   **BAKE:** 10 minutes at 450°F

Nonstick cooking spray
¾ cup panko bread crumbs
½ cup shredded or flaked coconut
1 egg
¼ cup unsweetened light coconut milk
2 teaspoons ground coriander
1 teaspoon salt
1 18-ounce package firm, tub-style tofu (fresh bean curd)
2½ cups packaged shredded broccoli (broccoli slaw mix)
1 15-ounce can no-salt-added black beans, rinsed and drained
1 8.25-ounce can mandarin orange sections, undrained
¼ cup rice vinegar
2 tablespoons unsweetened light coconut milk
¼ teaspoon crushed red pepper

1. Preheat oven to 450°F. Line a baking sheet with foil; coat foil with cooking spray. Set baking sheet aside. In a blender or food processor combine panko and coconut. Cover and blend or process until coconut is finely chopped. Transfer to a shallow dish. In another shallow dish whisk together egg, ¼ cup coconut milk, coriander, and salt.

2. Drain tofu; cut crosswise into four slices. Cut each slice in half diagonally to make two triangles. Pat dry with paper towels. Dip tofu triangles into egg mixture, then into panko mixture, turning to coat all sides. Place on the prepared baking sheet. Coat tops of tofu with cooking spray. Bake about 10 minutes or until golden and heated through.

3. Meanwhile, for slaw, in a large bowl combine broccoli and black beans. Drain mandarin oranges, reserving 2 tablespoons juice. Add the reserved juice, rice vinegar, 2 tablespoons coconut milk, and crushed red pepper to broccoli mixture; toss to coat. Gently stir in mandarin oranges.

4. Divide slaw among serving plates. Top with tofu.
Makes 4 servings.

PER SERVING: 328 cal., 11 g fat (5 g sat. fat), 47 mg chol., 711 mg sodium, 39 g carb., 9 g fiber, 21 g pro.

make it a meal

Brown rice with cilantro
Clementines
Sparkling lemon water

To maximize the amount of juice you extract from a fresh lime (or lemon), warm it in microwave for 10 seconds, then roll it on the counter under your palm a few times before cutting it in half.

vegetarian citrus-corn tacos

START TO FINISH: 30 minutes

½   cup orange juice
¼   cup snipped fresh cilantro
1   teaspoon finely shredded lime peel
2   tablespoons lime juice
1   fresh jalapeño pepper, seeded and finely chopped*
3   cloves garlic, minced
1½ teaspoons cornstarch
⅛   teaspoon salt
⅛   teaspoon ground black pepper
2   teaspoons cooking oil
1   medium red sweet pepper, cut into thin strips
1   12-ounce package frozen cooked and crumbled ground meat substitute (soy protein)
1   cup frozen whole kernel corn
8   6-inch corn tortillas
½   cup light sour cream

1. For the sauce, in a small bowl combine orange juice, cilantro, lime peel, lime juice, jalapeño pepper, garlic, cornstarch, salt, and black pepper. Set aside.

2. In a large nonstick skillet heat oil over medium-high heat. Add sweet pepper strips; cook and stir until crisp-tender. Remove from skillet; set aside.

3. Add ground meat crumbles to skillet. Cook, stirring occasionally, for 3 to 4 minutes or until heated through. Stir in corn. Stir sauce; add to skillet. Cook and stir until thickened and bubbly. Reduce heat; cook and stir for 2 minutes more. Return sweet pepper strips to skillet; stir to combine.

4. Wrap tortillas in microwave-safe paper towels. Microwave on 100-percent-power (high) for 45 to 60 seconds or until warm. Divide the pepper mixture among tortillas and top with sour cream. Fold tortillas over filling. **Makes 4 servings.**

PER SERVING: 361 cal., 11 g fat (2 g sat. fat), 8 mg chol., 490 mg sodium, 47 g carb., 10 g fiber, 21 g pro.

*tip: Fresh chile peppers contain volatile oils that can burn your skin and eyes, so avoid contact with them as much as possible. When working with fresh chile peppers, wear plastic or rubber gloves. If your bare hands do touch the chiles, wash your hands and nails thoroughly with soap and hot water.

make it a meal

Fruit salsa
Lowfat guacamole and veggies
Refried black beans

This pizza makes an excellent breakfast as well as dinner. Eating protein such as tofu, eggs or lean meat or dairy in the morning helps prevent the crashing and hunger pangs brought on by a carb-heavy breakfast.

veggie-tofu pita pizza

PREP: 20 minutes   **BAKE:** 8 minutes at 375°F

½   cup sliced fresh mushrooms
½   cup chopped red or green sweet pepper (1 medium)
1   teaspoon olive oil
3   ounces firm tub-style tofu (fresh bean curd), drained and crumbled (about ½ cup)
1   green onion, thinly sliced
1   clove garlic, minced
⅛   teaspoon ground black pepper
1   whole wheat pita bread round, split horizontally
½   cup shredded reduced-fat cheddar cheese (2 ounces)

1. Preheat oven to 375°F. In a medium skillet cook mushrooms and sweet pepper in hot oil over medium heat for 5 to 8 minutes or until tender, stirring occasionally. Stir in tofu, green onion, garlic, and black pepper.

2. Place pita halves, cut sides down, on a baking sheet; sprinkle with ¼ cup of the cheese. Top with mushroom mixture. Sprinkle the remaining ¼ cup cheese over mushroom mixture. Bake for 8 to 10 minutes or until heated through and cheese melts. **Makes 2 servings.**

PER SERVING: 256 cal., 11 g fat (5 g sat. fat), 20 mg chol.,417 mg sodium, 24 g carb., 4 g fiber, 15 g pro

make it a meal

Minestrone soup
Roasted red pepper hummus and veggies
Chocolate-Sesame Cookies, recipe page 276

Evaporated fat-free milk is an excellent base for creamy, rich-tasting sauces that actually are low in fat and calories. Sub it for whole milk, half-and-half, or heavy cream in your favorite cream soups as well.

whole grain farfalle with walnuts and arugula

START TO FINISH: 25 minutes

6	ounces dried whole grain farfalle (bow-tie) pasta
1	tablespoon walnut oil or olive oil
⅓	cup finely chopped walnuts
1	clove garlic, minced
1	tablespoon all-purpose flour
¼	teaspoon salt
⅛	teaspoon ground black pepper
1	cup evaporated fat-free milk
4	cups lightly packed arugula
2	tablespoons broken walnuts, toasted*
2	tablespoons shaved Parmesan cheese

1. Cook pasta according to package directions; drain. Return pasta to pan; cover and keep warm.

2. Meanwhile, for sauce, in a medium skillet heat oil over medium heat. Add ⅓ cup walnuts and garlic; cook and stir for 1 minute. Stir in flour, salt, and pepper. Gradually stir in evaporated milk. Cook and stir until slightly thickened and bubbly.

3. Pour sauce over pasta; toss gently to coat. Stir in arugula. Divide pasta mixture among warm shallow serving bowls and top with 2 tablespoons walnuts and cheese. **Makes 4 servings.**

PER SERVING: 339 cal., 14 g fat (2 g sat. fat), 4 mg chol., 270 mg sodium, 44 g carb., 5 g fiber, 15 g pro.

*tip: To toast whole nuts or large pieces, spread them in a shallow pan. Bake in a 350°F oven for 5 to 10 minutes, shaking the pan once or twice. Toast coconut in the same way, watching it closely to avoid burning. Toast small amounts of nuts, finely chopped or ground nuts, cumin seeds or sesame seeds in a dry skillet over medium heat for 2 minutes or until golden and fragrant, stirring often.

make it a meal

Roasted radicchio
Whole wheat ciabatta
Apple-Date Cake, recipe page 270

cook smart *Ever wonder why all the fuss about whole grains? Eating them is associated with a healthier weight and lower cholesterol. A grain is "whole" when all of the natural parts of its kernel are still present.*

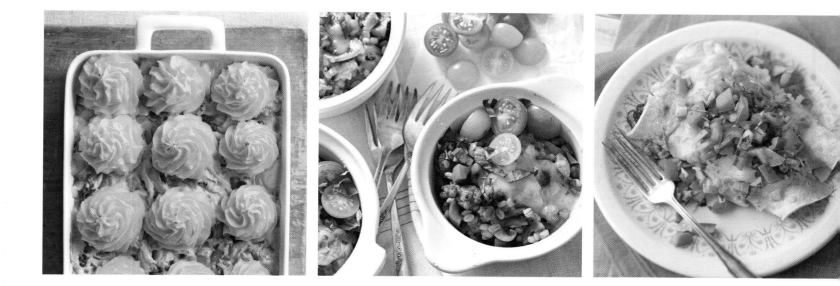

casseroles

Get comfort—without the usual high calorie counts—from these bubbling hot dishes that will please the whole family.

A mandoline makes quick and consistent work of very thinly slicing the potatoes for this dish. You don't have to spend a fortune on a fancy French model, either. There are quality products for less than $25.

caramelized onion and potato casserole

PREP: 45 minutes **BAKE:** 45 minutes at 350°F **STAND:** 15 minutes

4   cups sliced golden potatoes, cut ⅛ to ¼ inch thick (about 1½ pounds)
1   tablespoon olive oil
2   ounces pancetta, chopped
3   cups thinly sliced sweet onions, such as Vidalia or Maui Butter
6   eggs, lightly beaten
½   cup milk
1   cup shredded Gruyère cheese or Swiss cheese
1   teaspoon salt
1   teaspoon snipped fresh rosemary
½   teaspoon ground black pepper

1. Preheat oven to 350°F. In a large saucepan cook potatoes, covered, in boiling lightly salted water about 5 minutes or until slightly tender but still firm. Drain; set aside.

2. In a large skillet heat olive oil over medium-high heat. Add pancetta; cook until lightly browned. Using a slotted spoon, remove pancetta, reserving drippings in skillet. Set pancetta aside. Add onions to skillet. Cook and stir over medium-low heat about 20 minutes or until lightly browned and very tender. Remove from heat. Carefully stir potatoes and pancetta into onions in skillet.

3. Lightly butter a 2-quart rectangular baking dish. Spread potato mixture in the prepared dish. In a medium bowl whisk together eggs and milk. Stir in cheese, salt, rosemary, and pepper. Pour evenly over potato mixture in baking dish.

4. Bake, uncovered, for 45 to 50 minutes or until golden and a knife inserted in the center comes out clean. Let stand for 15 minutes before serving. **Makes 8 servings.**

PER SERVING: 250 cal., 13 g fat (5 g sat. fat), 180 mg chol., 535 mg sodium, 22 g carb., 3 g fiber, 13 g pro.

[make it a meal]

Sweet peppers and asparagus with hummus
Spinach salad with blueberries and walnuts
Green tea with mint

cook smart *Eat four to six small meals and snacks throughout the day. Studies show that eating less or more often than this can be a risk factor for extra pounds.*

Thin ribbons of zucchini stand in for pasta in this skinny version of everyone's favorite layered comfort food. Crush the fennel seeds—which give the dish a savory "sausagey" flavor—in a mortar and pestle.

zucchini-noodle lasagne

PREP: 15 minutes   **BROIL:** 12 minutes   **BAKE:** 30 minutes at 375°F   **STAND:** 10 minutes

2	pounds zucchini (about 2 large or 3 medium)
	Nonstick cooking spray
1	pound extra-lean ground beef
2	cups chopped fresh portobello mushrooms
2	cloves garlic, minced
1	24- to 26-ounce jar chunky-style pasta sauce
1	8-ounce can tomato sauce
1	teaspoon dried basil, crushed
1	teaspoon dried oregano, crushed
1	teaspoon fennel seeds, crushed
1	egg, lightly beaten
1	15-ounce container fat-free ricotta cheese
2	cups shredded part-skim mozzarella cheese

1. Preheat broiler. Trim ends off zucchini. Cut zucchini lengthwise into ¼-inch slices. Lightly coat both sides of zucchini slices with cooking spray; place half of the slices in a single layer on a wire rack set on a large baking sheet. Broil about 6 inches from the heat for 12 to 14 minutes or until lightly browned, turning once halfway through broiling. Repeat with remaining zucchini slices. Reduce oven temperature to 375°F.

2. In a large skillet cook ground beef, mushrooms, and garlic until meat is browned, using a wooden spoon to break up meat as it cooks. Drain. Remove from heat. Stir pasta sauce, tomato sauce, basil, oregano, and fennel seeds into mixture in skillet. In a small bowl combine egg and ricotta cheese.

3. To assemble lasagna, spread 1 cup of the sauce mixture on the bottom of a 13×9×2-inch baking pan. Top with enough of the zucchini slices to cover the sauce mixture. Drop half of the ricotta mixture by spoonfuls on top of the zucchini; use the back of the spoon to lightly spread ricotta mixture over zucchini. Sprinkle ¾ cup of the mozzarella cheese on top. Top with half of the remaining sauce mixture. Repeat layers once more, ending with sauce mixture.

4. Bake for 20 minutes. Sprinkle with the remaining ½ cup cheese. Bake for 10 to 15 minutes more or until cheese is melted. Let stand for 10 minutes before serving. **Makes 12 servings.**

PER SERVING: 209 cal., 8 g fat (3 g sat. fat), 58 mg chol., 565 mg sodium, 15 g carb., 3 g fiber, 20 g pro.

make it a meal

Hearts of romaine salad
Garlic-parsley bread toasts
Strawberries drizzled with balsamic vinegar

Nutrient-rich root vegetables—sweet potatoes, parsnips, and carrots—pack this Southern-style pot pie flavored with sweet and tangy barbecue sauce.

barbecue chicken pot pie

PREP: 45 minutes   **BAKE:** 15 minutes at 450°F   **STAND:** 5 minutes

½ **pound sweet potatoes or Yukon gold potatoes, peeled and cut into ¾-inch cubes**
¼ **teaspoon salt**
½ **cup chopped parsnips or carrots**
1¼ **pounds skinless, boneless chicken thighs, cut into ¾-inch pieces**
2 **teaspoons olive oil**
½ **cup chopped onion (1 medium)**
½ **cup chopped celery (1 stalk)**
1 **8-ounce package sliced button mushrooms (3 cups)**
⅔ **cup barbecue sauce**
½ **of a 14.1-ounce package rolled refrigerated unbaked piecrust (1 crust)**
1 **egg**
1 **tablespoon water**

1. Preheat oven to 450°F. In a medium saucepan combine potatoes and salt; add enough water to cover. Bring to boiling; reduce heat. Cover and simmer for 10 to 12 minutes or just until tender. Add the parsnips to the potatoes during the last 4 minutes of cooking. Drain; cool slightly.

2. Meanwhile, in a very large skillet cook chicken in hot oil over medium heat about 5 minutes or until brown, stirring occasionally. Remove chicken from skillet; set aside. Add onion, celery, and mushrooms to skillet. Cook and stir about 10 minutes or until vegetables are tender. Return chicken to skillet. Stir in barbecue sauce and cooked potatoes and parsnips; heat through. Divide filling evenly among six 10-ounce ramekins or custard cups.

3. Unroll piecrust. Press or roll piecrust into a 12-inch circle. Cut crust into ½-inch-wide strips. Cut long center strips in half. Arrange half of the strips 1 inch apart on filling (about 3 strips per ramekin). Turn each ramekin a quarter; arrange remaining strips perpendicular to the first half of the strips (about 3 strips per ramekin).

4. In a small bowl whisk together the egg and the water. Brush egg mixture on lattice crusts.

5. Bake, uncovered, for 15 to 20 minutes or until the filling is bubbly and crust is golden brown. Let stand for 5 minutes before serving. **Makes 6 servings.**

PER SERVING: 369 cal., 14 g fat (4 g sat. fat), 97 mg chol., 612 mg sodium, 38 g carb., 3 g fiber, 22 g pro.

[**make it a meal**

Sliced peaches with blueberries
Sauteed collard greens or kale
Lemonade with ginger]

cook smart *Stave off between-meal hunger by eating a lean protein at every meal—chicken, pork tenderloin, fat-free milk or yogurt, egg whites, fish, seafood or beans. Protein digests more slowly than carbs, keeping you full longer.*

Bake several bone-in chicken breasts at once, then cool and store in the refrigerator to be at the ready for dishes that call for cooked chicken, such as this one.

pumpkin, bean, and chicken enchiladas

PREP: 35 minutes   **BAKE:** 25 minutes at 400°F

Nonstick cooking spray
2   **teaspoons olive oil**
½   **cup chopped onion (1 medium)**
1   **fresh jalapeño pepper, seeded and finely chopped (see tip, page 62)**
1   **15-ounce can pumpkin**
1½   **to 1¾ cups water**
1   **teaspoon chili powder**
½   **teaspoon salt**
½   **teaspoon ground cumin**
1   **cup canned no-salt-added red kidney beans, rinsed and drained**
1½   **cups shredded cooked chicken breast**
½   **cup shredded part-skim mozzarella cheese (2 ounces)**
8   **6-inch white corn tortillas, softened***
Pico de gallo or salsa (optional)
Lime wedges (optional)

1. Preheat oven to 400°F. Lightly coat a 2-quart rectangular baking dish with cooking spray; set aside. In a medium saucepan heat oil over medium-high heat. Add onion and jalapeño; cook about 5 minutes or until onion is tender, stirring occasionally. Stir in pumpkin, 1½ cups of the water, the chili powder, salt, and cumin. Cook and stir until heated through. If necessary, stir in enough of the remaining ¼ cup water to reach desired consistency.

2. Place beans in a large bowl; mash slightly with a fork. Stir in half of the pumpkin mixture, the chicken, and ¼ cup of the cheese.

3. Spoon a generous ⅓ cup of the bean mixture onto each tortilla. Roll up tortillas; place, seam sides down, in the prepared baking dish. Pour the remaining pumpkin mixture over tortilla rolls.

4. Bake, covered, for 15 minutes. Sprinkle with the remaining ¼ cup cheese. Bake, uncovered, about 10 minutes more or until heated through. If desired, serve with pico de gallo and lime wedges. **Makes 4 servings.**

PER SERVING: 357 cal., 8 g fat (3 g sat. fat), 54 mg chol., 465 mg sodium, 44 g carb., 12 g fiber, 28 g pro.

***tip:** To soften tortillas, place tortillas between paper towels. Microwave on 100-percent-power (high) for 30 to 40 seconds.

make it a meal

Roasted beets with goat cheese
Green leaf and radicchio salad
Coconut macaroons

This appealing chicken-and-rice dish is positively packed with veggies—onions, bok choy, celery, carrots, and sweet peppers—and crowned with a crunchy topping of cashews and chow mein noodles.

garlic cashew chicken casserole

PREP: 35 minutes   **BAKE:** 24 minutes at 400°F

Nonstick cooking spray
1   cup reduced-sodium chicken broth
¼   cup hoisin sauce
2   tablespoons grated fresh ginger
4   teaspoons cornstarch
½   teaspoon crushed red pepper
⅛   teaspoon ground black pepper
1   pound skinless, boneless chicken breast halves, cut into 1-inch strips
2   medium onions, cut into thin wedges
2   cups sliced bok choy
1   cup sliced celery (2 stalks)
1   cup sliced carrots (2 medium)
¾   cup chopped green sweet pepper (1 medium)
6   cloves garlic, minced
2   cups cooked brown rice
1   cup chow mein noodles, coarsely broken
½   cup cashews
¼   cup thinly sliced green onions (2)

1. Preheat oven to 400°F. Lightly coat a 2-quart rectangular baking dish with cooking spray. Set aside.

2. For sauce, in a medium bowl whisk together broth, hoisin sauce, ginger, cornstarch, crushed red pepper, and black pepper; set aside.

3. Lightly coat an extra-large skillet with cooking spray; heat over medium-high heat. Add chicken to skillet; cook until lightly browned. Remove from skillet. Add onion wedges, bok choy, celery, carrots, and sweet pepper to the skillet. Cook for 3 to 4 minutes or until vegetables start to soften. Add garlic; cook for 30 seconds more. Stir in the sauce. Cook and stir about 3 minutes or until sauce is thickened and bubbly. Stir in cooked rice and browned chicken.

4. Spoon chicken mixture into the prepared baking dish. Cover and bake about 20 minutes or until casserole is bubbly and chicken is no longer pink (165°F). Sprinkle chow mein noodles and cashews over top. Bake, uncovered, for 4 to 5 minutes more or until noodles and cashews are golden brown. Sprinkle with green onions. **Makes 6 servings.**

PER SERVING: 340 cal., 10 g fat (2 g sat. fat), 49 mg chol., 480 mg sodium, 40 g carb., 4 g fiber, 23 g pro.

make it a meal

Carrot slaw

Sliced mango

Dark chocolate covered almonds

Sweet potatoes boost the nutritional value of the potato topping in this casserole. This version of the English classic features flavors of an American Thanksgiving—turkey, green beans, cranberries, and sage.

shepherd's pie *pictured on page 66*

PREP: 45 minutes   **BAKE:** 25 minutes at 375°F

1½   pounds sweet potatoes, peeled and cut into 2-inch pieces

1½   pounds Yukon gold or other yellow-flesh potatoes, peeled and cut into 2-inch pieces

4   cloves garlic, halved

½   cup milk

½   teaspoon salt

½   cup finely shredded Parmesan cheese (2 ounces)

1½   cups chopped carrots (3 medium)

1   cup chopped onion (1 large)

1   cup chopped red sweet pepper (1 large)

2   tablespoons olive oil

3   cups chopped or shredded cooked turkey or chicken

2   10.75-ounce cans condensed cream of mushroom soup

2   cups frozen cut green beans

½   cup dried cranberries

¼   cup water

3   tablespoons Worcestershire sauce

1   tablespoon snipped fresh sage or 1 teaspoon dried sage, crushed

1   teaspoon dry mustard

½   teaspoon ground black pepper

1. Preheat oven to 375°F. In a 4-quart Dutch oven cook potatoes and garlic, covered, in enough boiling lightly salted water to cover for 20 to 25 minutes or until potatoes are tender; drain. Using a potato masher, a ricer, or an electric mixer on low speed, mash potatoes and garlic. Gradually beat in milk and salt to make potatoes light and fluffy. Stir in Parmesan cheese. Cover and keep warm.

2. Meanwhile, in a large skillet cook carrots, onion, and sweet pepper in hot oil over medium heat until vegetables are tender, stirring occasionally. Stir in turkey, soup, beans, cranberries, the water, Worcestershire sauce, sage, mustard, and black pepper; heat through.

3. Transfer turkey filling to an ungreased 3-quart rectangular baking dish. Pipe or spoon mashed potatoes in 10 to 12 mounds on top of turkey mixture. Bake, uncovered, for 25 to 30 minutes or until heated through. **Makes 10 servings.**

PER SERVING: 335 cal., 10 g fat (3 g sat. fat), 36 mg chol., 719 mg sodium, 43 g carb., 5 g fiber, 19 g pro.

[make it a meal]

Red pear slices with toasted pecans
Spinach salad
Ginger-spice cake

Not all casseroles take hours to prep and bake. These individual casseroles are ready to eat in just 25 minutes, start to finish. The smaller size drastically cuts the baking time.

turkey-vegetable casserole

PREP: 15 minutes   **BAKE:** 10 minutes at 450°F

1   **16-ounce bag frozen stew vegetables (potatoes, carrots, onion, and celery)**

1   **18-ounce jar home-style gravy (1¾ cups)**

1   **teaspoon finely snipped fresh sage or ½ teaspoon ground sage**

2   **cups cooked turkey or chicken, cut into slices**

¼   **teaspoon ground black pepper**

¼   **teaspoon nutmeg**

1   **cooking apple, thinly sliced Fresh sage leaves (optional)**

2   **tablespoons butter, melted**

1. Preheat oven to 450°F. In a large microwave-safe bowl combine vegetables, gravy, and the 1 teaspoon sage. Cover with vented plastic wrap; microwave on 100-percent-power (high) for 5 minutes. Add turkey; cover and microwave 4 to 6 minutes more or until stew is heated through and vegetables are tender, stirring occasionally. In a small bowl combine pepper and nutmeg.

2. Spoon stew into four 14- to 16-ounce casseroles. Top with apple and, if desired, fresh sage. Drizzle with melted butter and sprinkle with nutmeg mixture. Bake uncovered, for 10 minutes or until bubbly and apple slices begin to brown. **Makes 4 servings.**

PER SERVING: 297 cal., 12 g fat (5 g sat. fat), 71 mg chol., 753 mg sodium, 23 g carb., 3 g fiber, 24 g pro.

[make it a meal

Quinoa pilaf
Mixed greens salad
Vanilla bean frozen yogurt with berries]

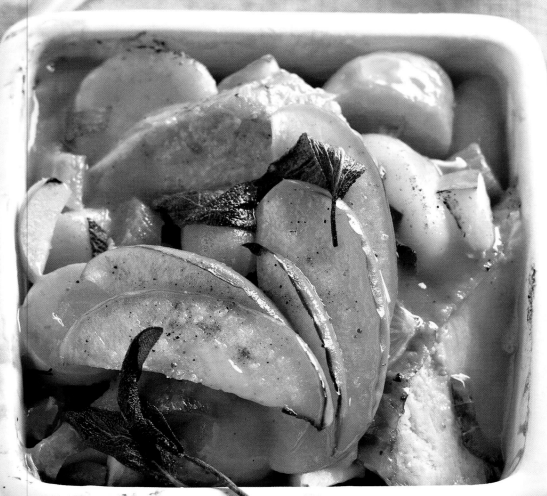

The rich, nutty flavor and chewy texture of barley is satisfying on many fronts—and barley is high in fiber, too. High-fiber foods help you stay feeling full, which means you'll likely eat fewer calories in a day.

italian barley and sausage casserole

PREP: 45 minutes   **BAKE:** 40 minutes at 350°F

Nonstick cooking spray
4   ounces uncooked bulk turkey Italian sausage or smoked turkey Italian sausage link, halved lengthwise and thinly sliced crosswise
3   cups sliced fresh button mushrooms (8 ounces)
½   cup chopped onion (1 medium)
2   cloves garlic, minced
2   cups cooked barley*
1½   cups no-salt-added tomato pasta sauce
1½   cups shredded part-skim mozzarella cheese (6 ounces)
½   cup bottled roasted red sweet pepper, chopped
¼   cup pitted green olives, chopped
2   tablespoons snipped fresh basil
½   cup red and/or yellow grape or cherry tomatoes, halved

1. Preheat oven to 350°F. Coat four 12- to 14-ounce individual casseroles with cooking spray; set aside. Coat a large nonstick skillet with cooking spray; heat skillet over medium heat. Add sausage, mushrooms, onion, and garlic. Cook for 8 to 10 minutes or until bulk sausage (if using) is no longer pink and vegetables are tender, using a wooden spoon to break up bulk sausage as it cooks. Drain off fat.

2. Stir barley, pasta sauce, 1 cup of the cheese, the roasted pepper, olives, and 1 tablespoon of the basil into sausage mixture. Divide filling among the prepared casseroles. Cover with foil.

3. Bake for 30 minutes. Sprinkle with the remaining ½ cup cheese. Bake, uncovered, about 10 minutes more or until heated through and cheese is melted. Top casseroles with tomatoes and remaining basil. **Makes 4 servings.**

PER SERVING: 346 cal., 13 g fat (6 g sat. fat), 42 mg chol., 704 mg sodium, 40 g carb., 7 g fiber, 20 g pro.

*tip: For 2 cups cooked quick-cooking barley, in a medium saucepan bring 1⅓ cups water to boiling; stir in ¾ cup quick-cooking barley. Return to boiling; reduce heat. Simmer, covered, for 10 to 12 minutes or until barley is tender; drain.

[make it a meal

Sauteed broccoli
Bananas Foster Mini Pies, recipe page 280
Decaf flavored coffee or tea
]

Meaty chunks of roasted eggplant add heft to this Mediterranean-style melange infused with the flavors of Greece, including lemon, garlic, oregano, olives, and feta cheese.

greek tuna casserole

PREP: 20 minutes   **ROAST:** 15 minutes at 425°F   **BAKE:** 40 minutes at 350°F

Nonstick cooking spray
⅓ cup dried whole wheat orzo pasta
1 medium eggplant, ends trimmed, cut into 1-inch-thick slices
1 large red sweet pepper, stemmed, quartered, and seeded
2 tablespoons olive oil
1½ teaspoons finely shredded lemon peel
2 tablespoons lemon juice
1 clove garlic, minced
4 tablespoons snipped fresh oregano
½ teaspoon salt
¼ teaspoon ground black pepper
½ cup panko bread crumbs
3 5-ounce cans very-low-sodium tuna (water pack), undrained, large pieces broken up
1 9-ounce package frozen artichoke hearts, thawed and quartered
½ cup ripe olives, halved
¼ cup crumbled feta cheese (1 ounce)
Lemon wedges

1. Preheat oven to 425°F. Coat a 1½-quart gratin dish with cooking spray; set aside. Cook pasta according to package directions. Drain and set aside.

2. Line a 15×10×1-inch baking pan with foil. Lightly coat both sides of each eggplant slice with cooking spray. Place coated eggplant slices in the baking pan; add sweet pepper. Roast, uncovered, for 15 to 20 minutes or until eggplant begins to brown and peppers are just tender. Remove from oven. When cool, cut into ¾-inch cubes. Reduce oven temperature to 350°F.

3. For lemon dressing, in a small bowl whisk together olive oil, 1 teaspoon of the lemon peel, the lemon juice, and garlic. Whisk in 3 tablespoons of the oregano, the salt, and black pepper; set aside. In another small bowl stir together panko, the remaining 1 tablespoon oregano, and the remaining ½ teaspoon lemon peel; set aside.

4. In a large bowl combine cooked orzo, eggplant, sweet pepper, tuna, artichoke hearts, olives, and feta cheese. Stir in the lemon dressing. Spoon into baking dish. Cover with foil. Bake for 35 to 40 minutes or until heated through. Sprinkle panko on top. Bake, uncovered, for 5 to 8 minutes more or until golden brown. Serve with lemon wedges. **Makes 6 servings.**

PER SERVING: 239 cal., 8 g fat (2 g sat. fat), 37 mg chol., 436 mg sodium, 24 g carb., 9 g fiber, 20 g pro.

make it a meal

Cucumbers sprinkled with feta
Salted Caramel Pistachio-Apricot
Baklava, recipe page 279

cook smart *Bulk up a small portion of pasta by adding generous portions of cooked veggies—then top with sauce.*

It doesn't look or taste skinny, but this luxurious mac and cheese most certainly is. A combination of reduced-fat cheeses, fat-free milk, and vegetables for bulk all contribute to the guilt-free factor.

lobster mac and cheese casserole

PREP: 35 minutes   **BAKE:** 15 minutes at 375°F

1½ cups dried whole wheat rigatoni or rotini (6 ounces)
1 large lobster tail (8 to 10 ounces)
2 cups small broccoli florets
   Nonstick cooking spray
¾ cup chopped red sweet pepper (1 medium)
⅓ cup chopped onion (1 small)
1 6.5-ounce container light semisoft cheese with garlic and herb
2 cups fat-free milk
1 tablespoon all-purpose flour
1 cup shredded reduced-fat Italian-style cheese blend (4 ounces)
½ teaspoon finely shredded lemon peel
¼ teaspoon ground black pepper
⅓ cup whole wheat or regular panko bread crumbs

1. Preheat oven to 375°F. In a 4-quart Dutch oven cook pasta according to package directions, adding the lobster tail for the last 7 minutes of cooking and adding the broccoli for the last 3 minutes of cooking. Drain and set aside. When lobster tail is cool enough to handle, remove the lobster meat from shell and coarsely chop the meat; discard shell.

2. Meanwhile, coat a large nonstick skillet with cooking spray; heat skillet over medium heat. Add sweet pepper and onion to skillet. Cook about 5 minutes or until tender, stirring frequently. Remove skillet from heat. Stir in semisoft cheese until melted.

3. In a medium bowl whisk together milk and flour until smooth. Add all at once to sweet pepper mixture in skillet. Cook and stir over medium heat until thickened and bubbly. Reduce heat to low. Stir in Italian-style cheese blend until melted. Stir in cooked pasta, broccoli, chopped lobster, lemon peel, and black pepper.

4. Transfer mixture to a 2-quart casserole. Sprinkle with panko. Bake for 15 to 20 minutes or until heated through and top is golden brown. **Makes 6 servings.**

PER SERVING: 322 cal., 10 g fat (6 g sat. fat), 68 mg chol., 402 mg sodium, 35 g carb., 4 g fiber, 25 g pro.

make it a meal

Arugula salad
Sliced strawberries sprinkled with minced crystallized ginger

To safely quick-thaw shrimp, place them in a bowl of cold water in the sink. Let a small trickle of cold water run into the bowl while the overflow goes down the drain. They'll be thawed in about 15 minutes.

spicy shrimp casserole

PREP: 20 minutes   **BAKE:** 52 minutes at 350°F   **STAND:** 10 minutes

6   6-inch corn tortillas, cut into bite-size strips
1   cup bottled green salsa
1   cup shredded reduced-fat Monterey Jack cheese (4 ounces)
½   cup light sour cream
3   tablespoons flour
¼   cup snipped fresh cilantro
1   12-ounce package frozen cooked, peeled, and deveined shrimp, thawed
1   cup frozen yellow and white whole kernel corn
1   medium tomato, coarsely chopped
¼   cup light sour cream (optional)

1. Preheat oven to 350°F. Lightly grease a 2-quart baking dish. Place half of the tortilla strips in the bottom of the prepared dish; set aside. Arrange remaining tortilla strips on a baking sheet; bake for 12 to 14 minutes or until crisp.

2. Meanwhile, in a large bowl stir together salsa, cheese, the ½ cup sour cream, the flour, and 2 tablespoons of the cilantro. Stir in shrimp and corn. Spoon shrimp mixture over tortilla strips in baking dish.

3. Bake, uncovered, for 40 to 45 minutes or until heated through. Let stand for 10 minutes before serving. Sprinkle with baked tortilla strips, tomato, and the remaining 2 tablespoons cilantro. If desired, serve with the ¼ cup sour cream. **Makes 6 servings.**

PER SERVING: 242 cal., 8 g fat (4 g sat. fat), 129 mg chol., 564 mg sodium, 25 g carb., 3 g fiber, 20 g pro.

make it a meal

Black bean salsa with baked chips
Asparagus with lemon
Sparkling water with fresh berries

If you're out of buttermilk, it's easy to make a sour milk substitute: Place 2 tablespoons vinegar or lemon juice in a glass measuring cup. Add enough milk to make 2 cups total liquid and let stand for 5 minutes.

chilaquile casserole

PREP: 20 minutes **BAKE:** 35 minutes at 375°F **STAND:** 15 minutes

1	tablespoon vegetable oil
1	cup chopped onion (1 large)
2	cloves garlic, minced
	Nonstick cooking spray
12	6-inch corn tortillas, cut into 1-inch pieces
1¾	cups shredded reduced-fat Monterey Jack cheese (6 ounces)
2	4-ounce cans diced green chile peppers, undrained
4	eggs, lightly beaten
2	cups low-fat buttermilk or sour milk
½	teaspoon salt
¼	teaspoon ground black pepper
⅛	teaspoon ground cumin
⅛	teaspoon dried oregano, crushed
	Salsa (optional)

1. Preheat oven to 375°F. In a large skillet heat oil over medium heat. Add onion and garlic; cook until onion is tender.

2. Spray a 2-quart rectangular baking dish with cooking spray. Spread half the tortilla pieces in the baking dish. Top with half the cheese and one can of chile peppers. Sprinkle with onion mixture. Top with remaining tortilla pieces, cheese, and chile peppers.

3. In a large bowl combine eggs, buttermilk, salt, black pepper, cumin, and oregano. Pour evenly over ingredients in baking dish.

4. Bake for 35 to 40 minutes or until center is set and edges are browned. Let stand for 15 minutes before serving. If desired, serve with salsa. **Makes 8 servings.**

PER SERVING: 269 cal., 14 g fat (6 g sat. fat), 125 mg chol., 532 mg sodium, 23 g carb., 3 g fiber, 14 g pro.

make it a meal

Spinach-mixed greens salad with
light Caesar dressing
Lemon sorbet

The more you use a cast-iron skillet (and properly care for it), the more nonstick its cooking surface gets. A well-seasoned cast-iron skillet cooks very evenly and requires the use of very little oil for frying.

cajun shrimp and corn bread casserole

PREP: 35 minutes   **BAKE:** 12 minutes at 400°F

1 pound fresh or frozen large shrimp in shells
1 teaspoon salt-free Cajun seasoning
1½ cups coarsely chopped green and/or red sweet peppers (2 medium)
½ cup sliced celery (2 stalks)
½ cup chopped onion (1 medium)
1 tablespoon canola oil
2 cloves garlic, minced
1 15-ounce can no-salt-added black-eyed peas, rinsed and drained
1 14.5-ounce can no-salt-added stewed tomatoes, undrained and cut up
1 recipe Corn Bread Dumplings
Snipped fresh parsley (optional)

1. Thaw shrimp, if frozen. Preheat oven to 400°F. Peel and devein shrimp, leaving tails intact, if desired. Rinse shrimp; pat dry with paper towels. In a large bowl combine shrimp and ½ teaspoon of the Cajun seasoning; toss gently to coat. Set aside.

2. In a large cast-iron skillet or oven-going skillet cook sweet peppers, celery, and onion in hot oil over medium-high heat for 5 to 7 minutes or until vegetables are tender, stirring frequently. Add shrimp and garlic. Cook and stir for 2 minutes.

3. Stir in black-eyed peas, tomatoes, and the remaining ½ teaspoon Cajun seasoning. Bring to boiling. Drop Corn Bread Dumplings into six mounds on top of shrimp mixture.

4. Bake, uncovered, for 12 to 15 minutes or until a wooden toothpick inserted in centers of dumplings comes out clean. If desired, sprinkle with parsley. **Makes 6 servings.**

PER SERVING: 311 cal., 9 g fat (1 g sat. fat), 137 mg chol., 340 mg sodium, 37 g carb., 5 g fiber, 21 g pro.

corn bread dumplings: In a medium bowl stir together ¾ cup flour, ⅓ cup cornmeal, 1 tablespoon sugar, 1½ teaspoons baking powder, and ¼ teaspoon salt; set aside. In a small bowl combine 1 lightly beaten egg, ⅓ cup fat-free milk, and 2 tablespoons oil. Add egg mixture all at once to flour mixture. Stir just until combined.

[**make it a meal**

Cajun-spiced broccoli
Fresh peaches with minced basil
Raspberry iced tea]

cook smart *When cooking at home, note the number of servings in a recipe so you can make a mental picture of a proper portion size.*

"Eat more kale" has become a mantra of the health-conscious. A cup of chopped kale has just 33 calories, and packs a powerful punch of potential cancer-fighting and anti-aging antioxidants.

vegetable-loaded pasta bake

PREP: 40 minutes   **BAKE:** 40 minutes at 350°F

8	ounces dried whole wheat penne pasta (2¾ cups)
2½	cups cauliflower florets (½ of a medium head)
½	cup chopped onion (1 medium)
2	cloves garlic, minced
1	tablespoon olive oil
1	cup sliced carrots (2 medium)
½	cup chopped celery (1 stalk)
12	ounces fresh kale, stems removed, leaves torn (12 cups)
½	cup frozen peas
½	cup frozen whole kernel corn
2	tablespoons butter
2	tablespoons all-purpose flour
¼	teaspoon salt
¼	teaspoon ground black pepper
1	cup fat-free milk
1	cup shredded extra-sharp cheddar cheese (4 ounces)
2	tablespoons finely shredded or grated Parmesan cheese

1. Preheat oven to 350°F. In a large Dutch oven cook pasta according to package directions, except add cauliflower for the last 4 minutes of cooking. Drain and rinse. Set aside.

2. In the same Dutch oven cook onion and garlic in hot oil over medium heat for 2 minutes. Add carrots and celery; cook just until carrots are tender. Add kale; cook just until wilted. Stir in pasta mixture, peas, and corn.

3. For cheese sauce, in a small saucepan melt butter; stir in flour, salt, and pepper. Add milk all at once; cook and stir until thickened and bubbly. Reduce heat; add cheddar cheese. Cook and stir until melted. Stir sauce into pasta and vegetables. Transfer to a 2½-quart casserole. Bake, covered, for 35 minutes. Sprinkle with Parmesan. Bake, uncovered, for 5 minutes more. **Makes 6 servings.**

PER SERVING: 365 cal., 14 g fat (7 g sat. fat), 32 mg chol., 355 mg sodium, 47 g carb., 4 g fiber, 15 g pro.

make it a meal

Almonds and dried cherries
Minced herb bruschetta
Sparkling lemon water

Lasagna doesn't have to be off the list when you're trying to lose or maintain weight. This lovely layered casserole is constructed with whole grain noodles, low-fat cheese, light Alfredo, and lots of vegetables.

spinach alfredo lasagna

PREP: 25 minutes **BAKE:** 1 hour 15 minutes at 350°F **STAND:** 20 minutes

Nonstick cooking spray
1 egg, lightly beaten
1 15-ounce carton part-skim ricotta cheese
1 10-ounce package frozen chopped spinach, thawed and well drained
4 cloves garlic, minced
¼ teaspoon freshly ground black pepper
1 15-ounce jar light Alfredo sauce
½ cup fat-free milk
6 whole grain lasagna noodles
2 cups shredded carrots (4 medium)
2 cups sliced fresh mushrooms
½ cup shredded part-skim mozzarella cheese (2 ounces)
¼ cup finely shredded Parmesan cheese (1 ounce)

1. Preheat oven to 350°F. Lightly coat a 2-quart rectangular baking dish with cooking spray.

2. In a medium bowl stir together egg, ricotta cheese, spinach, garlic, and pepper. In a separate bowl combine Alfredo sauce and milk.

3. Spread about ½ cup of the Alfredo sauce mixture into the bottom of the prepared baking dish. Arrange three of the uncooked noodles in a layer over the sauce. Spread half of the spinach mixture over the noodles; top with half of the carrots and half of the mushrooms. Arrange the remaining three uncooked noodles over the vegetables. Top noodles with the remaining spinach mixture. Top with the remaining carrots and the remaining mushrooms. Cover with the remaining Alfredo sauce mixture. Sprinkle with the mozzarella cheese and Parmesan cheese.

4. Lightly coat a sheet of foil with cooking spray. Cover dish with foil, coated side down.

5. Bake for 60 to 70 minutes. Uncover. Bake for 15 to 20 minutes more or until top is lightly browned. Let stand for 20 minutes before serving. **Makes 8 servings.**

PER SERVING: 262 cal., 12 g fat (7 g sat. fat), 69 mg chol., 527 mg sodium, 24 g carb., 4 g fiber, 16 g pro.

[make it a meal

Melon with honey and mint
Upside-down cake]

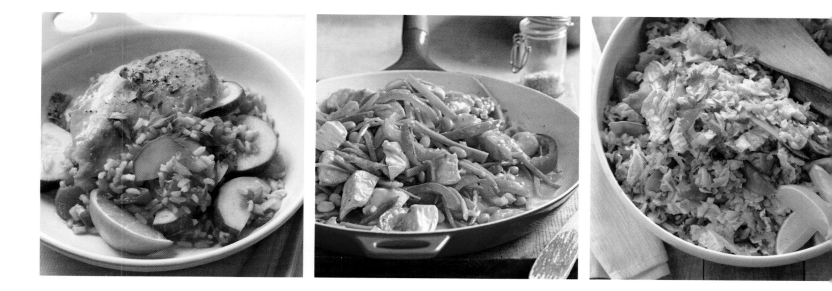

skillets
& stir-fries

These flash-in-the pan entrées are packed with lean proteins, legumes, fresh vegetables and grains.

Even small shifts in ingredient choices can make a big difference in flavor when you can't rely on fat for it. Fire-roasted tomatoes, for instance, are fat-free but add a nice, smoky flavor to dishes such as this one.

hungarian-style pork paprikash

PREP: 15 minutes   **COOK:** 15 minutes

- 2 tablespoons all-purpose flour
- 1 tablespoon paprika
- ¼ teaspoon ground black pepper
- ¼ teaspoon cayenne pepper
- 1 pound natural pork tenderloin, trimmed and cut into 1-inch cubes
- 1 tablespoon olive oil
- 2 medium carrots
- 2 14.5-ounce cans fire-roasted diced tomatoes, undrained
- 1 8-ounce can no-salt-added tomato sauce
- 1 medium yellow pepper, cut into thin strips (1 cup)
- 8 ounces dried whole grain fettuccine
- ¼ cup light sour cream or plain Greek fat-free yogurt
  Snipped fresh Italian parsley (optional)

1. In a resealable plastic bag combine flour, paprika, black pepper, and cayenne pepper. Add the pork; seal bag. Toss to coat pork with flour mixture. In a large skillet heat oil over medium-high heat. Add pork; cook about 5 minutes or until browned on all sides.

2. Cut carrots in half crosswise. Cut each piece, lengthwise into quarters, making a total of 16 carrot sticks. Add carrots, undrained tomatoes, tomato sauce, and yellow pepper to skillet; stir to combine. Bring to boiling; reduce heat. Cover and simmer for 10 minutes, stirring occasionally.

3. Meanwhile, cook pasta according to package directions; drain. Add pasta to pork mixture in skillet; toss to combine. Top each serving with sour cream, and, if desired, sprinkle with parsley. **Makes 6 servings.**

PER SERVING: 315 cal., 6 g fat (1 g sat. fat), 52 mg chol., 379 mg sodium, 44 g carb., 8 g fiber, 23 g pro.

[
make it a meal
Sauteed Cabbage with Bacon, recipe page 260
Cucumber-shallot-dill salad
Mini poppy seed cookies
]

cook smart *For healthy eating white is often not the best choice. Make your rice brown, your potatoes orange, and your breads and pasta whole grain.*

Use a cooking apple that will keep its shape when exposed to heat. A good choice for this dish is the sturdy Granny Smith, which also has a pleasing tart flavor that works well in savory dishes.

apple pork stir-fry

START TO FINISH: 25 minutes

2	tablespoons unsweetened apple juice
1½	tablespoons apple jelly
2	teaspoons reduced-sodium soy sauce
2	teaspoons reduced-sodium teriyaki sauce
⅛	to ¼ teaspoon crushed red pepper Nonstick cooking spray
½	cup red sweet pepper cut into bite-size strips
¼	cup sliced onion
¼	cup sliced celery
¼	cup matchstick-size apple strips
2	tablespoons canned sliced water chestnuts, drained
2	tablespoons shredded carrot
1	teaspoon grated fresh ginger
1	clove garlic, minced
2	teaspoons sesame oil
6	ounces boneless pork top loin chops, cut into thin bite-size strips
⅔	cup hot cooked brown rice

1. For the sauce, in a small bowl combine apple juice, apple jelly, soy sauce, teriyaki sauce, and crushed red pepper; set aside.

2. Meanwhile, coat an unheated large nonstick skillet or wok with cooking spray. Preheat over medium-high heat. Add sweet pepper, onion, and celery to hot skillet. Cover and cook for 3 minutes, stirring occasionally. Add apple, water chestnuts, carrot, ginger, and garlic; cover and cook for 3 to 4 minutes more or until vegetables and apple are crisp-tender, stirring occasionally. Remove vegetables from skillet.

3. Add sesame oil to the same skillet. Add pork strips. Cook and stir over medium-high heat for 2 to 3 minutes or until cooked through. Return vegetables to skillet along with sauce. Cook and stir for 1 to 2 minutes or until heated through. Serve stir-fry with hot cooked rice. **Makes 2 servings.**

PER SERVING: 294 cal., 7 g fat (1 g sat. fat), 35 mg chol., 498 mg sodium, 39 g carb., 4 g fiber, 20 g pro.

make it a meal

Radishes with creamy fat-free ricotta
Brothy mushroom soup
Skillet-wilted savoy cabbage with cumin

Mustard such as the brown mustard used in this dish is a terrific ingredient in healthful cooking because it adds so much flavor with no dietary repercussions. A tablespoon contains just 15 calories.

irish stout beef and cabbage stir-fry

START TO FINISH: 18 minutes

12	ounces extra-stout beer
2	to 3 tablespoons honey
2	tablespoons tomato paste
1	tablespoon brown mustard
1	teaspoon caraway seeds, crushed
½	teaspoon salt
½	teaspoon cracked black pepper
8	1-inch wedges cabbage
1	cup peeled baby carrots, cut in ½-inch chunks
2	tablespoons water
2	tablespoons olive oil
1	pound beef top sirloin steak, cut into ¾-inch-thick slices
1	small onion, halved and thinly sliced
2	tablespoons water
1	tablespoon all-purpose flour Snipped fresh parsley (optional)

1. In a medium bowl whisk together beer, honey, tomato paste, mustard, caraway seeds, salt, and pepper; set aside.

2. Place cabbage and carrots in a 2-quart baking dish; add 2 tablespoons water. Microwave, covered, on 100-percent-power (high) for 8 to 10 minutes or until crisp-tender, stirring once. Set aside; keep warm.

3. Meanwhile, in a very large nonstick skillet heat olive oil over medium-high heat. Add beef. Cook, stirring frequently, 3 to 4 minutes or until just slightly pink in the center. Remove beef from skillet; keep warm.

4. Add onion to skillet. Cook, stirring occasionally, for 4 to 5 minutes or until tender. Pour beer mixture into skillet. In a small bowl stir together 2 tablespoons water and flour; stir into onion and beer mixture. Return beef to skillet; cook and stir 3 minutes or until bubbling.

5. Serve beef mixture with cabbage wedges and carrots. Sprinkle with parsley, if desired. **Makes 4 servings.**

PER SERVING: 365 cal., 12 g fat (3 g sat. fat), 68 mg chol., 532 mg sodium, 30 g carb., 6 g fiber, 29 g pro.

[## make it a meal

Mixed greens with balsamic vinaigrette
Crusty bread
Apple-Date Cake, recipe page 270]

cook smart *Lean red meat is a rich source of many important nutrients, including protein, vitamin B12, iron, and zinc just to name a few.*

Beans add bulk.. Adding beans to a meat dish means you can get by with using less meat—and still feel completely satisfied when you leave the dinner table. That's a savings in both calories and dollars.

fusilli with beef and beans

PREP: 15 minutes   **COOK:** 20 minutes

1	cup chopped onion (1 large)
1	tablespoon olive oil
2	cloves garlic, minced
1¼	pounds boneless beef sirloin steak, trimmed and cut into bite-size strips
2	to 3 teaspoons chili powder
1½	teaspoons dried Italian seasoning, crushed
½	teaspoon ground black pepper
1	14.5-ounce can 50% less sodium beef broth
1	14.5-ounce can no-salt-added diced tomatoes
1	8-ounce can no-salt-added tomato sauce
½	teaspoon salt
6	ounces dried multigrain fusilli or rotini pasta
1	15.5-ounce can red kidney beans, rinsed and drained
10	ounces frozen corn, thawed
	Shredded reduced-fat sharp cheddar cheese (optional)
	Snipped fresh Italian parsley (optional)

1. In a large skillet cook onion in hot oil over medium-high heat for 3 minutes. Add garlic; cook and stir for 1 minute. Add beef, chili powder, Italian seasoning, and pepper. Cook for 3 to 4 minutes or until beef is browned.

2. Stir in broth, undrained tomatoes, tomato sauce, and salt. Bring to boiling. Stir in pasta; reduce heat. Simmer, uncovered, about 10 minutes or until pasta is just tender, stirring frequently. Stir in beans and corn. Cover and simmer for 3 to 4 minutes or until heated through. If desired, sprinkle each serving with cheddar cheese and/or parsley. **Makes 6 servings.**

PER SERVING: 399 cal., 9 g fat (2 g sat. fat), 63 mg chol., 629 mg sodium, 50 g carb., 10 g fiber, 33 g pro.

[**make it a meal**

Wilted escarole with light Parmesan dressing
Orange-fennel salad
Dark chocolate mini squares]

Classic chili mac never goes out of style. This version is homey and lean—and most of the ingredients are in your pantry or refrigerator most of the time, making it a great last-minute meal.

chili-pasta skillet

PREP: 20 minutes   **COOK:** 20 minutes

1	pound lean ground beef
¾	cup chopped onion
1	15- to 15.5-ounce can red kidney beans, black beans, or red beans, rinsed and drained
1	14.5-ounce can diced tomatoes, undrained
1	8-ounce can tomato sauce
½	cup dried elbow macaroni
1	4-ounce can diced green chile peppers, drained
2	to 3 teaspoons chili powder
½	teaspoon garlic salt
½	cup shredded Monterey Jack or cheddar cheese (2 ounces)

1. In a large skillet cook meat and onion until meat is brown and onion is tender, using a wooden spoon to break up meat as it cooks. Drain off fat.

2. Stir beans, tomatoes, tomato sauce, macaroni, chile peppers, chili powder, and garlic salt into meat mixture in skillet. Bring to boiling; reduce heat. Simmer, covered, about 20 minutes or until macaroni is tender, stirring often. Top each serving with some of the cheese. **Makes 6 servings.**

PER SERVING: 289 cal., 11 g fat (5 g sat. fat), 56 mg chol., 622 mg sodium, 27 g carb., 5 g fiber, 23 g pro.

[make it a meal

Bibb lettuce with fresh avocado and onions
Fresh corn salad with basil and tomatoes
Brownie bites]

Mangoes are the world's most popular fruit. They're available year-round and each cup is rich in vitamin A, folate, vitamin C, and a good source of fiber.

mango-chicken stir-fry

START TO FINISH: 30 minutes

1	cup orange juice
8	teaspoons reduced-sodium soy sauce
4	cloves garlic, minced
1	teaspoon Chinese five-spice powder
½	teaspoon crushed red pepper
12	ounces skinless, boneless chicken breast cut into bite-size pieces
8	teaspoons cornstarch
7	teaspoons vegetable oil
3	cups pre-cut fresh stir-fry vegetables
2	cups cubed fresh or bottled mango
1⅓	cups hot cooked brown rice
8	teaspoons cashews

1. For sauce, in a small bowl combine orange juice, soy sauce, garlic, five-spice powder, and crushed red pepper; set aside.

2. In a small bowl toss together chicken and cornstarch. In a large nonstick skillet heat oil over medium-high heat. Add chicken; cook and stir for 4 minutes. Add stir-fry vegetables; cook and stir for 1 minute. Add sauce. Cook and stir about 2 minutes or until thickened. Stir in mango. Serve stir-fry over rice and sprinkle with cashews. **Makes 4 servings.**

PER SERVING: 423 cal., 14 g fat (2 g sat. fat), 54 mg chol., 550 mg sodium, 48 g carb., 5 g fiber, 25 g pro.

[make it a meal]

Roasted almonds with rosemary and thyme
Skillet-roasted baby bok choy
Upside-Down Pineapple-Ginger Carrot
Cake, recipe page 271

Fatah ("crushed" or "crumbs" in Arabic) was originally developed as a way to use up stale flatbread but in parts of the Middle East has come to include couscous or rice as well.

lamb fatah with asparagus

PREP: 10 minutes   **COOK:** 15 minutes

1	tablespoon olive oil
1	medium onion, halved and sliced
4	cloves garlic, minced
12	ounces boneless lamb leg or beef sirloin steak, trimmed and cut into 2×½-inch pieces
1	14.5-ounce can 50% less sodium beef broth
1	cup whole wheat Israeli couscous
½	teaspoon dried oregano, crushed
½	teaspoon ground cumin
¼	teaspoon salt
¼	teaspoon ground black pepper
1	pound thin asparagus spears, bias-sliced into 2-inch pieces
¾	cup chopped red sweet pepper (1 medium)
	Snipped fresh oregano
	Lemon wedges

1. In a large skillet heat oil over medium-high heat. Add onion; cook and stir for 3 minutes. Add garlic; cook and stir for 1 minute. Add lamb; cook for 3 to 5 minutes or until brown on all sides.

2. Stir in broth, couscous, oregano, cumin, salt, and black pepper. Bring to boiling; reduce heat. Cover and simmer for 10 minutes, stirring occasionally.

3. Stir in asparagus and sweet pepper. Cover and simmer for 3 to 5 minutes more or until vegetables are crisp-tender. Fluff lamb mixture lightly with a fork. Sprinkle with oregano and serve with lemon wedges. **Makes 4 servings.**

PER SERVING: 334 cal., 9 g fat (3 g sat. fat), 54 mg chol., 390 mg sodium, 39 g carb., 6 g fiber, 26 g pro.

make it a meal

Mustard green chips
Brothy tomato-basil soup
Gingered Pears, recipe page 289

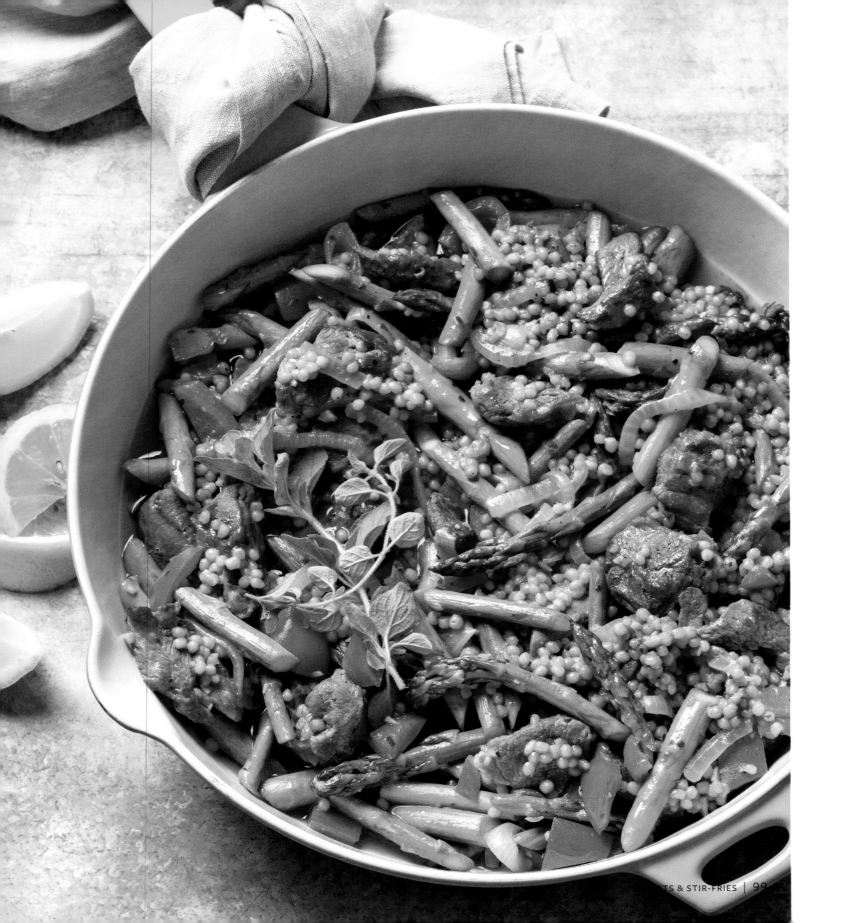

An extra-large skillet—nonstick or not—is a very good investment if you like to make a lot of healthful one-dish meals such as this light and fresh Italian-style dish.

basil-tomato chicken skillet

START TO FINISH: 25 minutes

1 **pound skinless, boneless chicken breast halves, cut into bite-size pieces**
2 **cloves garlic, minced**
1 **tablespoon olive oil**
½ **teaspoon salt**
¼ **teaspoon ground black pepper**
1 **cup quartered fresh mushrooms**
½ **cup chopped onion (1 medium)**
4 **cups fresh spinach**
¼ **cup snipped fresh basil**
3 **cups red and/or yellow cherry tomatoes, halved**
2 **tablespoons finely shredded Parmesan cheese**

1. In an extra-large skillet cook and stir chicken and garlic in hot oil over medium-high heat for 4 to 5 minutes or until chicken is no longer pink. Sprinkle with salt and pepper. Remove from skillet; keep warm.

2. Add mushrooms and onion to hot skillet. Cook for 3 to 5 minutes or until mushrooms and onion are tender and lightly browned, stirring occasionally.

3. Return chicken to skillet; heat through. Add spinach and basil to skillet; toss gently until spinach is wilted. Stir in tomatoes; cook about 2 minutes or until slightly softened and heated through. Top each serving with some of the cheese. **Makes 4 servings.**

PER SERVING: 212 cal., 6 g fat (1 g sat. fat), 68 mg chol., 425 mg sodium, 10 g carb., 3 g fiber, 30 g pro.

make it a meal

Pesto, radish, sea salt on gluten-free crostini
Asparagus and Wild Mushrooms, recipe page 242
Whole wheat orzo

Low carb, high protein quinoa stands in for rice in this Asian-inspired stir fry. If you're in a bit of a hurry, look for the packages of julienne carrots in the produce section in place of cutting your own.

orange-ginger chicken stir-fry

START TO FINISH: 45 minutes

3 tablespoons olive oil
1 pound carrots, cut into thin strips
1 medium red sweet pepper, seeded and cut into thin bite-size strips
1 pound skinless, boneless chicken breast halves, cut into 1-inch pieces
1 cup frozen shelled edamame (sweet soybeans), thawed
1 tablespoon grated fresh ginger
3 cloves garlic, minced
½ teaspoon crushed red pepper (optional)
1½ cups reduced-sodium chicken broth
¼ cup frozen orange juice concentrate, thawed
2 tablespoons reduced-sodium soy sauce
2 tablespoons cornstarch
2 tablespoons water
3 cups hot cooked quinoa
1 tablespoon sesame seeds, toasted (see tip, page 64)

1. In a large skillet heat 1 tablespoon of the oil over medium heat. Add carrots; cook and stir for 5 minutes. Add sweet pepper; cook and stir about 3 minutes more or until carrots are tender. Transfer to a medium bowl. In the same skillet heat 1 tablespoon of the oil over medium-high heat. Add chicken; cook and stir for 4 to 5 minutes or until chicken is no longer pink. Transfer to the bowl with carrot mixture. Stir in edamame.

2. In the same skillet heat the remaining 1 tablespoon oil over medium heat. Add ginger, garlic, and, if desired, crushed red pepper; cook and stir for 30 seconds. Stir in broth, orange juice concentrate, and soy sauce. Bring to boiling.

3. In a small bowl combine cornstarch and the water; stir into broth mixture. Simmer, uncovered, for 2 minutes. Stir in chicken mixture. Cook and stir until heated through.

4. Serve chicken mixture over quinoa. Sprinkle with sesame seeds.
Makes 6 servings.

PER SERVING: 373 cal., 13 g fat (2 g sat. fat), 48 mg chol., 481 mg sodium, 39 g carb., 7 g fiber, 26 g pro.

make it a meal
Vegetable spring rolls
Snow pea-radish-green onion salad
Almond-Tangerine Panna Cotta, recipe page 290

cook smart *Fiber is only one of the nutritional perks found in whole grains which have abundant quantities of vitamins and minerals, as well as antioxidants.*

If you're having a hard time finding 4- to 5-ounce boneless, skinless chicken breasts, buy two 8- to 10-ounce breasts and cut them in half.

mexican chicken and rice

PREP: 25 minutes   **COOK:** 25 minutes

4 skinless, boneless chicken breast halves (1 to 1¼ pounds total)
½ teaspoon salt
¾ teaspoon ground black pepper
2 teaspoons olive oil
½ cup chopped onion (1 medium)
2 cloves garlic, minced
¼ cup reduced-sodium chicken broth
1 14.5-ounce can no-salt-added diced tomatoes
3 to 4 tablespoons finely chopped fresh jalapeño pepper (see tip, page 62)
2 teaspoons lime juice
1 medium zucchini, halved lengthwise and sliced ½ inch thick (2 cups)
2 8.8-ounce packages cooked whole grain brown rice
¼ cup snipped fresh cilantro
   Lime wedges

1. Sprinkle chicken breast halves with ¼ teaspoon of the salt and ¼ teaspoon of the pepper. In a large nonstick skillet heat 1 teaspoon of the oil over medium-high heat. Brown chicken breasts in hot oil for 5 minutes, turning once.

2. Add the remaining 1 teaspoon oil to the skillet. Add the onion and garlic; cook and stir for 2 minutes. Stir in broth, undrained tomatoes, jalapeño, lime juice, the remaining ½ teaspoon pepper, and the remaining ¼ teaspoon salt. Bring to boiling; reduce heat. Cover and simmer for 10 minutes. Stir in zucchini. Cover and simmer for 3 to 4 minutes more or until zucchini is crisp-tender and chicken is no longer pink (170°F). Stir in rice, heat through. Sprinkle each serving with cilantro and serve with lime wedges. **Makes 4 servings.**

PER SERVING: 414 cal., 8 g fat (1 g sat. fat), 73 mg chol., 518 mg sodium, 47 g carb., 5 g fiber, 31 g pro.

make it a meal

Summer Corn and Tomatoes, recipe page 258
Green and red leaf salad
Sectioned and chopped grapefruit with mint

Chile bean sauce is a salty brown sauce made from fermented soybeans, similar to miso. If you can't find it at your supermarket, look for it at an Asian market (where you will also find the banh pho noodles).

chicken-peanut stir-fry

PREP: 30 minutes **COOK:** 10 minutes

4 ounces banh pho (Vietnamese wide rice noodles)
½ teaspoon finely shredded lime peel
3 tablespoons lime juice
2 tablespoons peanut butter
1 tablespoon fish sauce
1 tablespoon water
4 cloves garlic, minced
2 teaspoons Asian chile bean sauce or ½ teaspoon crushed red pepper
3 teaspoons canola oil
1 pound skinless, boneless chicken breast, cut into bite-size strips
1 medium red sweet pepper, cut into thin bite-size strips
3 green onions, thinly sliced, with green tops separated from white bottoms
2 cups packaged shredded broccoli (broccoli slaw mix)
2 tablespoons unsalted peanuts, finely chopped

1. Fill a large saucepan half full with water; bring to boiling. Remove saucepan from heat. Add noodles; let stand for 8 minutes. Drain well in a colander.

2. Meanwhile, for sauce, in a small bowl combine lime peel, lime juice, peanut butter, fish sauce, the water, garlic, and bean sauce; whisk together well until smooth. Set aside.

3. In a very large nonstick skillet or large nonstick wok heat 2 teaspoons of the oil over medium-high heat. Add chicken; cook and stir for 4 to 6 minutes or until chicken is no longer pink. Transfer chicken to a bowl.

4. Add the remaining 1 teaspoon oil to the skillet. Add sweet pepper and stir-fry for 2 minutes. Add drained noodles and white bottoms of green onions. Stir-fry for 2 minutes. Add broccoli, sauce, and chicken. Cook and stir until heated through. To serve, divide stir-fry among four plates. Sprinkle with green onion tops and peanuts. **Makes 4 servings.**

PER SERVING: 368 cal., 11 g fat (2 g sat. fat), 66 mg chol., 556 mg sodium, 34 g carb., 3 g fiber, 32 g pro.

[**make it a meal**

Roasted leeks with thyme and garlic
Mango salad
Honey-ginger tea]

If your cutlets are thicker than ½-inch, lay them on a flat surface and cover them with plastic wrap. Pound lightly with the flat side of a meat mallet until they reach the desired thickness.

turkey cutlets with barley

PREP: 15 minutes   **COOK:** 25 minutes

2 teaspoons olive oil
6 ½-inch-thick turkey breast slices (cutlets) (about 1½ pounds)
3 cups sliced fresh button or cremini mushrooms (8 ounces)
½ cup chopped onion (1 medium)
½ cup chopped carrot (1 medium)
½ cup chopped red sweet pepper (1 small)
2 cups reduced-sodium chicken broth
1 cup quick-cooking barley
2 teaspoons snipped fresh thyme or oregano, or 1 teaspoon dried thyme or oregano, crushed
½ teaspoon finely shredded lemon peel
¼ teaspoon ground black pepper
Salt and ground black pepper
Snipped fresh thyme or oregano (optional)
Lemon wedges (optional)

1. In an extra-large nonstick skillet heat 1 teaspoon of the oil over medium-high heat. Add turkey and cook for 4 to 8 minutes or until browned and no longer pink, turning once. Remove turkey from skillet; set aside.

2. Add the remaining 1 teaspoon oil to the skillet. Add the mushrooms, onion, carrot, and sweet pepper; cook and stir for 3 to 4 minutes or until tender. Stir in broth, barley, and dried thyme (if using). Bring to boiling; reduce heat. Cover and simmer for 10 to 12 minutes or until barley is tender and liquid is nearly absorbed.

3. Stir in fresh thyme (if using), lemon peel, and ¼ teaspoon black pepper. Return turkey to skillet. Cover and cook for 1 to 3 minutes or until heated through. Season to taste with salt and pepper. If desired, sprinkle each serving with additional fresh thyme and serve with lemon wedges. **Makes 6 servings.**

PER SERVING: 241 cal., 4 g fat (1 g sat. fat), 50 mg chol., 318 mg sodium, 23 g carb., 4 g fiber, 31 g pro.

[make it a meal]

Tricolor Summer Squash, recipe page 248
Ginger poached pears
Low-fat shortbread cookies

To remove the tough string that runs along the inside curve of the pea pod, use a paring knife to cut off the very tip of the stem end of the pod, then pull the string down the length of it.

sauteed shrimp and bok choy

START TO FINISH: 25 minutes

1 pound fresh or frozen large shrimp in shells
3 cups bok choy, cut into 2-inch-thick slices
2 cloves garlic, minced
1 tablespoon toasted sesame oil
1 cup fresh snow pea pods
2 teaspoons reduced-sodium soy sauce
¼ teaspoon ground black pepper
1 tablespoon sesame seeds, toasted (see tip, page 64)
2 cups hot cooked whole grain spaghetti or udon noodles

1. Thaw shrimp, if frozen. Peel and devein shrimp, leaving tails intact if desired. Rinse shrimp; pat dry with paper towels.

2. In an extra-large skillet cook and stir shrimp, bok choy, and garlic in hot sesame oil over medium-high heat for 4 to 6 minutes or just until shrimp are opaque. Carefully add pea pods, soy sauce, and pepper to skillet. Cook and stir for 1 minute more.

3. Sprinkle with sesame seeds. Serve with hot cooked whole grain spaghetti. **Makes 4 servings.**

PER SERVING: 228 cal., 6 g fat (1 g sat. fat), 143 mg chol., 648 mg sodium, 23 g carb., 4 g fiber, 21 g pro.

make it a meal

Hot and sour soup
Ginger-soy glazed edamame
Lemon balm tea

cook smart *To reduce the amount of sodium in cooking, substitute with products such as reduced-sodium canned broth, and no-salt-added diced tomatoes.*

Because the anchovies, olives, capers, and cheese are high in sodium, be sure to use no-salt-added tomatoes to keep the sodium level in check.

cod and potatoes puttanesca

PREP: 25 minutes **COOK:** 20 minutes

2   **teaspoons olive oil**

3   **cloves garlic, minced**

2   **to 3 anchovy fillets, drained well and chopped**

2   **14.5-ounce cans no-salt-added diced tomatoes**

1¼   **pounds yellow potatoes, unpeeled and cut into ¾- to 1-inch pieces**

2   **teaspoons dried oregano, crushed**

¼   **teaspoon ground black pepper**

¼   **teaspoon crushed red pepper**

¼   **teaspoon salt**

¼   **cup pitted kalamata olives, quartered lengthwise**

1   **tablespoon capers, rinsed and drained**

1   **pound cod fillets, cut into 1½-inch cubes**

2   **tablespoons snipped fresh Italian parsley**

2   **tablespoons finely shredded Parmesan cheese**

1. In a large skillet heat oil over medium-high heat. Add garlic and anchovy fillets; cook and stir for 30 seconds. Add undrained tomatoes, potatoes, oregano, black pepper, red pepper, and salt. Bring to boiling; reduce heat. Cover and simmer for 10 minutes, stirring once.

2. Stir in olives and capers. Place the cod on top of the potato mixture. Cover and simmer about 10 minutes or until potatoes are tender and fish flakes easily when tested with a fork. Stir together parsley and Parmesan; sprinkle over potato mixture in skillet. **Makes 4 servings.**

PER SERVING: 286 cal., 5 g fat (1 g sat. fat), 52 mg chol., 582 mg sodium, 35 g carb., 8 g fiber, 26 g pro.

make it a meal

Broccoli with Peas and Seared Lemons,
recipe page 244
Tangerine-orange tea

Frittatas are economical, fast to fix, and versatile. They're a great way to use up leftover roasted or fresh vegetables, whatever fresh herbs you have on hand, and small amounts of cheese and/or meats.

potato frittata

PREP: 25 minutes   **COOK:** 10 minutes   **BAKE:** 15 minutes at 375°F   **STAND:** 5 minutes

1   **pound Yukon gold or russet potatoes, scrubbed and thinly sliced**
2   **tablespoons olive oil**
1½   **cups thinly sliced carrots (2 large)**
12   **eggs, lightly beaten**
½   **cup chopped green onions (4)**
½   **teaspoon salt**
¼   **teaspoon ground black pepper**
½   **cup halved yellow cherry tomatoes**
1   **clove garlic, minced**
     Snipped fresh Italian parsley and/or cilantro

1. Preheat oven to 375°F. In a large ovenproof nonstick skillet cook potatoes in hot oil over medium heat for 5 minutes. Add carrots; cook about 5 minutes more or until potatoes and carrots are tender and lightly browned, turning occasionally.

2. In a medium bowl whisk together the eggs, half of the green onions, the salt, and pepper. Pour egg mixture over potato mixture in skillet. Place skillet in oven. Bake, uncovered, for 15 to 18 minutes or until frittata appears dry on top. Remove from oven. Let stand on a wire rack for 5 minutes.

3. Meanwhile, for topper, in a small bowl gently toss together the remaining green onions, the cherry tomatoes, garlic, and parsley. Set aside.

4. With a spatula, loosen edges of frittata from skillet. Place a large serving platter over the skillet. Using two hands, invert platter and skillet to release frittata onto platter. Cut frittata into wedges. Serve with green onion topper. **Makes 6 servings.**

PER SERVING: 259 cal., 14 g fat (4 g sat. fat), 372 mg chol., 362 mg sodium, 18 g carb., 3 g fiber, 15 g pro.

[*make it a meal*

Roasted chickpeas
Kale-herb salad
Brown Sugar Peaches, recipe page 287]

cook smart *Going meatless just one dinner a week is an easy way to ease into a more plant-based, economical way of eating. Plus it decreases overall saturated fat intake.*

The grains of rice will separate best to incorporate the other ingredients if the rice is cold or cool when you use it. Make ahead and chill in the refrigerator or use an 8.8-ounce pouch of precooked rice.

spicy vegetable fried rice

START TO FINISH: 30 minutes

4 eggs
2 tablespoons water
  Nonstick cooking spray
1 tablespoon finely chopped, peeled fresh ginger
2 cloves garlic, minced
1 tablespoon olive oil
2 cups chopped napa cabbage
1 cup coarsely shredded carrots (2 medium)
1 cup fresh snow pea pods, trimmed
2 cups cooked brown rice, chilled
⅓ cup sliced green onions
2 tablespoons reduced-sodium soy sauce
1 to 2 teaspoons Asian chile sauce (Sriracha sauce)
2 tablespoons snipped fresh cilantro
  Lime slices or wedges

1. In a small bowl whisk together eggs and the water. Coat an extra-large nonstick skillet with cooking spray. Heat skillet over medium heat. Pour in egg mixture. Cook, without stirring, until mixture begins to set on the bottom and around the edges. Using a spatula or large spoon, lift and fold the partially cooked eggs so the uncooked portion flows underneath. Continue cooking over medium heat for 2 to 3 minutes or until egg mixture is cooked through but still glossy and moist, keeping eggs in large pieces. Carefully transfer eggs to a medium bowl; set aside.

2. In the same skillet cook and stir ginger and garlic in hot oil over medium-high heat for 30 seconds. Add cabbage, carrots, and pea pods; cook and stir for 2 minutes. Stir in cooked eggs, brown rice, green onions, soy sauce, and chile sauce; cook and stir about 2 minutes or until heated through. Top with cilantro. Serve with lime slices. **Makes 4 servings.**

PER SERVING: 250 cal., 9 g fat (2 g sat. fat), 212 mg chol., 367 mg sodium, 31 g carb., 4 g fiber, 11 g pro.

make it a meal

Jicama-radish salad
Plum halves with lemon zest
Chilled cucumber water

● HIGH FIBER   ● VEGETARIAN

Toasted sesame oil adds terrific, nutty flavor to this Asian-style dish. Sesame oil is high in heart-healthy omega-3 fatty acids, which help regulate blood pressure and may reduce your risk of type 2 diabetes.

spring green fried rice

PREP: 15 minutes   **COOK:** 12 minutes

2	**eggs**
1	**teaspoon soy sauce**
1	**teaspoon toasted sesame oil**
1	**tablespoon vegetable oil**
1	**clove garlic, minced**
1	**teaspoon minced fresh ginger**
2	**cups shredded green cabbage**
¾	**cup frozen shelled edamame (sweet soybeans), thawed**
½	**cup frozen peas, thawed**
2	**cups cooked brown rice, chilled**
2	**tablespoons soy sauce**
¼	**cup sliced green onion**
	Crushed red pepper (optional)

1. In a small bowl beat eggs and 1 teaspoon soy sauce; set aside. In a wok or large skillet heat toasted sesame oil over medium heat. Add egg mixture; stir gently until set. Remove egg; cool slightly. Using your hands, roll the cooked eggs into a log and slice into strips; set aside.

2. In the same skillet heat vegetable oil over medium-high heat. Add garlic and ginger, cook 30 seconds. Add cabbage; cook and stir 2 minutes. Add edamame and peas; cook for 2 minutes. Add rice and 2 tablespoons soy sauce. Cook and stir for 2 to 4 minutes or until heated through. Add egg mixture and green onion; cook and stir about 1 minute or until heated through. Top with crushed red pepper, if desired. **Makes 4 servings.**

PER SERVING: 251 cal., 9 g fat (2 g sat. fat), 93 mg chol., 669 mg sodium, 32 g carb., 5 g fiber, 11 g pro.

[make it a meal]

Egg drop soup
Carrot-apple slaw
Green tea

An acidic element such as citrus or vinegar in a dish adds lots of great flavor with virtually no calories—and without contributing fat or salt.

whole wheat tortellini with broccoli

START TO FINISH: 25 minutes

9 ounces refrigerated whole wheat or regular three cheese-filled tortellini

2 cups small broccoli florets

1 15- to 19-ounce can cannellini (white kidney beans), rinsed and drained

¼ cup slivered pitted kalamata olives

2 tablespoons olive oil

2 tablespoons white balsamic vinegar

½ teaspoon crushed red pepper

1 cup quartered cherry or grape tomatoes

½ cup crumbled reduced-fat feta cheese

¼ cup snipped fresh basil

1. In a deep large skillet bring 1 to 2 inches water to boiling. Add tortellini; cook for 7 to 8 minutes or until tender, stirring occasionally. Stir in broccoli; cook for 1 to 2 minutes or until broccoli is crisp-tender. Drain in colander. Return tortellini and broccoli to skillet.

2. Stir in beans, olives, oil, vinegar, and red pepper. Heat through. Sprinkle with tomatoes, feta, and basil. **Makes 4 servings.**

PER SERVING: 397 cal., 14 g fat (4 g sat. fat), 44 mg chol., 665 mg sodium, 49 g carb., 11 g fiber, 19 g pro.

make it a meal

Shaved carrot, fennel, and tangerine salad
Butter lettuce with light creamy Italian dressing
Sparkling water with raspberries

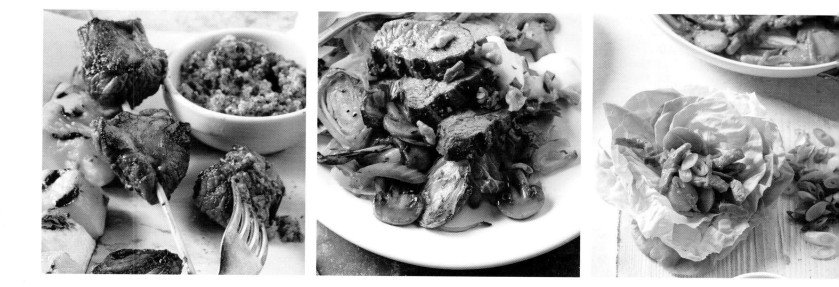

low carb, high protein

These high-protein entrees with very few carbs will keep energy up and hunger at bay.

Most pork tenderloin comes in a package of two tenderloins that generally weigh about 1 to 1¼ pounds each. Cook one, then wrap the other one in plastic wrap and seal in a freezer bag. Freeze until needed.

pork tenderloin with lemon-thyme cream and cabbage-apple slaw

PREP: 20 minutes   **COOK:** 12 minutes   **ROAST:** 25 minutes at 425°F   **STAND:** 3 minutes

1¼	pounds natural pork tenderloin, trimmed of fat
¼	teaspoon salt
¼	teaspoon ground black pepper
1	tablespoon olive oil
2	teaspoons butter
3	cups napa cabbage, cut in ¼-inch-thick slices
1	medium apple, cored and chopped
1	teaspoon cider vinegar
⅛	teaspoon salt
⅛	teaspoon ground black pepper
¼	cup reduced-sodium chicken broth
2	tablespoons lemon juice
½	teaspoon snipped fresh thyme
2	ounces reduced-fat cream cheese (Neufchâtel), softened
	Fresh thyme sprigs (optional)

1. Preheat oven to 425°F. Sprinkle pork with ¼ teaspoon salt and ¼ teaspoon pepper. In a large nonstick skillet heat oil over medium-high heat. Sear pork for about 5 minutes, browning on all sides. Place pork on a rack in a roasting pan and roast for 25 to 35 minutes, or until it reaches an internal temperature of 145°F when tested with a thermometer. Remove from oven and cover with foil. Allow to stand for at least 3 minutes.

2. Meanwhile, in the same skillet melt butter over medium heat into the drippings remaining in the skillet. Add sliced cabbage and cook until just starting to wilt. Add apple and cook 3 minutes more or until apple is tender and cabbage is cooked. Transfer to a medium bowl, stir in vinegar, and season with the ⅛ teaspoon salt and ⅛ teaspoon black pepper; keep warm.

3. In a small bowl stir together chicken broth, lemon juice, and thyme. Pour broth mixture into the drippings in the hot skillet. Add cream cheese and whisk until smooth and heated through.

4. Slice pork and serve over warm cabbage apple slaw. Top with lemon thyme cream. Garnish with fresh thyme sprigs, if desired. **Makes 4 servings.**

PER SERVING: 274 cal., 12 g fat (5 g sat. fat), 108 mg chol., 398 mg sodium, 9 g carb., 2 g fiber, 32 g pro.

make it a meal

Greens and sweet onion saute
Butternut squash
Lemon-ginger tea

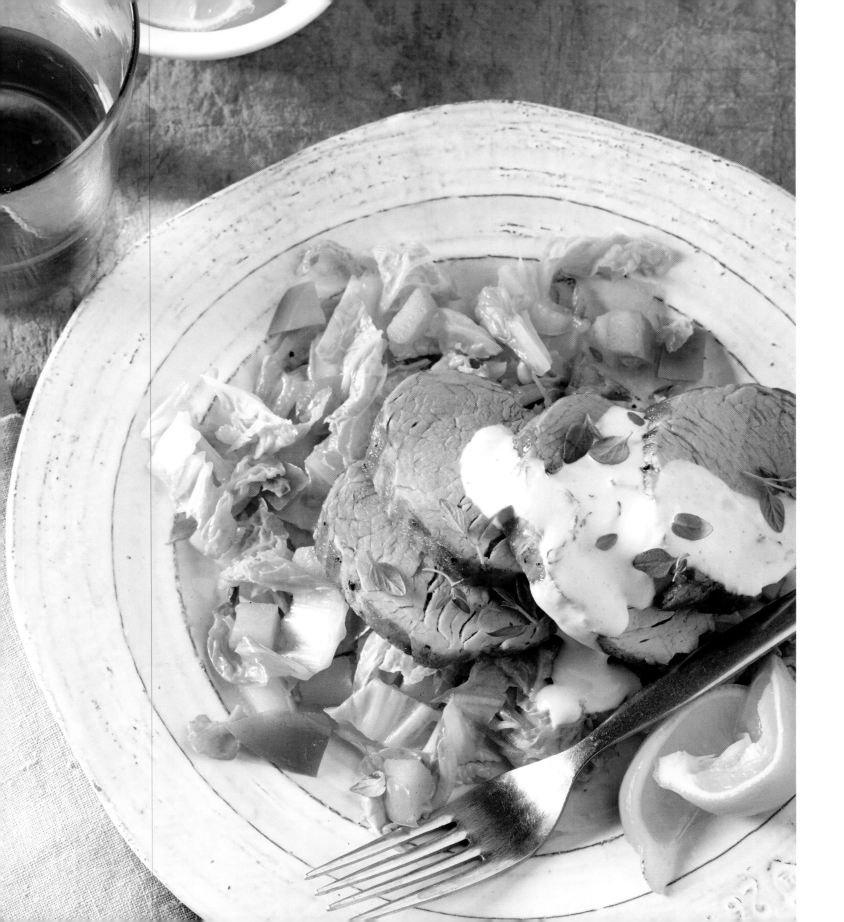

The cool crunch of the lettuce wrap is a nice contrast to the zippy peanut sauce. If you like your peanut sauce hotter, add a little more chili sauce or ⅛ teaspoon crushed red pepper.

crunchy peanut pork lettuce wraps

START TO FINISH: 25 minutes

Nonstick cooking spray
1 teaspoon canola oil
1 clove garlic, minced
1 pound natural pork loin, trimmed of fat and cut into thin strips
⅛ teaspoon ground black pepper
2 tablespoons water
2 tablespoons peanut butter
2 tablespoons reduced-sodium soy sauce
½ tablespoon grated fresh ginger
1 teaspoon Asian chili sauce (Sriracha sauce)
½ teaspoon apple cider vinegar
1 8-ounce can sliced water chestnuts, drained, rinsed, and chopped
¼ cup shredded carrot
¼ cup thinly sliced green onions
3 tablespoons roasted and salted peanuts, chopped
12 large butterhead (Boston or Bibb) lettuce leaves

1. Coat a large nonstick skillet with cooking spray; add oil and heat over medium high heat.

2. Cook garlic in the hot oil for 30 seconds. Add pork to the skillet and sprinkle with the black pepper. Cook for about 5 minutes, turning once, until pork is no longer pink.

3. In a small bowl whisk together the water, peanut butter, soy sauce, ginger, chili sauce, and vinegar; pour over the pork in the hot skillet. Stir in the water chestnuts, and carrot. Heat through.

4. Spoon ¼ cup of pork mixture onto each lettuce leaf. Top with onions and peanuts and roll up. **Makes 4 servings.**

PER SERVING: 274 cal., 14 g fat (3 g sat. fat), 63 mg chol., 391 mg sodium, 7 g carb., 2 g fiber, 30 g pro.

make it a meal

Chinese dumpling soup
Cucumbers marinated in vinegar and dill
Ginger tea

Any dry red wine—such as Cabernet Sauvignon, Merlot, Pinot Noir, Shiraz, or Zinfandel—works well in this richly flavored mushroom-shallot pan sauce.

sirloin steak with red wine pan sauce

START TO FINISH: 30 minutes

20	to 24 ounces beef top sirloin steak, ¾ to 1 inch thick, cut into 4 pieces
½	teaspoon cracked black pepper
¼	teaspoon salt
2	tablespoons butter
1	cup sliced mushrooms
½	cup thin shallot wedges
⅔	cup dry red wine
½	cup 50% less sodium beef broth
1	tablespoon balsamic vinegar
2	cups stemmed watercress

1. Trim fat from beef. Sprinkle both sides of beef with pepper and salt. In a very large nonstick skillet heat 1 tablespoon of the butter over medium-high heat until bubbly. Reduce heat to medium and add steaks. Cook for 8 to 10 minutes or until medium-rare doneness (145°F), turning once. Transfer steaks to a plate and cover with foil while preparing the sauce.

2. Add mushrooms and shallots to skillet. Cook and stir for 2 minutes. Remove skillet from heat. Add wine, broth, and vinegar to the hot skillet. Return skillet to heat. Cook and stir to scrape up the browned bits from the bottom of the pan. Bring to boiling. Boil gently, uncovered, for 5 to 8 minutes or until liquid is slightly thickened and reduced. Add the remaining 1 tablespoon butter, stirring until butter is melted.

3. Transfer steaks to serving plates. Top with sauce and watercress. **Makes 4 servings.**

PER SERVING: 302 cal., 13 g fat (6 g sat. fat), 110 mg chol., 337 mg sodium, 6 g carb., 1 g fiber, 32 g pro.

make it a meal

Brothy onion soup
Apple-shaved celery salad with pecans and blue cheese
Sparkling water with pomegranate juice

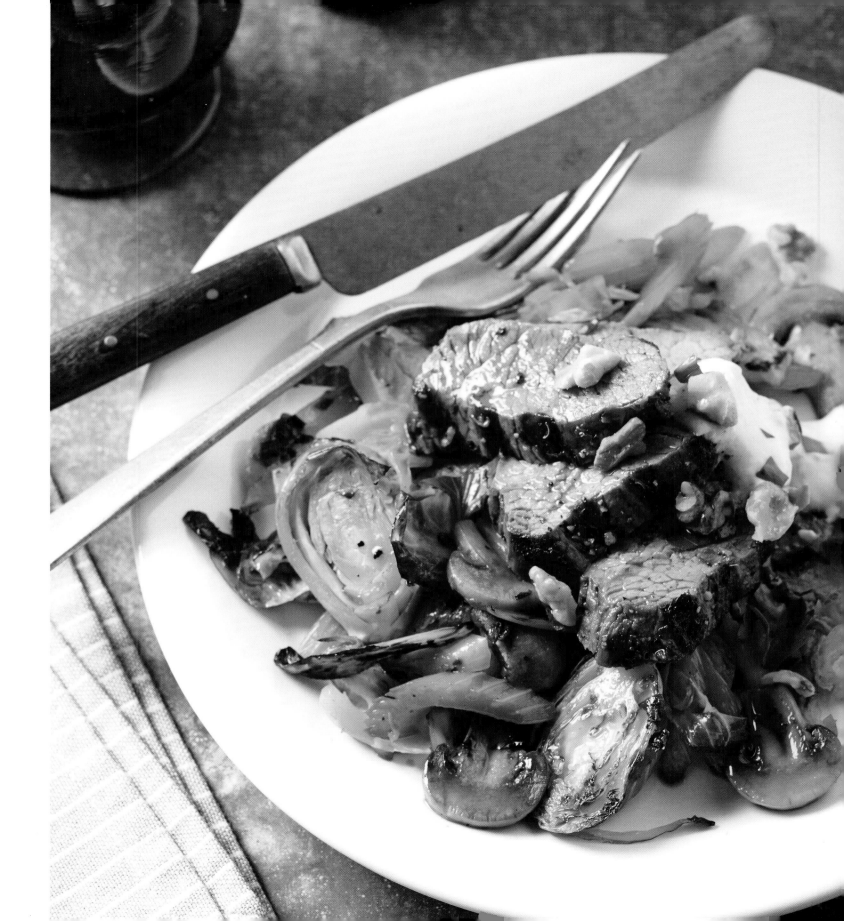

Beef shoulder petite tender, also called beef shoulder tender, is cut from the chuck of the animal. Petite tenders are similar in shape to beef tenderloin but smaller. They're tender, flavorful, and economical.

beef medallions with horseradish sauce, celery, and mushrooms

START TO FINISH: 35 minutes

4   5-ounce beef shoulder petite tenders, cut 1 inch thick
½   teaspoon Montreal steak seasoning
     Nonstick cooking spray
½   cup fat-free plain Greek yogurt
1   tablespoon prepared horseradish
1   tablespoon olive oil
1   clove garlic, minced
8   ounces fresh Brussels sprouts, trimmed and sliced
¾   cup celery, cut into ¼-inch diagonal slices
⅛   teaspoon salt
8   ounces fresh button mushrooms, sliced (2½ cups)
2   tablespoons chopped walnuts, toasted (see tip, page 64)
1   tablespoon chopped fresh Italian parsley

1. Sprinkle beef with steak seasoning. Coat a grill pan with nonstick spray. Heat pan over medium heat. Add beef to grill pan and grill 10 to 12 minutes for medium-rare (145°F), turning once.

2. For the sauce, in a small bowl whisk together the yogurt and the horseradish.

3. Meanwhile, in a large skillet heat oil over medium-high heat. Cook garlic for 30 seconds; add Brussels sprouts, celery, and salt; cook and stir for 2 minutes. Add mushrooms and continue to cook 2 to 3 minutes more or until celery is crisp-tender.

4. Spoon vegetable mixture onto serving plates. Slice steak, if desired, and place on vegetables. Top with horseradish sauce. Sprinkle with walnuts and chopped parsley. **Makes 4 servings.**

PER SERVING: 310 cal., 14 g fat (3 g sat. fat), 80 mg chol., 286 mg sodium, 9 g carb., 3 g fiber, 36 g pro.

make it a meal

Red and green leaf lettuce salad
Caramelized Balsamic Onions, recipe page 255
Fresh apricots drizzled with honey

Trim the core end of the lettuce head to make it more attractive, but be sure to leave a portion of the core attached to the leaves so the head stays intact when cut in half.

grilled flank steak and romaine

PREP: 25 minutes   **MARINATE:** 2 hours   **GRILL:** 17 minutes   **STAND:** 5 minutes

1	pound beef flank steak
¼	cup freshly squeezed lemon juice
2	tablespoons red wine vinegar
2	tablespoons reduce-sodium soy sauce
1	tablespoon Worcestershire sauce
5	teaspoons olive oil
½	teaspoon ground dry mustard
½	teaspoon celery salt
¼	teaspoon garlic powder
¼	teaspoon ground black pepper
2	8-ounce hearts of romaine, halved lengthwise
1	ounce crumbled blue cheese (optional)

1. Trim fat from meat. Score both sides of the flank steak in a diamond pattern with shallow diagonal cuts spaced 1 inch apart. Place steak in a large resealable plastic bag set in a shallow dish.

2. For marinade, in a small bowl combine 2 tablespoons of the lemon juice, the vinegar, soy sauce, Worcestershire sauce, 2 teaspoons of the oil, the dry mustard, celery salt, garlic powder, and black pepper. Reserve 2 tablespoons of the marinade and pour the rest over the steak. Seal bag and turn to coat. Marinate in the refrigerator, for 2 to 4 hours, turning the bag occasionally.

3. In a small bowl combine the remaining 2 tablespoons of lemon juice with the remaining olive oil and the reserved marinade. Brush this mixture on the cut sides of the romaine.

4. Drain steak, discarding marinade. For a charcoal or gas grill, place steak on the grill rack directly over medium heat. Cover and grill for 17 to 20 minutes for medium (160°F), turning once halfway through grilling. Let steak stand for 5 minutes. Thinly slice steak across the grain to serve.

5. Grill romaine, cut sides down, about 2 minutes, until edges char.

6. Serve flank steak with grilled romaine. If desired, sprinkle with crumbled blue cheese. **Makes 4 servings.**

PER SERVING: 251 cal., 14 g fat (4 g sat. fat), 53 mg chol., 275 mg sodium, 5 g carb., 2 g fiber, 26 g pro.

make it a meal

Herbed Dijon-Marinated Veggies, recipe page 249
Minted poached peaches

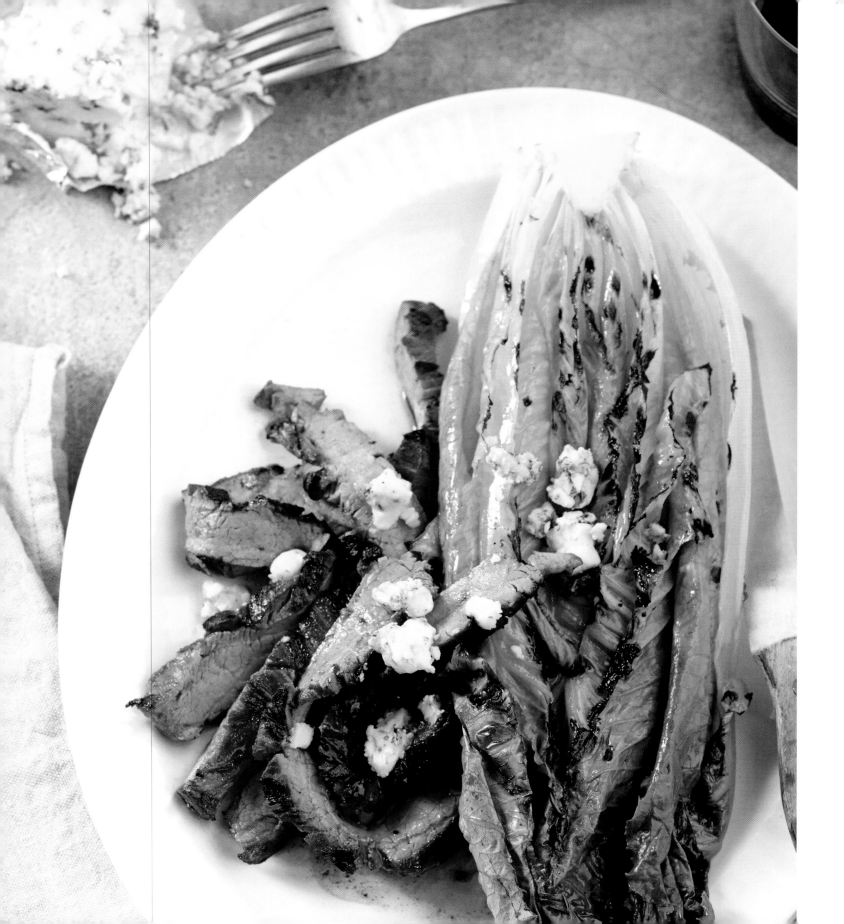

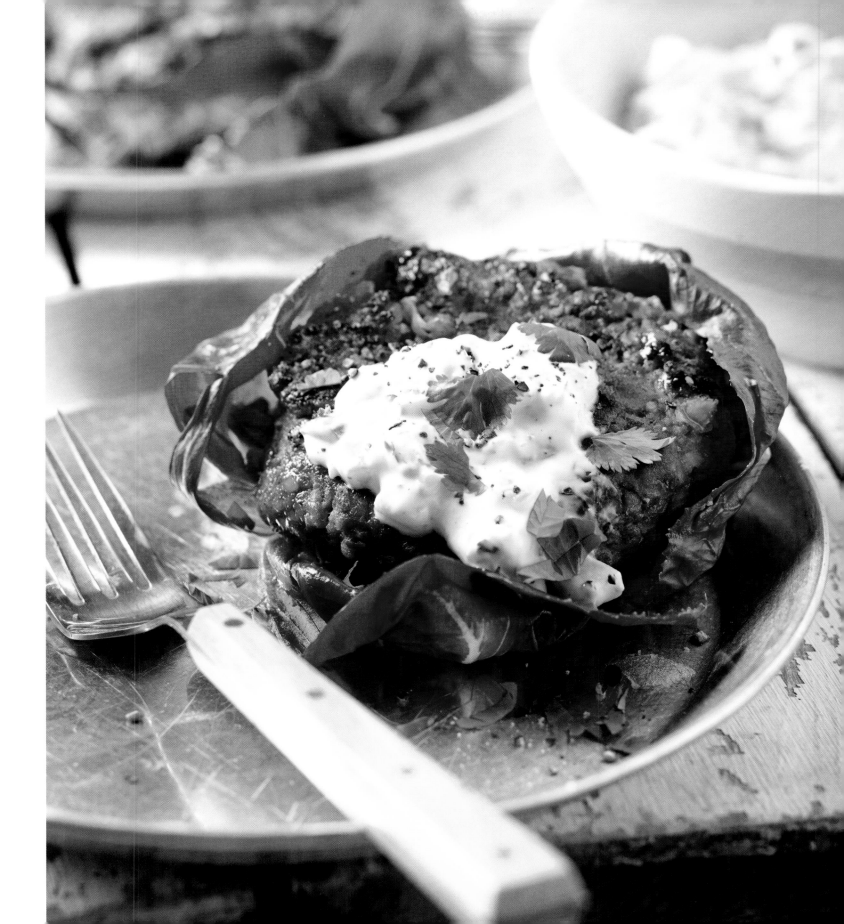

Radicchio has a natural bitterness that is pleasing when combined with other flavors.. To get the best-tasting radicchio, look for firm, medium-size heads that have crisp, glossy, fresh-looking leaves.

indian-spiced burgers with cilantro cucumber sauce

PREP: 25 minutes   **GRILL:** 14 minutes

1 5.3- to 6-ounce container fat-free plain Greek yogurt
⅔ cup finely chopped cucumber
¼ cup snipped fresh cilantro
2 cloves garlic, minced
⅛ teaspoon salt
¼ teaspoon ground black pepper
½ cup canned garbanzo beans (chickpeas), rinsed and drained
1 pound lean ground beef
¼ cup finely chopped red onion
2 tablespoons finely chopped fresh jalapeño pepper; seeded, if desired (see tip, page 62)
½ teaspoon salt
¼ teaspoon ground cumin
¼ teaspoon ground coriander
⅛ teaspoon cinnamon
4 to 8 radicchio leaves
   Coarsely ground black pepper (optional)
   Fresh cilantro leaves (optional)

1. For sauce, in a small bowl stir together yogurt, cucumber, cilantro, garlic, the ⅛ teaspoon salt, and ⅛ teaspoon of the ground black pepper. Cover and chill until ready to serve.

2. In a medium bowl using a potato masher or fork, mash garbanzo beans. Add the beef, onion, jalapeño, ½ teaspoon salt, cumin, coriander, cinnamon, and remaining ground black pepper; mix well. Form meat mixture into four ¾-inch-thick patties.

3. For a charcoal or gas grill, place patties on the grill rack directly over medium heat. Cover and grill for 14 to 18 minutes or until patties are done (160°F), turning once halfway through grilling.

4. Serve burgers on radicchio leaves topped with sauce. If desired, sprinkle with coarsely ground black pepper and cilantro leaves. **Makes 4 servings.**

PER SERVING: 258 cal., 12 g fat (5 g sat. fat), 75 mg chol., 539 mg sodium, 8 g carb., 2 g fiber, 29 g pro.

make it a meal

Kale, sweet pepper, carrot slaw with peanut dressing
Tangerines with shaved celery, walnuts, and honey

It's important to leave ¼-inch between the chunks of meat and vegetables on this—or any—kabob. It allows heat to circulate around the food to ensure that it will be properly and evenly cooked.

lamb and zucchini kabobs with mint-parsley pesto

PREP: 25 minutes   **MARINATE:** 1 hour   **GRILL:** 12 minutes

¼   cup packed fresh Italian parsley
¼   cup packed fresh mint leaves
3   tablespoons slivered almonds, toasted (see tip, page 64)
2   tablespoons shredded Parmesan cheese (½ ounce)
2   cloves garlic, minced
3   tablespoons lemon juice
1   to 2 tablespoons water
2   tablespoons olive oil
⅛   teaspoon kosher salt
2   tablespoons balsamic vinegar
¼   teaspoon kosher salt
⅛   teaspoon ground black pepper
1   pound boneless leg of lamb, trimmed of fat and cut into 1½-inch pieces
8   ounces zucchini, cut into 1-inch pieces
8   ounces yellow summer squash, cut into 1-inch pieces

1. For the pesto, in a blender or mini food processor combine parsley, mint, almonds, Parmesan cheese, and garlic. Pulse until coarsely chopped. Add 1 tablespoon of the lemon juice, the water, 2 teaspoons of the olive oil, and ⅛ teaspoon salt. Process until very finely chopped and fully combined. Transfer to a small bowl; cover and refrigerate.

2. For marinade, in a small bowl whisk together the remaining 2 tablespoons of the lemon juice, the vinegar, 2 teaspoons of the olive oil, ¼ teaspoon salt, and ⅛ teaspoon black pepper.

3. Place lamb in a large resealable plastic bag set in a shallow dish. Add marinade to lamb in bag. Seal bag and turn to coat lamb evenly. Marinate in the refrigerator for 1 to 4 hours, turning occasionally.

4. Drain lamb, discarding marinade. Thread meat onto four 8- to 10-inch skewers (see tip, page 19), leaving ¼-inch space between pieces.

5. Thread squash onto another four wooden skewers (see tip, page 19), alternating zucchini and yellow squash, leaving ¼-inch space between pieces. Brush vegetables with the remaining 2 teaspoons of the olive oil.

6. For a charcoal or gas grill, place kabobs on the rack of a grill directly over medium heat. Cover and grill for 12 to 14 minutes or until lamb reaches desired doneness and vegetables are tender, turning occasionally.

7. Serve lamb and zucchini kabobs with the mint-parsley pesto. **Makes 4 servings.**

PER SERVING: 272 cal., 15 g fat (3 g sat. fat), 74 mg chol., 291 mg sodium, 8 g carb., 2 g fiber, 27 g pro.

[
make it a meal
Orange, fennel, and olive salad
Moroccan mint tea
]

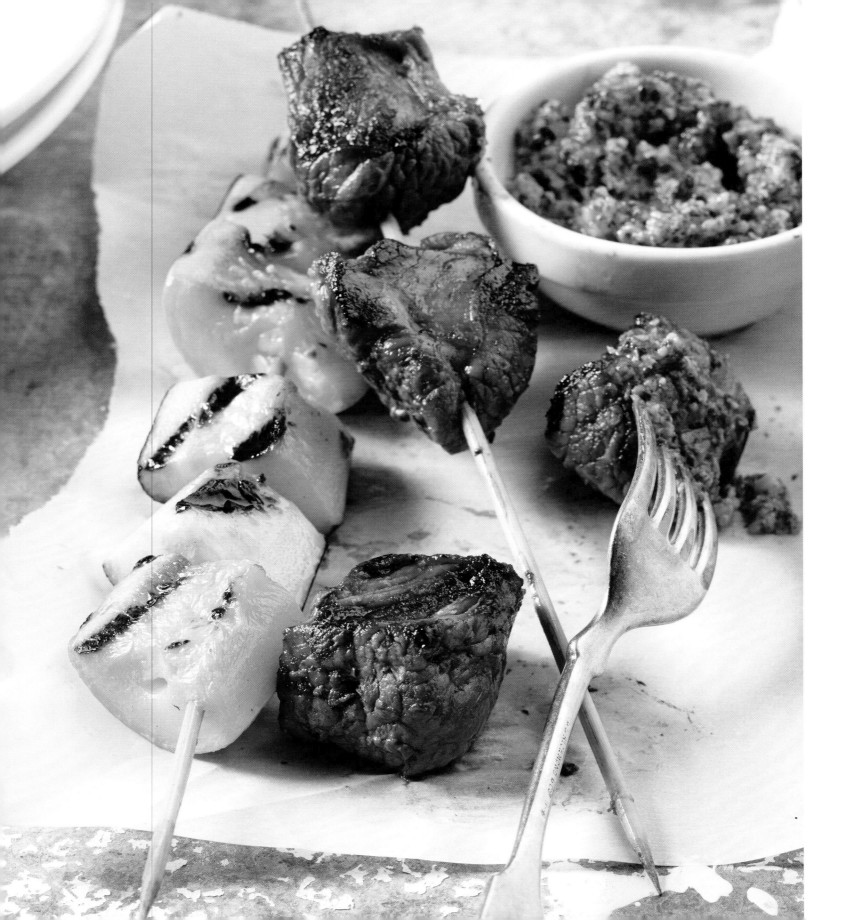

Lamb loin chops have a T-bone running through them and are usually a little larger than rib chops, which have a delicate and attractive rib bone that extends out of the meat.

lamb chops with blackberry-peach chutney

PREP: 20 minutes   **GRILL:** 12 minutes

1   peach, peeled, halved, pitted, and coarsely chopped (about 1⅓ cups)
¼   cup sliced green onions (2)
⅛   teaspoon ground cloves
2   teaspoons vegetable oil
1   cup fresh blackberries
1   tablespoon red wine vinegar
½   teaspoon ground allspice
¼   teaspoon salt
¼   teaspoon coarsely ground black pepper
8   lamb loin chops or rib chops, cut 1 inch thick

1. For chutney, in a large skillet cook peach, green onions, and cloves in hot oil over medium heat about 3 minutes or just until peach is tender, stirring occasionally. Add blackberries; reduce heat to medium-low. Cook and stir for 3 minutes; remove from heat. Stir in vinegar. Set aside to cool.

2. In a small bowl stir together allspice, salt, and pepper. Sprinkle evenly over all sides of the chops; rub in with your fingers.

3. For a charcoal or gas grill, place chops on the grill rack directly over medium heat. Cover and grill until desired doneness, turning once halfway through grilling time. Allow 12 to 14 minutes for medium-rare (145°F) or 15 to 17 minutes for medium (160°F).

4. Serve lamb with chutney. **Makes 4 servings.**

PER SERVING: 152 cal., 8 g fat (3 g sat. fat), 40 mg chol., 197 mg sodium, 8 g carb., 3 g fiber, 13 g pro.

[make it a meal

Grilled cauliflower steaks
Frisee and endive salad
Green tea with lemon]

Allow these cheese-and-veggie-stuffed breasts to stand 5 to 10 minutes after grilling so the filling (the best part!) doesn't squish out when they're cut.

grillers stuffed with spinach and smoked gouda

PREP: 30 minutes   **GRILL:** 12 minutes

⅓   **cup finely chopped onion (1 small)**
2   **cloves garlic, minced**
1   **tablespoon olive oil**
1   **cup chopped fresh mushrooms**
1   **cup shredded smoked Gouda cheese (4 ounces)**
½   **of a 10-ounce package frozen chopped spinach, thawed and squeezed dry**
¼   **teaspoon ground nutmeg**
4   **skinless, boneless chicken breast halves**
    Cooked whole wheat fettucine with fresh snipped Italian parsley (optional)

1. For filling, in a large skillet cook onion and garlic in hot oil over medium heat about 5 minutes or until onion is tender. Add mushrooms. Cook and stir about 5 minutes more or until mushrooms are tender. Remove from heat. Stir in cheese, spinach, and nutmeg. Set aside.

2. Using a sharp knife, cut a 2-inch pocket into the thickest part of each chicken breast half by cutting horizontally toward, but not through, the opposite side. Divide filling evenly among pockets in chicken. If necessary, secure openings with wooden toothpicks.

3. For a charcoal or gas grill, place chicken on the grill rack of directly over medium heat. Cover and grill for 12 to 15 minutes or until chicken is no longer pink (170°F), turning once halfway through grilling. Remove and discard any toothpicks. If desired, serve with fettuccine. **Makes 4 servings.**

PER SERVING: 328 cal., 13 g fat (6 g sat. fat), 121 mg chol., 578 mg sodium, 6 g carb., 2 g fiber, 47 g pro.

make it a meal

Sliced avocado and red onion salad
Grilled zucchini and summer squash
Grilled fresh pineapple slices

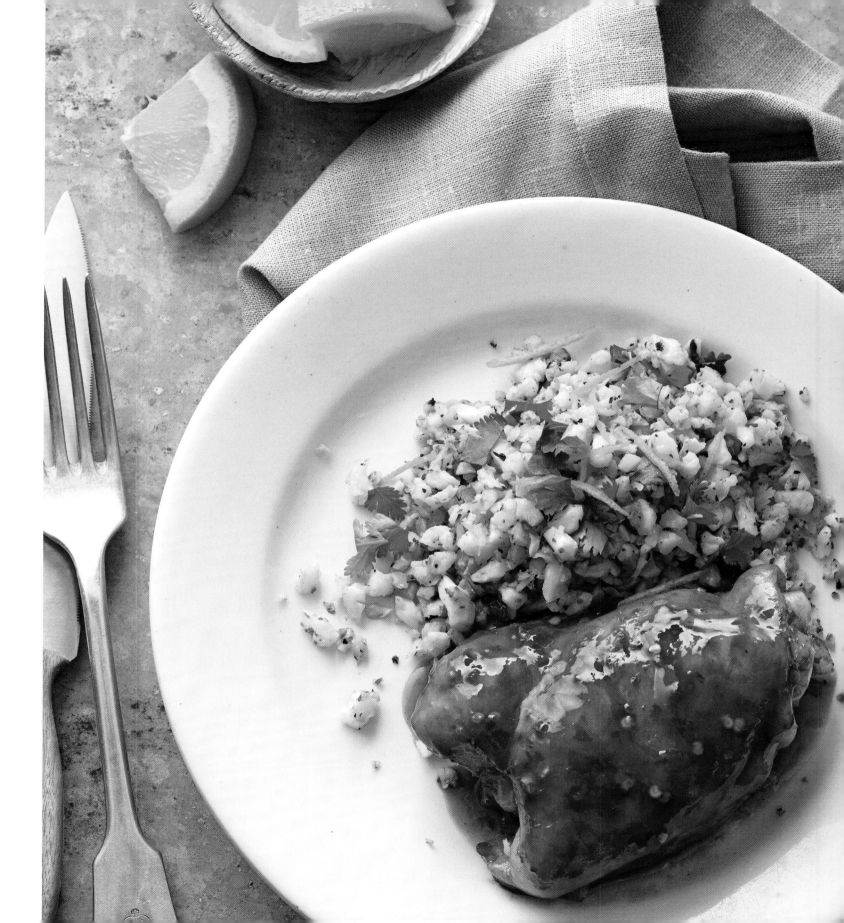

One cup of regular cooked white rice has about 200 calories and 44 grams of carbohydrates, while cauliflower rice has about 30 calories and 6 grams of carbohydrates for the same amount.

asian orange chicken thighs with cauliflower rice

PREP: 25 minutes   **BAKE:** 30 minutes at 375°F   **COOK:** 18 minutes

Nonstick cooking spray
2 tablespoons sesame oil (not toasted)
4 large bone-in chicken thighs (about 2¼ pounds total), skin removed
1 tablespoon reduced-sodium soy sauce
1 teaspoon finely shredded orange peel
1 tablespoon freshly squeezed orange juice
1 tablespoon rice vinegar
1 tablespoon brown sugar
¼ teaspoon crushed red pepper
2 tablespoons cold water
1 teaspoon cornstarch
4 cups coarsely chopped cauliflower florets
½ teaspoon kosher salt
⅛ teaspoon ground black pepper
Snipped fresh cilantro (optional)
Finely shredded orange peel (optional)

1. Preheat oven to 375°F. Coat a 2-quart square baking dish with cooking spray. In a very large nonstick skillet heat 1 tablespoon of the sesame oil over medium-high heat. Add chicken to hot oil; cook about 10 minutes, turning to brown evenly. Transfer chicken to prepared dish, arranging in a single layer. Drain and discard drippings from the skillet.

2. In a small bowl whisk together soy sauce, orange peel, orange juice, vinegar, brown sugar, crushed red pepper, the cold water, and cornstarch; add to the skillet. Cook and stir until thickened and bubbly; pour sauce over chicken thighs in dish.

3. Bake, uncovered, about 30 minutes or until chicken is done (175°F).

4. Meanwhile, place cauliflower in a large food processor. Cover and pulse several times until cauliflower is evenly chopped into rice-size pieces.

5. Wipe out the skillet and add the remaining 1 tablespoon oil. Heat the oil over medium-high heat; add the cauliflower, salt, and pepper. Cook the cauliflower, stirring occasionally for 8 to 10 minutes, until you begin to see caramelized flecks throughout. If desired, sprinkle cauliflower with cilantro and orange peel and serve with chicken thighs. **Makes 4 servings.**

PER SERVING: 285 cal., 13 g fat (3 g sat. fat), 145 mg chol., 526 mg sodium, 9 g carb., 2 g fiber, 32 g pro.

[make it a meal

Lemony Green Beans and Arugula, recipe page 256
Roasted red pepper salad]

LOW CARB, HIGH PROTEIN

To make it easier to cut the turkey tenderloins in half evenly, be sure to use a very sharp chef's knife and press down lightly on the tenderloin with the palm of your hand as you cut from end to end horizontally.

turkey-spinach medley

START TO FINISH: 20 minutes

2   **8-ounce turkey breast tenderloins, cut in half horizontally**
½   **teaspoon coarsely ground black pepper**
2   **tablespoons butter**
2   **ounces thinly sliced deli ham, cut into bite-size strips**
½   **cup orange juice**
2   **9- to 10-ounce packages fresh spinach**
1   **orange, cut into wedges**
¼   **teaspoon salt**

1. Sprinkle turkey with ¼ teaspoon of the black pepper. In a very large skillet melt butter over medium-high heat; add turkey. Cook for 12 to 15 minutes or until no pink remains (170°F), turning once halfway through cooking. Remove turkey from skillet. Cover to keep warm.

2. Add ham to hot skillet; cook and stir for 1 to 2 minutes or until ham is heated through and starting to crisp. Using a slotted spoon, remove ham from skillet.

3. Add orange juice to skillet; bring to boiling. Add half of the spinach; cook about 1 minute or just until wilted. Transfer wilted spinach to a bowl. Repeat with remaining spinach and orange wedges; transfer to the bowl with spinach and season with salt and remaining black pepper. Reserve juices in skillet.

4. Divide spinach among four serving plates. Top with a piece of turkey and some of the ham. Drizzle with the juices in the skillet. **Makes 4 servings.**

PER SERVING: 244 cal., 8 g fat (4 g sat. fat), 94 mg chol., 528 mg sodium, 9 g carb., 3 g fiber, 34 g pro.

[**make it a meal**

Heirloom tomato salad
Sparkling water with mint]

The lime juice not only adds great flavor to the marinade but also helps tenderize the meat. Avoid marinating the tenderloins much more than the recommended 2 hours, as they will start to get mushy.

chili lime turkey tenderloin with peppers and arugula

PREP: 25 minutes   **MARINATE:** 1 hour   **GRILL:** 8 minutes

¼ cup bottled Italian salad dressing
2 tablespoons freshly squeezed lime juice
½ teaspoon chili powder
¼ teaspoon ground black pepper
2 10- to 12-ounce all-natural turkey tenderloins
2 medium red and/or yellow sweet peppers, quartered with stems and seeds removed
1 medium onion, cut in ½-inch slices
1 tablespoon olive oil
4 cups arugula
⅓ cup crumbled feta cheese
Lime wedges (optional)

1. In a small bowl whisk together the salad dressing, lime juice, chili powder, and black pepper.

2. Cut turkey tenderloins in half horizontally. Place turkey in a resealable plastic bag. Pour ¼ cup of the marinade over the turkey. Seal bag and turn several times so turkey becomes evenly coated with the marinade. Refrigerate for 1 to 2 hours, turning occasionally. Remove turkey from marinade, discarding marinade.

3. For a charcoal or gas grill, grill turkey, sweet peppers, and onion on the rack of a covered grill directly over medium heat for 8 to 10 minutes or until turkey is no longer pink (165°F) and vegetables are crisp-tender, turning once. Slice sweet peppers into strips and separate onion into rings.

4. For dressing, in a small bowl whisk together the remaining marinade and olive oil. Add dressing to arugula; toss to coat. Top arugula with pepper strips, onions, and turkey. Top with feta and serve with lime wedges, if desired. **Makes 4 servings.**

PER SERVING: 267 cal., 9 g fat (2 g sat. fat), 96 mg chol., 333 mg sodium, 8 g carb., 2 g fiber, 39 g pro.

make it a meal

Fava bean salad with garlic vinaigrette
Strawberries with minced candied ginger

Leaving some pink in the center of the tuna is not only OK, but desirable. Cooking the pink out of tuna means cooking the flavor and moisture out of it as well!

tuna salad with wonton crisps

START TO FINISH: 30 minutes

12 **ounces fresh or frozen tuna steaks**
1 **recipe Wonton Crisps (optional)**
 Salt
 Ground black pepper
 Nonstick cooking spray
¼ **cup cider vinegar**
2 **tablespoons olive oil**
1 **tablespoon sugar**
1 **teaspoon finely shredded lime peel**
½ **of a medium head napa cabbage, torn (6 cups)**
½ **of a medium seedless cucumber, sliced and/or cut into strips**

1. Thaw tuna, if frozen. Prepare Wonton Crisps, if desired; set aside.

2. Rinse tuna with cold water; pat dry with paper towels. Sprinkle tuna lightly with salt and pepper. Coat a large skillet with cooking spray. Cook tuna for 6 to 8 minutes over medium heat or until some pink remains in center, turning once. Transfer tuna to a cutting board; cut into thin slices.

3. For dressing, in a small bowl whisk together vinegar, olive oil, sugar, and lime peel.

4. Divide cabbage, tuna, and cucumber among shallow bowls. Drizzle with dressing and top with Wonton Crisps, if desired. **Makes 4 servings.**

PER SERVING: 193 cal., 7 g fat (1 g sat. fat), 33 mg chol., 196 mg sodium, 8 g carb., 2 g fiber, 22 g pro.

wonton crisps: Cut 8 wonton wrappers into strips. In an extra-large skillet heat 3 tablespoons olive oil over medium-high heat. Cook wonton strips in the hot oil until browned, stirring occasionally. Using a slotted spoon, transfer wonton crisps to paper towels to drain; set aside.

make it a meal

Asparagus with garlic
Sectioned oranges with fresh basil
Sparkling water with a splash of fruit juice

cook smart *Know what's for dinner before you get to the kitchen to start cooking. Otherwise it is too easy to mindlessly munch while trying to decide what to make.*

LOW CARB, HIGH PROTEIN

A hot, healthy, home cooked meal doesn't get any quicker than this. This flavorful fish dish can be ready to eat just 17 minutes from the start time.

lemon-ginger fish

PREP: 10 minutes   **COOK:** 7 minutes

1	pound fresh or frozen cod or other firm whitefish
2	small lemons
1	tablespoon grated fresh ginger
2	teaspoons sugar
¼	cup butter
2	5-ounce packages fresh baby spinach
2	tablespoons water
¼	teaspoon salt
¼	teaspoon ground black pepper

1. Thaw fish, if frozen. Rinse fish with cold water; pat dry with paper towels. Cut fish into four pieces; set fish aside. Thinly slice 1 lemon; set aside. Finely shred peel from the remaining lemon; juice the lemon. In a small bowl combine the lemon peel and juice, ginger, and sugar. Set aside.

2. In a large skillet melt butter over medium heat. Add fish to skillet. Cook for 1 to 2 minutes or until browned. Turn fish and add lemon juice mixture. Cover and cook for 2 to 3 minutes or until fish flakes easily when tested with a fork. Using a slotted spatula, transfer fish to platter; cover to keep warm.

3. Add lemon slices to the skillet. Cook about 2 minutes or until lemon slices are softened and sauce is slightly thickened.

4. Meanwhile, place spinach in a very large microwave-safe bowl. Sprinkle with the water. Microwave on 100-percent-power (high) about 2 minutes or just until wilted, tossing once after 1 minute.

5. To serve, divide spinach among four shallow serving bowls. Top with fish and sauce. Add lemon slices and sprinkle with salt and pepper. **Makes 4 servings.**

PER SERVING: 228 cal., 12 g fat (7 g sat. fat), 79 mg chol., 344 mg sodium, 9 g carb., 3 g fiber, 22 g pro.

make it a meal

Shaved Brussels sprouts and apple salad
Sauteed leeks with lemon, thyme, and garlic
Raspberries with mint

Shrimp is labeled by the number of shrimp per pound. Extra-large shrimp will likely be labeled somewhere in the range of 16⁄20, which means there are between 16 and 20 shrimp per pound.

orange-balsamic marinated shrimp

PREP: 20 minutes   **MARINATE:** 1 hour   **BROIL:** 4 minutes

1   **pound fresh or frozen extra-large shrimp in shells**
2   **tablespoons white balsamic vinegar**
½   **teaspoon finely shredded orange peel**
2   **tablespoons orange juice**
2   **tablespoons finely chopped shallot or onion**
1   **tablespoon olive oil**
¼   **teaspoon salt**
    Finely shredded orange peel

1. Thaw shrimp, if frozen. Peel and devein shrimp, leaving tails intact, if desired. Rinse shrimp and pat dry with paper towels. Place shrimp in a large resealable plastic bag set in a shallow bowl.

2. In a small bowl combine vinegar, ½ teaspoon orange peel, orange juice, shallot, olive oil, and salt. Pour over shrimp. Seal bag and toss gently to coat shrimp. Marinate in the refrigerator for 1 to 4 hours.

3. Preheat broiler. Remove shrimp from marinade, discarding marinade. Arrange shrimp on the unheated rack of a broiler pan. Broil 4 to 5 inches from the heat for 4 to 6 minutes or until shrimp are opaque, turning once halfway through broiling. Sprinkle shrimp with additional orange peel. **Makes 4 servings.**

PER SERVING: 114 cal., 3 g fat (1 g sat. fat), 129 mg chol., 181 mg sodium, 3 g carb., 3 g fiber, 17 g pro.

[make it a meal]

Butter lettuce with avocado and onions
Shaved carrot and asparagus salad
Iced pomegranate tea

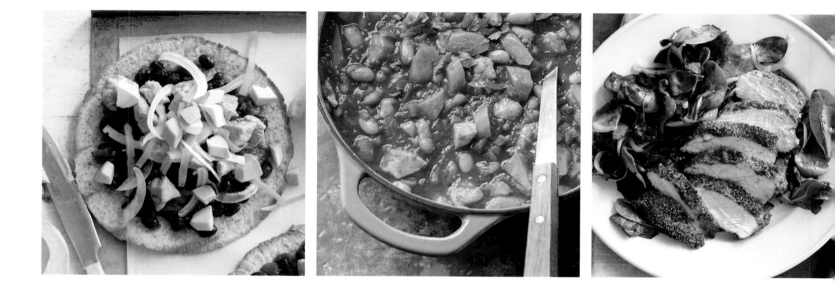

from the pantry

Stock up with our list of recommended ingredients and you'll be able to make 15 different recipes without a trip to the store. Sound good?

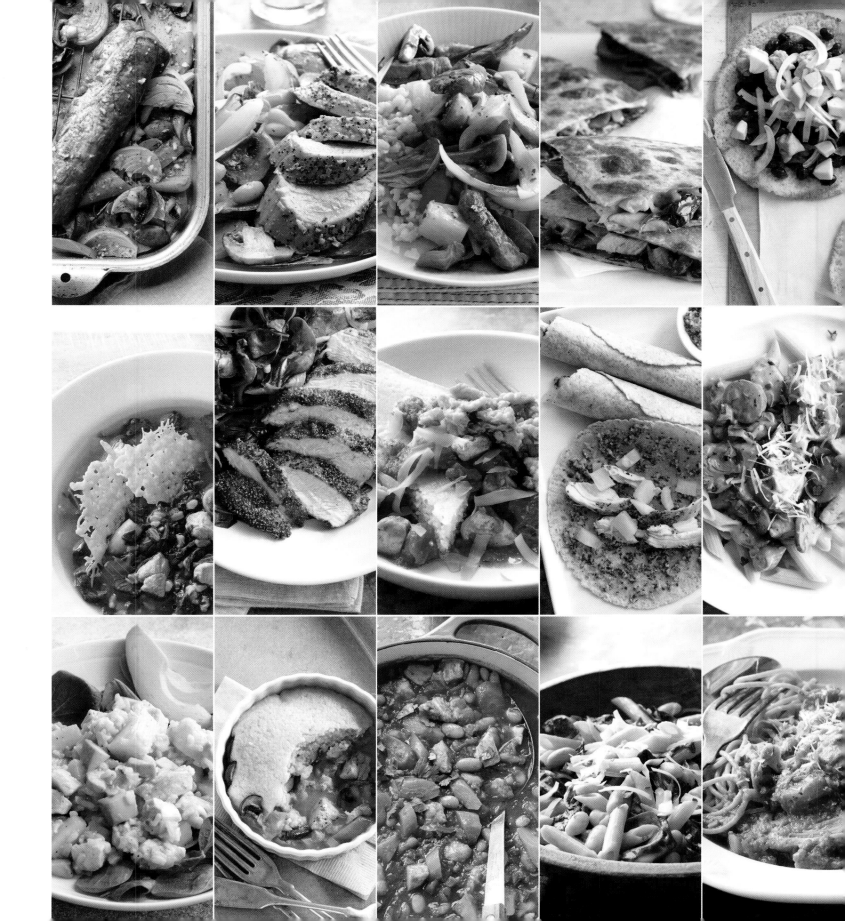

Sticking to a healthy-eating plan means making it easy to eat within your own personally established guidelines every day of the week. Our busy lives can make that difficult, but with just a little bit of preparation, it can be easy—and delicious too. Stock your pantry and refrigerator with all of the ingredients below—plus staples such as salt, pepper, flour, and oil—and you will able to treat yourself and your family to an amazingly diverse array of entrées, including Lime-Glazed Pork Tenderloin and Roasted Vegetables, Spicy Cornmeal-Crusted Chicken with Garlic Spinach, and Pasta with White Beans and Greens.

1 grocery list = 15 recipes

the list

1. Skinless, boneless chicken breasts
2. Natural pork tenderloin
3. Whole grain or multigrain pasta
4. Fresh carrots
5. Canned broth
6. Canned beans
7. Fresh or canned tomatoes
8. Fresh onions
9. Brown rice
10. Cheese

11. Fresh limes or bottled juice
12. Low carb, whole wheat tortillas
13. Fresh pineapple or canned pineapple chunks in juice
14. Dried Italian blend herbs or fresh herbs
15. Chili powder
16. Fresh garlic or bottled minced
17. Canned or frozen artichoke hearts
18. Crushed red pepper
19. Fresh spinach or frozen spinach

20. Fresh avocado or refrigerated mashed avocado
21. Fresh or canned mushrooms
22. Ginger
23. Eggs
24. Evaporated fat-free milk or fat-free milk
25. Corn muffin mix
26. Butter
27. Brown sugar

Quick-cooking pork tenderloin allows you to enjoy juicy, flavorful pork roast any night of the week. Just a few minutes of prep, pop it in the oven for just about 30 minutes, and dinner is done!

lime-glazed pork tenderloin and roasted vegetables

PREP: 20 minutes   **COOK:** 5 minutes   **ROAST:** 25 minutes at 425°F   **STAND:** 3 minutes

Nonstick cooking spray

6	**medium carrots, cut in half and quartered lengthwise**
8	**ounces fresh sliced mushrooms**
1	**cup thin onion wedges**
1	**tablespoon vegetable oil**
1	**to 1½ pounds natural pork tenderloin, trimmed of fat**
¼	**cup chicken broth**
1	**teaspoon finely shredded lime peel**
¼	**cup lime juice**
2	**tablespoons butter, melted**
2	**tablespoons packed brown sugar**
3	**cloves garlic, minced**
½	**teaspoon salt**
¼	**teaspoon ground black pepper**

1. Preheat oven to 425°F. Coat a roasting pan with nonstick cooking spray. Place a small rack in the roasting pan. Arrange carrots, mushrooms, and onion around the rack. Roast, uncovered, for 10 minutes.

2. Meanwhile, heat oil in an extra-large skillet over medium-high heat. Add pork and cook 5 minutes, turning to brown on all sides. Place pork on the rack in the roasting pan.

3. For the glaze, in a small bowl whisk together chicken broth, lime peel, lime juice, butter, brown sugar, garlic, salt, and pepper.

4. Brush glaze over pork and drizzle over vegetables. Stir vegetables to coat.

5. Roast, uncovered, for 25 to 35 minutes or until pork is 145°F when tested with a thermometer and vegetables are tender, stirring vegetables once halfway through cooking. Remove from oven and cover; let stand for 3 minutes. **Makes 4 servings.**

PER SERVING: 305 cal., 12 g fat (5 g sat. fat), 89 mg chol., 514 mg sodium, 23 g carb., 4 g fiber, 27 g pro.

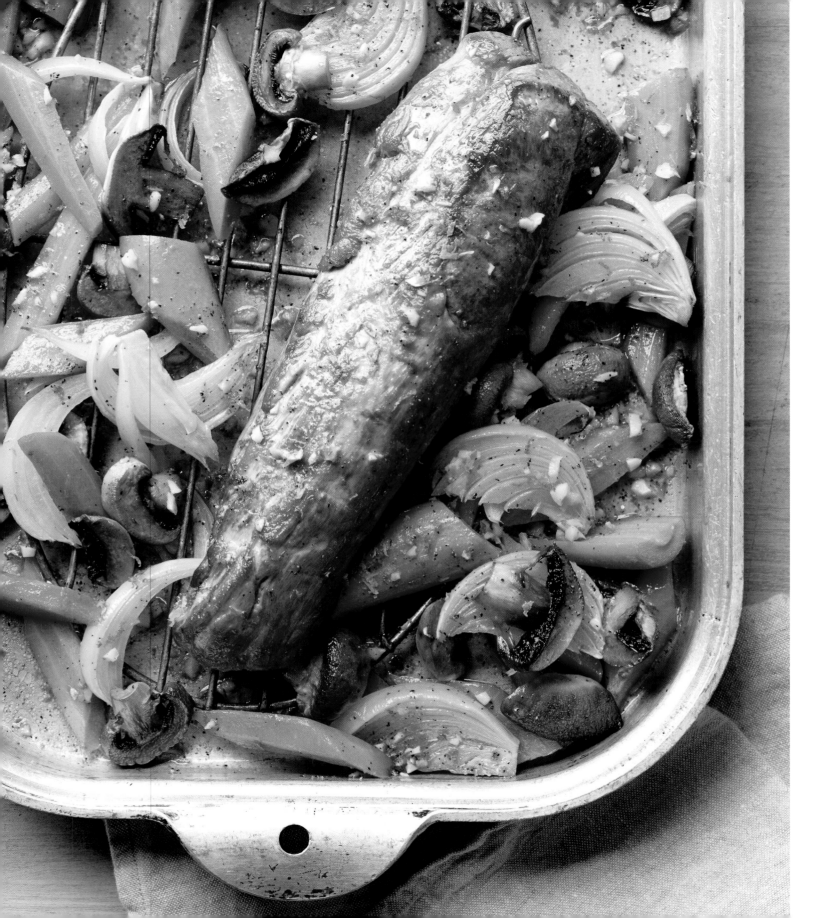

If you can't find cannellini beans—also called white kidney beans—substitute Great Northern beans. Great Northern beans are slightly smaller than cannellini beans, but they have a similar flavor and texture.

pork tenderloin with white bean and veggie saute

PREP: 30 minutes   **ROAST:** 30 minutes at 425°F   **COOK:** 18 minutes   **STAND:** 3 minutes

2	tablespoons canola oil
2	cloves garlic, minced
½	teaspoon ground black pepper
1	pound natural pork tenderloin, trimmed of fat
2	cups thinly sliced onions
1½	cups thinly sliced carrots
1	cup sliced white mushrooms
1	15-ounce can cannellini beans, rinsed and drained
2	teaspoons dried Italian seasoning, crushed
½	teaspoon salt
4	cups fresh spinach
1	to 2 tablespoons fresh lime juice

1. Preheat oven to 425°F. In a small bowl combine 1 tablespoon of the oil, the garlic, and ¼ teaspoon of the ground black pepper. Rub mixture onto the pork with your fingers. Place pork in a shallow roasting pan. Roast 30 to 40 minutes or until an instant-read thermometer inserted in the center of the pork registers 145°F. Remove pork from oven, cover and let stand 3 minutes.

2. Meanwhile, in a large nonstick skillet heat the remaining 1 tablespoon of oil over medium-high heat. Add onions and cook for 6 minutes or until tender and starting to brown. Add carrots and mushrooms. Cook and stir for 10 minutes more or until carrots are crisp-tender. Add beans, Italian seasoning, salt, and the remaining ¼ teaspoon pepper; heat through.

3. Stir in spinach. Cook and stir until spinach is wilted. Add lime juice; stir to combine. Slice pork and serve with vegetable mixture. **Makes 4 servings.**

PER SERVING: 330 cal., 10 g fat (1 g sat. fat), 73 mg chol., 624 mg sodium, 28 g carb., 8 g fiber, 32 g pro.

Sweet and spicy flavors pair particularly well with pork. If you'd like more heat with the sweet, add an additional ¼ teaspoon crushed red pepper to the pineapple mixture, for a total of ½ teaspoon.

pineapple pork and rice

START TO FINISH: 45 minutes

⅔	cup uncooked long grain brown rice
¾	teaspoon salt
½	teaspoon crushed red pepper
1	pound natural pork tenderloin, trimmed of fat
1	tablespoon vegetable oil
½	cup onion wedges
½	cup thinly sliced carrots
8	ounces fresh button mushrooms, quartered
1	20-ounce can pineapple chunks (juice pack)
4	teaspoons grated fresh ginger
2	cups fresh spinach

1. In a small saucepan prepare rice according to package directions except add ½ teaspoon of the salt and ¼ teaspoon of the crushed red pepper with the water.

2. Meanwhile, slice the pork tenderloin into ½-inch slices. Cut each slice into 3 bite-size strips. In a 12-inch nonstick skillet cook the pork in hot oil over medium-high heat until pork is no longer pink.

3. With a slotted spoon remove pork and set aside; keep warm. In the same skillet cook and stir the onion and carrots over medium heat for 3 minutes. Add the mushrooms. Cook and stir for 2 minutes more or until vegetables are crisp tender.

4. Meanwhile, drain pineapple, reserving the juice. In a medium bowl whisk together ⅔ cup of the reserved pineapple juice (add water to make ⅔ cup if needed), ginger, the remaining ¼ teaspoon salt, and the remaining ¼ teaspoon crushed red pepper. Push vegetables to the side of skillet. Add sauce to center of skillet; bring to boiling. Cook until slightly thickened, about 1 minute. Add reserved pork and pineapple chunks to the skillet; toss to coat and heat through. Stir in spinach just before serving.

5. Serve pork mixture over rice. **Makes 4 servings.**

PER SERVING: 388 cal., 8 g fat (1 g sat. fat), 74 mg chol., 528 mg sodium, 50 g carb., 4 g fiber, 29 g pro.

cook smart *Journaling what you eat is a form of self-monitoring as you track your weight loss journey. Download an app from your smart phone to help you.*

If you happen to have leftover roast or grilled pork, use it—thinly sliced—in these toasty quesadillas. If that's the case, start with Step 2.

pork and veggie quesadillas

PREP: 20 minutes   **COOK:** 4 minutes

10	ounces natural pork tenderloin or lean boneless pork, trimmed of fat
	Ground black pepper
	Nonstick cooking spray
1	tablespoon vegetable oil
8	ounces sliced mushrooms
¼	cup thinly sliced onion
1	clove garlic, minced
10	ounces fresh baby spinach
8	6½-inch fajita-size low-carb whole wheat flour tortillas
½	cup shredded Italian-blend cheese

1. Thinly slice pork. Sprinkle with pepper.

2. Coat a large nonstick skillet with cooking spray. Add 2 teaspoons of the oil. Heat over medium-high heat. Add pork to skillet. Cook and stir, about 3 to 4 minutes or until no longer pink. Remove pork from the skillet; set aside.

3. To the same skillet, add the mushrooms, onion, and garlic. Cook and stir for about 3 minutes until onion is tender. Stir in spinach. Cook and stir for 1 minute more or just until spinach is wilted.

4. Coat one side of each of the tortillas with cooking spray. Place 4 of the tortillas, coated side down on a sheet of waxed paper. Evenly sprinkle 1 tablespoon of shredded cheese on each. Evenly place pork slices on top of the cheese. Spread an equal amount of the vegetable mixture onto each quesadilla, followed by another tablespoon of cheese. Top with the last 4 tortillas, coated sides up.

5. Add 1 or 2 quesadillas to the same skillet. Cook over medium-high heat for 2 to 3 minutes per side, until tortillas are crisp and brown and cheese is melting inside. Remove from heat. Repeat with remaining quesadillas. To serve, cut quesadillas into quarters. **Makes 4 servings.**

PER SERVING: 347 cal., 12 g fat (5 g sat. fat), 56 mg chol., 599 mg sodium, 32 g carb., 22 g fiber, 28 g pro.

Fresh and light pico de gallo makes a flavorful topping for these tostadas. Toss together 1 cup chopped tomatoes, 2 tablespoons chopped red onion, 2 tablespoons snipped fresh cilantro, 1 tablespoon minced fresh jalapeño, 1 tablespoon lime juice, 2 cloves minced garlic, and a dash of salt.

pork and black bean tostadas

PREP: 10 minutes   **BAKE:** 5 minutes at 400°F   **COOK:** 15 minutes

Nonstick cooking spray

4   6½-inch low-carb whole wheat flour tortillas

1   teaspoon cooking oil

12   ounces natural pork tenderloin, cut into ½- to ¾-inch cubes

2   cloves garlic, minced

1   14.5-ounce can diced tomatoes, undrained

1   15-ounce can no-salt-added black beans, rinsed and drained

2   teaspoons chili powder

½   teaspoon dried Italian seasoning, crushed

⅛   teaspoon salt

½   cup shredded cheddar cheese (2 ounces)

¼   cup onion slivers

1   ripe avocado, halved, seeded, peeled, and chopped

1. Preheat oven to 400°F. Lightly coat both sides of each tortilla with cooking spray. Place tortillas directly on oven rack and bake for 5 minutes or until crisp and starting to brown, turning once halfway through baking. Remove from oven.

2. Coat a large nonstick skillet with cooking spray. Add oil to the skillet and heat over medium-high heat. Add pork to skillet. Cook, stirring occasionally, for about 5 minutes or until pork is no longer pink. Using a slotted spoon, remove meat from skillet; keep warm.

3. Add garlic to the same skillet and cook for 30 seconds. Add tomatoes; reduce heat. Simmer for about 5 minutes, stirring frequently, until tomatoes thicken. Crush tomatoes with the spoon as they cook.

4. Stir black beans, chili powder, Italian seasoning, and salt into the tomatoes. Heat through.

5. To serve, top baked tortillas with bean mixture, pork, cheese, onions, and avocado. **Makes 4 servings.**

PER SERVING: 404 cal., 15 g fat (5 g sat. fat), 70 mg chol., 611 mg sodium, 36 g carb., 18 g fiber, 31 g pro.

tip: Cook with less oil—it's easy to cut back. Start with a nonstick skillet coated with cooking spray, and then use just 1 teaspoon of oil to sauté. Add a splash of broth if more moisture is needed.

The lacy cheese crisps made of Parmesan are an Italian invention called *fricos*. They make a crispy, low-carb—and very tasty—addition to soups and salads. They can be made from Asiago and cheddar as well.

pork, spinach, and rice soup

PREP: 25 minutes   **COOK:** 20 minutes   **BAKE:** 10 minutes at 350°F

2   tablespoons canola oil
1   pound natural pork tenderloin, trimmed of fat and cut into bite-size pieces
8   ounces fresh sliced mushrooms
1   cup coarsely chopped onion
2   cloves garlic, minced
4   cups no-salt-added vegetable broth
2   cups cooked brown rice
¾   teaspoon salt
½   teaspoon crushed red pepper
2   5-ounce packages fresh spinach, coarsely chopped
3   ounces shredded Parmesan cheese

1. Preheat oven to 350°F. Heat 1 tablespoon of the oil in a Dutch oven over medium-high heat. Cook pork in hot oil until brown on all sides (about 5 minutes). Remove pork from pan; keep warm.

2. Add remaining oil to the Dutch oven. Add the mushrooms, onion, and garlic. Cook and stir until onion is tender, scraping up the browned bits on the bottom of the pan.

3. Add broth, rice, salt, and crushed red pepper; stir. Bring to boiling, reduce heat and simmer 10 minutes. Stir in spinach and pork; cook until spinach wilts and pork is cooked through.

4. Meanwhile, line a large baking sheet with parchment paper. Spoon shredded cheese into six 2 tablespoon mounds at least 2 inches apart. Using the back of a spoon, carefully pat each mound into a 3-inch circle. Bake 10 to 12 minutes or until golden brown. Remove from oven and cool crisps on baking sheet.

5. Serve one Parmesan crisp on top of each serving of soup. **Makes 6 servings.**

PER SERVING: 295 cal., 11 g fat (4 g sat. fat), 59 mg chol., 708 mg sodium, 23 g carb., 4 g fiber, 26 g pro.

The volume of fresh spinach used in this recipe is quite large. If it won't all fit in the pot at once, add it in stages as each previous addition wilts and makes room. Toss and stir with tongs to ensure even cooking.

spicy cornmeal-crusted chicken with garlic spinach

PREP: 15 minutes   **COOK:** 24 minutes   **BAKE:** 10 minutes at 375°F

3	tablespoons all-purpose flour
2	tablespoons packaged corn muffin mix
2	teaspoons chili powder
½	teaspoon Italian seasoning, crushed
½	teaspoon ground black pepper
4	teaspoons butter, melted
4	5-ounce skinless, boneless chicken breast halves
1	tablespoon canola oil
2	cups thinly sliced onion
4	cloves garlic, minced
2	10-ounce packages fresh spinach
½	teaspoon salt

1. Preheat oven to 375°F.

2. In a small shallow bowl combine flour, corn muffin mix, chili powder, Italian seasoning, and ¼ teaspoon of the black pepper. Place melted butter in another shallow bowl.

3. Place chicken in melted butter and turn to coat. Dip in corn muffin mixture, turning to coat evenly. Shake off any excess corn muffin mixture.

4. In a large nonstick skillet heat 1½ teaspoons of the oil over medium-high heat. Cook chicken for 8 minutes or until browned on both sides, turning once halfway through cooking.

5. Place chicken on a rack placed in a shallow baking pan. Bake, uncovered, for 10 to 12 minutes or until cooked through (165°F). Cut into ½-inch-thick slices.

6. Meanwhile, in a 6-quart Dutch oven heat remaining 1½ teaspoons of the oil over medium-low heat. Stir in onion and garlic. Cook, covered, for 13 to 15 minutes or until onions are tender, stirring occasionally. Uncover; cook and stir over medium-high heat for 3 to 5 minutes or until golden. Add spinach, salt, and remaining ¼ teaspoon pepper. Cook and stir spinach just until wilted.

7. Using a slotted spoon, place some of the spinach on each of four serving plates. Top with chicken slices. **Makes 4 servings.**

PER SERVING: 332 cal., 15 g fat (4 g sat. fat), 77 mg chol., 515 mg sodium, 19 g carb., 5 g fiber, 29 g pro.

cook smart Always keep a bag of cleaned spinach or mixed greens in the fridge to pile on sandwiches, an omelet, or soup.

Avocado adds creaminess—and a dose of healthy fat—to this Tex-Mex-style dish. Avocado is rich in monounsaturated fat, which can help lower cholesterol and your chances of stroke and heart disease.

tex-mex chicken-topped corn bread

PREP: 20 minutes   **BAKE:** 14 minutes at 400°F   **COOK:** 15 minutes

Nonstick cooking spray
1   6.5-ounce package corn muffin mix
⅓   cup evaporated fat-free milk or fat-free milk
2   tablespoons vegetable oil
1   egg, lightly beaten
1   pound skinless, boneless chicken breast halves, cut into bite-size pieces
1   cup chopped onion
2   cloves garlic, minced
2   14.5-ounce cans canned diced tomatoes, undrained
1   tablespoon chili powder
1   teaspoon dried Italian seasoning, crushed
½   teaspoon sugar
⅛   to ¼ teaspoon ground black pepper
1   ripe avocado, halved, seeded, and peeled
2   teaspoons lime juice
½   cup shredded cheddar cheese (2 ounces)

1. Preheat oven to 400°F. Coat an 8×8×2-inch square baking dish with cooking spray.

2. In a medium bowl stir together the corn muffin mix, evaporated milk, oil, and egg until blended (batter will be lumpy). Pour batter into prepared dish and bake for 14 to 15 minutes, until a wooden toothpick inserted near the center comes out clean.

3. Meanwhile coat a large nonstick skillet with cooking spray. Heat over medium-high heat. Add chicken and cook for 8 to 10 minutes or until cooked through (165°F). Remove chicken from skillet; set aside.

4. If needed, coat skillet again with cooking spray. Add onion and garlic; cook and stir about 5 minutes or until tender.

5. Place half of the tomatoes in a blender or food processor. Cover and process until smooth. Add the blended tomatoes, the remaining tomatoes, chili powder, Italian seasoning, sugar, and black pepper to the skillet. Simmer, uncovered, for 5 to 10 minutes or until slightly thickened. Stir in chicken. Cook and stir until chicken is heated through.

6. In a small bowl mash avocado with the lime juice. To serve, cut corn bread into six pieces. Top each piece of cornbread with chicken mixture, cheese, and mashed avocado. **Makes 6 servings.**

PER SERVING: 381 cal., 15 g fat (4 g sat. fat), 90 mg chol., 629 mg sodium, 36 g carb., 4 g fiber, 25 g pro.

To warm the tortillas, stack on a plate and cover with plastic wrap. Heat in the microwave on high power for 30 seconds or just until warmed. Use immediately.

pineapple pesto chicken wraps

PREP: 15 minutes **COOK:** 25 minutes

2	8- to 10-ounce skinless, boneless chicken breast halves, halved crosswise
1	tablespoon dried Italian seasoning, crushed
¼	teaspoon salt
¼	teaspoon ground black pepper
	Nonstick cooking spray
2	tablespoons vegetable oil
1	cup packed spinach leaves
1	cup drained juice pack pineapple chunks
2	tablespoons shredded Parmesan cheese
2	cloves garlic, minced
8	6½-inch low-carb whole wheat flour tortillas, warmed

1. Sprinkle chicken on both sides with the Italian seasoning, salt, and pepper.

2. Coat a large nonstick skillet with cooking spray. Add 2 teaspoons of the oil and heat over medium-high heat. Cook chicken breasts in the hot oil about 6 minutes per side or until browned. Reduce heat slightly, cover, and cook for 10 to 12 minutes or until cooked through (165°F) turning once halfway through cooking. Remove from heat and coarsely shred.

3. For the pesto, in a food processor combine spinach, ½ cup of the pineapple, Parmesan, garlic, and remaining 4 teaspoons of oil. Cover and process until pesto ingredients are finely chopped. Coarsely chop reserved ½ cup pineapple; set aside.

4. Spread pesto evenly on tortillas. Place chicken on the pesto and top with chopped pineapple. Roll up. **Makes 4 servings.**

PER SERVING: 392 cal., 15 g fat (4 g sat. fat), 75 mg chol., 695 mg sodium, 34 g carb., 21 g fiber, 32 g pro.

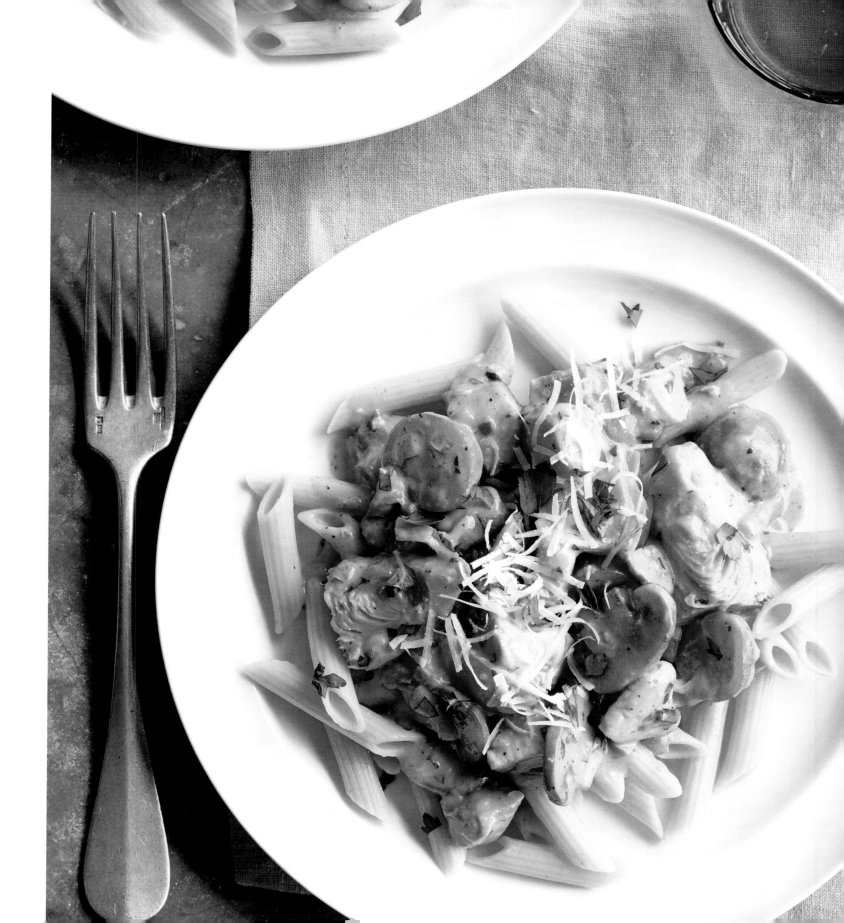

The Alfredo-style sauce in this veggie-packed pasta dish is made with a tiny bit of butter for flavor and lightly thickened evaporated fat-free milk. Tastes indulgent but isn't a bit!

creamy chicken artichoke and mushroom pasta

START TO FINISH: 40 minutes

4 ounces dried multigrain penne pasta
2 tablespoons butter
12 ounces skinless, boneless chicken breast halves, cut into ¾- to 1-inch cubes
½ cup chopped onion
2 cloves garlic, minced
1 8-ounce package fresh button mushrooms, sliced
1 tablespoon all-purpose flour
¼ teaspoon salt
⅛ teaspoon ground black pepper
⅛ teaspoon crushed red pepper
1 12-ounce can evaporated fat-free milk
1 14-ounce can quartered artichoke hearts, drained
1 cup cherry tomatoes, halved
4 tablespoons coarsely chopped fresh Italian parsley
1 ounce shredded Parmesan cheese

1. Cook pasta according to package directions.

2. In a large nonstick skillet heat 1 tablespoon of the butter over medium heat. Add the chicken and cook until no longer pink, about 5 minutes. Remove chicken from skillet; keep warm.

3. Add remaining 1 tablespoon butter to the skillet. Add onion and garlic. Cook for 5 minutes or until tender. Add mushrooms and cook for 5 minutes more, or until nearly all of the liquid has evaporated. Sprinkle with flour, salt, pepper, and crushed red pepper; stir to combine.

4. Whisk in evaporated milk. Cook and stir until reduced by nearly half and thickened. Add artichokes, tomatoes, 3 tablespoons of the parsley, and chicken; heat through.

5. Serve chicken sauce over pasta. Sprinkle with cheese and remaining 1 tablespoon parsley. **Makes 4 servings.**

PER SERVING: 406 cal., 11 g fat (5 g sat. fat), 75 mg chol., 715 mg sodium, 42 g carb., 5 g fiber, 35 g pro.

tip: Substitute evaporated fat-free milk for higher fat ingredients in Alfredo-type dishes. It's a sneaky way to keep that delicious creaminess while slashing fat calories.

To get perfectly ripe, unblemished avocados, buy when they are still green and firm, then ripen on the counter for a couple of days before using. Ripe avocados bruise when transported, but green ones don't.

chicken, pineapple, avocado, and rice salad

START TO FINISH: 30 minutes

5   tablespoons lime juice
5   teaspoons canola oil
2   cloves garlic, minced
⅛   teaspoon crushed red pepper
1   pound skinless, boneless chicken breast, cut into ½- to ¾-inch chunks
    Nonstick cooking spray
1   teaspoon sugar
½   teaspoon ground ginger
½   teaspoon salt
¼   teaspoon ground black pepper
1   ripe avocado, halved, seeded, and peeled
2   cups cooked brown rice or one 8.8-ounce package cooked brown rice
2   cups fresh or juice pack canned pineapple chunks, drained
4   cups torn fresh spinach

1. In a medium bowl whisk together 1 tablespoon of the lime juice, 2 teaspoons of the oil, the garlic, and the crushed red pepper. Add chicken and toss to coat.

2. Coat a large nonstick skillet with cooking spray. Add chicken and marinade to the skillet and cook over medium-high heat until browned and cooked through (165°F), about 5 to 7 minutes. Remove from heat; set aside.

3. For the dressing, in a medium bowl whisk together the remaining lime juice, oil, sugar, ginger, salt, and black pepper. Chop half of the avocado. Gently stir chopped avocado into the dressing.

4. In a large bowl combine cooked rice, pineapple, cooled chicken, and avocado. Serve over fresh spinach and top with avocado. **Makes 4 servings.**

PER SERVING: 402 cal., 15 g fat (2 g sat. fat), 72 mg chol., 429 mg sodium, 40 g carb., 6 g fiber, 29 g pro.

A cross between a chicken pot pie and chicken and dumplings, these homey individual chicken-and-veggie casseroles only need a crisp green salad to round out the meal.

corn muffin-topped chicken stew

PREP: 25 minutes   **BAKE:** 30 minutes at 400°F   **STAND:** 15 minutes

Nonstick cooking spray
1   pound skinless, boneless chicken breast halves, cut into 1-inch pieces
1   teaspoon dried Italian seasoning, crushed
¼   teaspoon ground black pepper
1   tablespoon unsalted butter
2   teaspoons canola oil
8   ounces sliced fresh button mushrooms
¾   cup chopped onion
2   cloves garlic, minced
2   tablespoons all-purpose flour
2¼ cups ½-inch-thick sliced carrots
1   14.5-ounce can reduced-sodium chicken broth
⅛   teaspoon salt
1   6.5-ounce package corn muffin mix
⅓   cup milk
1   egg, lightly beaten
2   tablespoons unsalted butter, melted

1. Preheat oven to 400°F. Coat five 12-ounce individual casserole dishes with nonstick spray; set aside. Sprinkle chicken with Italian seasoning and black pepper.

2. Coat a large nonstick skillet with cooking spray. Heat skillet over medium-high heat, add chicken and cook just until browned, about 5 minutes. Transfer chicken to the prepared dishes.

3. In the same skillet add 1 tablespoon butter and 2 teaspoons oil; stir to combine. Add the mushrooms, onion, and garlic. Cook and stir over medium heat until onion is crisp tender, about 5 minutes. Stir in flour; cook and stir for 1 minute more. Add the carrots, broth, and salt into the skillet. Cook and stir until the mixture is thickened and bubbly. Pour broth mixture over the chicken in the prepared dishes. Cover and bake for 20 minutes.

4. Meanwhile, for muffin topping, stir together the muffin mix, milk, egg, and 2 tablespoons melted butter. Spoon about ¼ cup batter on top of each casserole and return to the oven. Bake, uncovered, for 10 minutes or until a toothpick inserted near the center comes out clean. Let stand 15 minutes before serving. **Makes 5 servings.**

PER SERVING: 399 cal., 14 g fat (6 g sat. fat), 115 mg chol., 670 mg sodium, 41 g carb., 3 g fiber, 27 g pro.

The argument over whether or not beans belong in chili holds no sway when it comes to health-conscious takes on the Tex-Mex-style stew. Cannellini beans add fiber and heft to this hearty version.

thick chicken chili

PREP: 35 minutes   **COOK:** 30 minutes

2   14.5-ounce cans no-salt-added diced tomatoes, undrained
4   cups reduced-sodium chicken broth
2   15-ounce cans no-salt-added cannellini beans, rinsed and drained
2   cups ½-inch-thick sliced carrots
1   cup chopped onion
3   tablespoons chili powder
½   teaspoon salt
½   teaspoon crushed red pepper
1   tablespoon canola oil
1½ pounds skinless, boneless chicken breast halves, cut in ½- to ¾-inch chunks
    Fat-free sour cream (optional)
    Chopped fresh cilantro (optional)

1. Place tomatoes in a blender or food processor; cover and blend or process until smooth. In a 5- to 6-quart pot combine processed tomatoes, broth, beans, carrots, onion, chili powder, salt, and crushed red pepper. Bring to boiling; reduce heat. Simmer, uncovered, for 30 minutes or until carrots are tender and chili is thickened, stirring occasionally.

2. Meanwhile, heat 1½ teaspoons of the oil in a large nonstick skillet over medium-high heat. Add half of the chicken. Cook and stir over medium-high heat for 4 to 5 minutes or until chicken is no longer pink; remove from skillet. Repeat with remaining 1½ teaspoons oil and remaining chicken.

3. Stir cooked chicken into the thickened chili; heat through. If desired, top chili with sour cream and/or chopped cilantro. **Makes 8 servings.**

PER SERVING: 244 cal., 5 g fat (1 g sat. fat), 54 mg chol., 642 mg sodium, 24 g carb., 8 g fiber, 26 g pro.

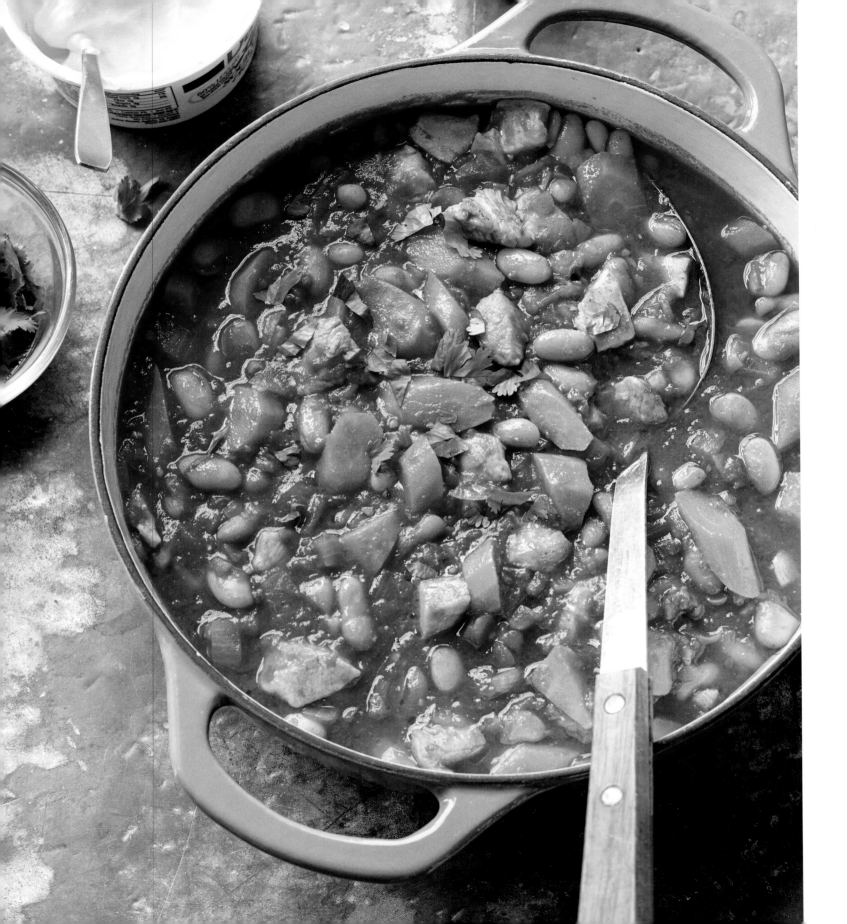

FROM THE PANTRY

White beans and nutrient-rich greens are a classic combination—particularly in Italian cooking. Substitute an equivalent amount of coarsely chopped kale or escarole in this dish, if you like.

pasta with white beans and greens

PREP: 15 minutes   **COOK:** 15 minutes

4   **ounces dried multigrain penne pasta**
1   **tablespoon canola oil**
2   **cloves garlic, minced**
¼   **teaspoon crushed red pepper**
1   **9-ounce package fresh spinach**
¼   **teaspoon salt**
¼   **teaspoon ground black pepper**
½   **cup evaporated fat-free milk**
2   **teaspoons all-purpose flour**
1   **15-ounce can cannellini beans, drained and rinsed**
¾   **cup shredded Parmesan cheese (3 ounces)**

1. Cook pasta according to package directions. Drain; set aside.

2. In an extra-large skillet heat oil over medium-high heat. Add garlic and crushed red pepper and cook for 30 seconds or until fragrant.

3. Add spinach, salt, and black pepper. Cook and toss spinach until spinach wilts.

4. In a small bowl whisk together evaporated milk and flour. Add milk mixture, beans, and pasta to the skillet. Cook and stir until thickened and bubbly. Stir in the Parmesan cheese and serve. **Makes 4 servings.**

PER SERVING: 322 cal., 9 g fat (3 g sat. fat), 11 mg chol., 745 mg sodium, 44 g carb., 9 g fiber, 19 g pro.

tip: Cook with fat-free or low fat (1%) dairy products to power up calcium levels without adding a lot of fat.

Evaporated fat-free milk adds a touch of creaminess to this tomatoey pasta dish. Artichokes impart meatiness without the addition of meat.

artichoke and tomato pasta

PREP: 25 minutes   **COOK:** 15 minutes

6   **ounces dried whole grain spaghetti**
¾   **cup shredded carrots**
½   **cup chopped onion**
2   **large cloves garlic, minced**
2   **tablespoons oil**
2   **14.5-ounce cans no-salt-added diced tomatoes, undrained**
1   **9-ounce package frozen artichoke hearts, thawed and quartered**
4   **teaspoons dried Italian seasoning, crushed**
½   **teaspoon salt**
¼   **teaspoon ground black pepper**
¼   **teaspoon crushed red pepper**
6   **tablespoons evaporated fat-free milk**
½   **cup shredded Parmesan cheese (2 ounces)**
    Crushed red pepper (optional)

1. Cook spaghetti according to package directions; drain and set aside.

2. In an extra-large skillet cook carrot, onion, and garlic in hot oil over medium heat for 3 to 5 minutes or until onion is tender.

3. Place one can of tomatoes in a blender or food processor. Blend or process until smooth. Add tomatoes to skillet. Add remaining can of tomatoes, artichoke hearts, Italian seasoning, salt, black pepper, and the ¼ teaspoon crushed red pepper. Bring to a simmer. Stir in the evaporated milk, ¼ cup of the Parmesan cheese, and spaghetti. Cook and stir until the cheese melts.

4. To serve, sprinkle individual servings with remaining Parmesan cheese and, if desired, additional crushed red pepper. **Makes 6 servings.**

PER SERVING: 245 cal., 8 g fat (2 g sat. fat), 6 mg chol., 453 mg sodium, 37 g carb., 7 g fiber, 11 g pro.

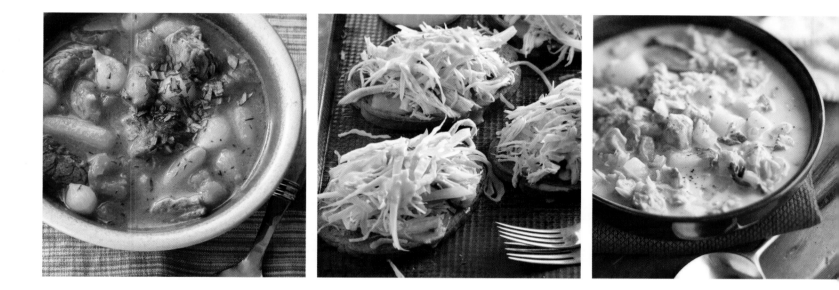

make-ahead
slow cooker

Assemble the recipe the night before, place in the cooker in the
morning, and come home to a hot, healthy, homemade meal.

Salsa verde is made from tomatillos, which have a bright, tangy, almost lemony taste. You can use regular salsa verde or—for a slightly smoky flavor—a fire-roasted version.

braised pork with salsa verde

PREP: 20 minutes   **SLOW COOK:** 6 hours (low) or 3 hours (high)

1	large onion, cut into thin wedges
1½	pounds natural boneless pork loin, cut into 1½-inch pieces
2	large tomatoes, coarsely chopped (1⅓ cups)
1	16-ounce jar salsa verde (green salsa)
½	cup reduced-sodium chicken broth
2	cloves garlic, minced
1	teaspoon ground cumin
¼	teaspoon ground black pepper
3	cups hot cooked brown rice
	Snipped fresh cilantro

1. Place a disposable slow cooker liner in a 3½- or 4-quart ceramic slow cooker liner. Place onion and pork in disposable liner. Top with tomatoes, salsa, broth, garlic, cumin, and black pepper. Using a twist tie close the disposable liner. Place the ceramic liner in the refrigerator overnight.

2. Place ceramic liner in the slow cooker. Remove the twist tie from the disposable liner. Cover and cook on low-heat setting for 6 to 6½ hours or on high-heat setting for 3 hours. Serve with hot cooked brown rice and top each serving with cilantro. **Makes 6 servings.**

PER SERVING: 297 cal., 6 g fat (1 g sat. fat), 78 mg chol., 231 mg sodium, 31 g carb., 3 g fiber, 29 g pro.

[make it a meal

Arugula salad with citrus dressing
Mango, tomato, onion salad
Sparkling water with ginger and lemon]

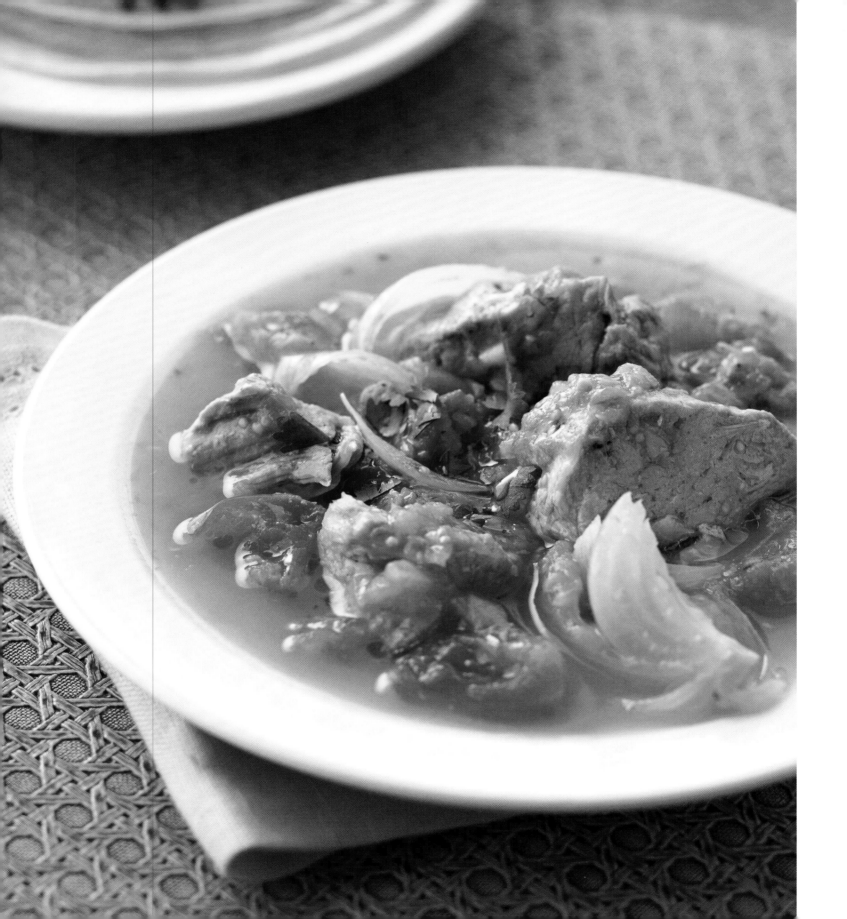

This recipe is ideal when you need to feed a crowd and but have no time to cook—and it's economical too. Pork shoulder is one of the most inexpensive cuts of meat, but turns fork tender in the slow cooker.

mexican-style roast sandwiches

PREP: 30 minutes   **COOK:** 18 minutes   **SLOW COOK:** 10 hours (low) or 5 hours (high)

1	3- to 3½-pound boneless pork shoulder roast
4	cloves garlic, thinly sliced
1½	cups vinegar
1	cup fresh cilantro leaves
1	medium onion, cut into wedges
¼	cup water
1	teaspoon dried oregano, crushed
1	teaspoon ground cumin
¼	teaspoon salt
¼	teaspoon ground black pepper
2	medium red onions, thinly sliced
1	tablespoon vegetable oil
¼	cup lime juice
10	multigrain ciabatta rolls, split and toasted
	Thinly sliced radishes (optional)
	Fresh cilantro sprigs (optional)
	Lime wedges (optional)

1. Place a disposable slow cooker liner in a 3½- or 4-quart ceramic slow cooker liner. Trim fat from roast. Using a sharp knife, make slits evenly on all sides of the roast. Insert garlic slices into slits. Place roast in the disposable liner.

2. In a blender combine vinegar, cilantro leaves, onion wedges, the water, oregano, cumin, salt, and pepper. Cover and blend until smooth. Pour over roast. Using a twist tie close the disposable liner. Place the ceramic liner in the refrigerator overnight.

3. Place ceramic liner back in the slow cooker. Remove the twist tie from the disposable liner. Cover and cook on low-heat setting for 10 to 12 hours or on high-heat setting for 5 to 6 hours.

4. Before serving, in a large skillet cook red onions in hot oil about 15 minutes or until tender. Carefully add lime juice to skillet. Cook and stir for 3 to 5 minutes or until lime juice is evaporated.

5. Meanwhile, using a slotted spoon, remove meat from slow cooker, reserving cooking liquid in cooker. Using two forks, shred meat; discard fat. Transfer shredded meat to a large bowl. Add 1 cup of the cooking liquid, tossing to coat.

6. Spoon about ⅔ cup shredded meat onto each roll bottom. If desired, drizzle with additional cooking liquid. Top each with about 2 tablespoons cooked red onions and, if desired, radishes and cilantro sprigs. Add roll tops. If desired, serve with lime wedges. **Makes 10 servings.**

PER SERVING: 378 cal., 10 g fat (3 g sat. fat), 88 mg chol., 496 mg sodium, 34 g carb., 3 g fiber, 32 g pro.

make it a meal

Tomato wedges with oregano and lime
Romaine with garlic vinaigrette
Vanilla Tres Leches Cake,
recipe page 268

BBQ pork sandwiches are always a hit. Almost everyone loves succulent shredded pork in a sweet, tangy, spicy sauce. This recipe makes a lot—12 servings—but leftovers freeze beautifully.

honey barbecue shredded pork wraps

PREP: 25 minutes   **SLOW COOK:** 10 hours (low) or 5 hours (high)

1	3- to 3½-pound boneless pork shoulder roast
1	cup ketchup
1	cup chopped celery (2 stalks)
1	cup chopped onion (1 large)
½	cup water
⅓	cup honey
¼	cup lemon juice
3	tablespoons white vinegar
2	tablespoons dry mustard
2	tablespoons Worcestershire sauce
½	teaspoon ground black pepper
12	8-inch whole wheat tortillas

1. Place a disposable slow cooker liner in a 4- or 5-quart ceramic slow cooker liner. Trim fat from roast. If necessary, cut roast to fit slow cooker. Place roast in liner. In a medium bowl stir together ketchup, celery, onion, the water, honey, lemon juice, vinegar, mustard, Worcestershire sauce, and pepper. Pour over roast in liner. Using a twist tie close the disposable liner. Place the ceramic liner in the refrigerator overnight.

2. Place ceramic liner in the slow cooker. Remove the twist tie from the disposable liner. Cover and cook on low-heat setting for 10 to 12 hours or on high-heat setting for 5 to 6 hours.

3. Remove meat from cooker, reserving sauce. Using two forks, shred meat; discard fat. Place meat in a large bowl.

4. Skim fat from sauce. Add enough of the reserved sauce to moisten meat (about 1 cup). Spoon about ⅔ cup pork on top of each tortilla; roll up and cut in half to serve. **Makes 12 servings.**

PER SERVING: 326 cal., 10 g fat (3 g sat. fat), 73 mg chol., 589 mg sodium, 24 g carb., 10 g fiber, 31 g pro.

[make it a meal

Sauteed spinach with golden raisins and pine nuts
Sliced mangoes and berries]

● HIGH FIBER ● GLUTEN FREE

Poblano peppers are the deep green, glossy chiles used most often in the decidedly not-skinny Mexican dish, chiles rellenos. Occasionally poblanos have a little heat but are usually very mildly flavored.

cheesy ham and veggie bowls

PREP: 15 minutes **SLOW COOK:** 6 hours (low) or 3 hours (high) **STAND:** 10 minutes

1½	cups chopped zucchini (1 small)
1½	cups frozen whole kernel corn
1	red sweet pepper, chopped (¾ cup)
½	of a medium fresh poblano chile pepper, seeded and thinly sliced (see tip, page 62)
1½	ounces reduced-sodium ham, chopped
½	teaspoon smoked paprika
2	tablespoons water
⅓	cup thinly sliced green onions
¼	cup shredded reduced-fat cheddar cheese (1 ounce)
2	tablespoons snipped fresh cilantro or parsley
1	tablespoon fat-free milk
2	tablespoons shredded reduced-fat cheddar cheese

1. Place a disposable slow cooker liner in a 2-quart ceramic slow cooker liner. Place the zucchini, corn, sweet pepper, poblano pepper, ham, and paprika in the liner. Using a twist tie close the disposable liner. Place the ceramic liner in the refrigerator overnight.

2. Place ceramic liner in the slow cooker. Remove the twist tie from the disposable liner. Drizzle the water over mixture in the liner. Cover and cook on low-heat setting for 6 to 7 hours or on high-heat setting for 3 to 3½ hours. Stir in the green onions, ¼ cup cheese, the cilantro, and milk. Remove liner from cooker. Let stand, covered, for 10 minutes. Serve in bowls; top with remaining cheese. **Makes 2 servings.**

PER SERVING: 251 cal., 7 g fat (4 g sat. fat), 26 mg chol., 364 mg sodium, 37 g carb., 5 g fiber, 16 g pro.

make it a meal

Mixed greens salad
Nectarines with vanilla yogurt

A topping of shredded carrots and lettuce adds freshness and crunch to this Mexican favorite. Optional salsa, guacamole, and light sour cream make it even better.

beef fajitas

PREP: 25 minutes   **SLOW COOK:** 7 hours (low) or 3½ hours (high)

1   **large onion, cut into thin wedges**
2   **pounds boneless beef sirloin steak**
1   **teaspoon ground cumin**
1   **teaspoon ground coriander**
½   **teaspoon ground black pepper**
¼   **teaspoon salt**
2   **medium red and/or green sweet peppers, cut into thin bite-size strips**
¼   **cup lower-sodium beef broth**
8   **7- to 8-inch whole wheat or plain flour tortillas**
1   **cup shredded carrots**
1   **cup coarsely shredded lettuce**

1. Place a disposable slow cooker liner in a 3½- or 4-quart ceramic slow cooker liner. Place onion in liner. Trim fat from steak. In a small bowl stir together cumin, coriander, black pepper, and salt. Sprinkle mixture over one side of the steak; rub in with your fingers. Cut steak across grain into thin bite-size strips. Add steak strips to cooker. Top with sweet peppers. Pour broth over all in liner. Using a twist tie close the disposable liner. Place the ceramic liner in the refrigerator overnight.

2. Place ceramic liner in the slow cooker. Remove the twist tie from the disposable liner. Cover and cook on low-heat setting for 7 to 8 hours or on high-heat setting for 3½ to 4 hours.

3. Using a slotted spoon, spoon ½ cup beef-vegetable mixture onto each tortilla. Top each serving with carrots and lettuce. Fold tortillas over filling. **Makes 8 servings.**

PER SERVING: 298 cal., 8 g fat (2 g sat. fat), 68 mg chol., 485 mg sodium, 20 g carb., 12 g fiber, 33 g pro.

make it a meal

Salsa, guacamole, and light sour cream
Mexican rice
Fresh strawberries

Dijon mustard is packed with flavor but is high in salt too. Be sure to use no-salt-added tomatoes and reduced sodium beef broth to keep the stew from being too salty.

dijon beef stew

PREP: 25 minutes   **SLOW COOK:** 8 hours (low) or 4 hours (high)

2 cups frozen small whole onions
2 cups packaged peeled fresh baby carrots
1 pound beef stew meat, cut into 1-inch cubes
1 14- to 14.5-ounce can no-salt-added diced tomatoes, undrained
1 14.5-ounce can reduced-sodium beef broth
2 tablespoons Dijon-style mustard
4 cloves garlic, minced
1 teaspoon dried thyme, crushed
½ teaspoon dried tarragon, crushed
¼ teaspoon ground black pepper
2 tablespoons snipped fresh parsley or tarragon

1. Place a disposable slow cooker liner in a 3½- or 4-quart ceramic slow cooker liner. Place onions and carrots in the disposable liner. Top with meat. In a small bowl stir together the tomatoes, broth, mustard, garlic, thyme, tarragon, and pepper. Pour over meat. Using a twist tie close the disposable liner. Place the ceramic liner in the refrigerator overnight.

2. Place the ceramic liner in the slow cooker. Remove the twist tie from the disposable liner. Cover and cook on low-heat setting for 8 to 10 hours or on high-heat setting for 4 to 5 hours. Sprinkle each serving with parsley. **Makes 6 servings.**

PER SERVING: 164 cal., 4 g fat (2 g sat. fat), 48 mg chol., 370 mg sodium, 14 g carb., 4 g fiber, 19 g pro.

[make it a meal]

Root vegetable mash
Frisee-radicchio salad
Chai

cook smart *Read healthful food and exercise blogs for added inspiration and motivation.*

Red jalapeño peppers are simply green jalapeños that have ripened further. They are not milder or hotter than green jalapeños, but do have a fruitier, less grassy taste.

steak sandwiches with spicy aïoli

PREP: 25 minutes   **SLOW COOK:** 9 hours (low) or 4½ hours (high)   **STAND:** 5 minutes

1	2- to 2½-pound boneless beef round steak, cut ¾ to 1 inch thick
¼	teaspoon salt
¼	teaspoon black pepper
1	onion, halved and thinly sliced
2	fresh red jalapeño peppers or red Thai chile peppers, stemmed, quartered, and seeded and finely chopped (see tip, page 62)
1	14.5-ounce can lower-sodium beef broth
⅓	cup light mayonnaise
½	teaspoon finely shredded lemon peel
1	tablespoon lemon juice
2	cloves garlic, minced
8	whole wheat sandwich thins, split and toasted
2	medium tomatoes, trimmed and cut into 8 slices total
3	cups lightly packed arugula or fresh spinach leaves

1. Place a disposable slow cooker liner in a 3½- or 4-quart ceramic slow cooker liner. Sprinkle steak with salt and black pepper. Place onion, steak, and one of the jalapeños in the disposable liner; add broth. Using a twist tie close the disposable liner. Place the ceramic liner in the refrigerator overnight.

2. Place ceramic liner in the slow cooker. Remove the twist tie from the disposable liner. Cover and cook on low-heat setting for 9 to 10 hours or on high-heat setting for 4½ to 5 hours.

3. Meanwhile, for the aïoli, in a small bowl combine mayonnaise, lemon peel, lemon juice, and garlic. Add the remaining jalapeño to the mayonnaise mixture. Cover and chill until ready to serve.

4. Transfer meat from cooker to a cutting board. Using two forks, shred meat or thinly slice meat against the grain. Place meat and ½ cup of the cooking liquid in a bowl; let stand for 5 minutes.

5. Spread aïoli on cut sides of sandwich thins. If desired, remove onion from cooker with a slotted spoon and divide among sandwich thin bottoms. Discard remaining cooking liquid. Top onion with shredded or sliced beef and tomato slices. To serve, top tomatoes with arugula and sandwich tops. **Makes 8 servings.**

PER SERVING: 314 cal., 11 g fat (3 g sat. fat), 73 mg chol., 551 mg sodium, 27 g carb., 6 g fiber, 30 g pro.

make it a meal

Sauteed kale, onion, and smoked paprika
Heirloom tomatoes with balsamic vinegar and basil
Baked apple halves

When the hot stew is ladled over the spinach on the serving platter, this wilts the spinach just slightly so that it stays fresh and flavorful but is just warmed through.

greek lamb with spinach and orzo

PREP: 25 minutes **SLOW COOK:** 8 hours (low) or 4 hours (high)

1	tablespoon dried oregano, crushed
1	tablespoon finely shredded lemon peel
4	cloves garlic, minced
½	teaspoon salt
3	pounds lamb stew meat
¼	cup lemon juice
12	ounces dried whole wheat orzo (2 cups dried)
1	10-ounce package fresh spinach, chopped
1	cup crumbled reduced-fat feta cheese (4 ounces)
	Lemon wedges

1. Place a disposable slow cooker liner in a 3½- or 4-quart ceramic slow cooker liner. In a small bowl stir together oregano, lemon peel, garlic, and salt. Sprinkle oregano mixture evenly over lamb; rub in with your fingers. Place lamb in liner. Sprinkle lamb with lemon juice. Using a twist tie close the disposable liner. Place the ceramic liner in the refrigerator overnight.

2. Place ceramic liner in the slow cooker. Remove the twist tie from the disposable liner. Cover and cook on low-heat setting for 8 to 10 hours or on high-heat setting for 4 to 5 hours.

3. Meanwhile, cook orzo according to package directions; drain. Stir cooked orzo into meat mixture in cooker. Place spinach on a large serving platter. Spoon lamb mixture over spinach. Sprinkle with feta cheese. Serve with lemon wedges. **Makes 10 servings.**

PER SERVING: 347 cal., 10 g fat (4 g sat. fat), 92 mg chol., 417 mg sodium, 28 g carb., 8 g fiber, 36 g pro.

make it a meal

Spiced almonds
Roasted asparagus
Salted Caramel Pistachio-Apricot Baklava,
recipe page 279

cook smart *Have a plan—especially when you are eating away from home. If you're closely watching your calories don't get caught in the moment and cave in to making choices you will regret.*

Boneless, skinless chicken thighs are a great choice for the slow cooker. They're flavorful and low fat, and they stay juicy—even over fairly long cooking times.

chicken tostadas

PREP: 25 minutes   **SLOW COOK:** 5 hours (low) or 2½ hours (high)

2	**fresh jalapeño peppers, seeded and finely chopped (see tip, page 62)**
8	**cloves garlic, minced**
3	**tablespoons chili powder**
3	**tablespoons lime juice**
¼	**teaspoon bottled hot pepper sauce**
1	**medium onion, sliced and separated into rings**
2	**pounds skinless, boneless chicken thighs**
1	**16-ounce can fat-free refried beans**
10	**purchased tostada shells**
¾	**cup shredded reduced-fat cheddar cheese (3 ounces)**
2	**cups shredded lettuce**
¾	**cup bottled salsa**
¾	**cup light sour cream**
½	**cup sliced ripe olives**
	Lime wedges (optional)

1. Place a disposable slow cooker liner in a 3½- or 4-quart ceramic slow cooker liner. Place jalapeños, garlic, chili powder, lime juice, and hot pepper sauce in liner. Add onion and chicken. Using a twist tie close the disposable liner. Place the ceramic liner in the refrigerator overnight.

2. Place ceramic liner in the slow cooker. Remove the twist tie from the disposable liner. Cover and cook on low-heat setting for 5 to 6 hours or on high-heat setting for 2½ to 3 hours.

3. Remove chicken and onion from cooker, reserving ½ cup of the cooking liquid. Using two forks, shred chicken. In a medium bowl combine chicken, onion, and the ½ cup cooking liquid.

4. Spread refried beans on tostada shells. Top with hot chicken mixture and shredded cheese. Serve with lettuce, salsa, sour cream, and olives. If desired, serve with lime wedges. **Makes 10 servings.**

PER SERVING: 285 cal., 11 g fat (4 g sat. fat), 86 mg chol., 606 mg sodium, 22 g carb., 5 g fiber, 25 g pro.

[**make it a meal**

Pineapple, jicama, avocado salad
Baby spinach salad with toasted almonds
Vanilla bean frozen yogurt]

A topping of snipped parsley and chopped pimiento-stuffed olives gives this Mexican-style dish a touch of fresh flavor after it emerges from the slow cooker.

chicken vera cruz

PREP: 25 minutes   **SLOW COOK:** 10 hours (low)

1	medium onion, cut into wedges
1	pound yellow-skin potatoes, cut into 1-inch pieces
6	skinless, boneless chicken thighs (about 1¼ pounds total)
2	14.5-ounce cans no-salt-added diced tomatoes
1	fresh jalapeño pepper, seeded and sliced (see tip, page 62)
2	tablespoons Worcestershire sauce
1	tablespoon chopped garlic
1	teaspoon dried oregano, crushed
¼	teaspoon ground cinnamon
⅛	teaspoon ground cloves
1	recipe Parsley-Olive Topping

1. Place a disposable slow cooker liner in a 3½- or 4-quart ceramic slow cooker liner. Place onion in the liner; top with potatoes and chicken thighs. Drain juices from one can of tomatoes and discard the juice. In a bowl stir together the drained and undrained tomatoes, the jalapeño, Worcestershire sauce, garlic, oregano, cinnamon, and cloves; pour over all in cooker. Using a twist tie close the disposable liner. Place the ceramic liner in the refrigerator overnight.

2. Place ceramic liner in the slow cooker. Remove the twist tie from the disposable liner. Cover and cook on low-heat setting for 10 hours. Sprinkle Parsley-Olive Topping over individual servings. **Makes 6 servings.**

PER SERVING: 228 cal., 5 g fat (1 g sat. fat), 78 mg chol., 287 mg sodium, 25 g carb., 5 g fiber, 22 g pro.

parsley-olive topping: In a small bowl stir together ½ cup snipped fresh Italian parsley and ½ cup chopped pimiento-stuffed olives. Makes about ¾ cup.

make it a meal

Summer squash saute
Black beans with cilantro and tomatoes
Grapefruit granita

A ragoût is a thick, long-simmered stew of French origin that is usually cooked on the stovetop or in the oven. This slow cooker adaptation allows you to walk away and let it bubble while you do other things.

chicken ragoût

PREP: 20 minutes   **SLOW COOK:** 8 hours (low)   **COOK:** 8 minutes

8	chicken thighs (about 3½ pounds total), skinned
2	14.5-ounce cans no-salt-added diced tomatoes, drained
3	cups 1-inch carrot slices or baby carrots
1	large onion, cut into wedges (1 cup)
⅓	cup reduced-sodium chicken broth
2	tablespoons white wine vinegar
1	teaspoon dried rosemary, crushed
1	teaspoon dried thyme, crushed
¼	teaspoon ground black pepper
8	ounces fresh button mushrooms, sliced
1	teaspoon olive oil
3	cups hot cooked whole wheat noodles
	Snipped fresh Italian parsley (optional)

1. Place a disposable slow cooker liner in a 3½- or 4-quart ceramic slow cooker liner. Place chicken thighs in the disposable liner. In a large bowl stir together tomatoes, carrots, onion, broth, vinegar, rosemary, thyme, and pepper. Pour over chicken. Using a twist tie close the disposable liner. Place the ceramic liner in the refrigerator overnight.

2. Place ceramic liner in the slow cooker. Remove the twist tie from the disposable liner. Cover and cook on low-heat setting for 8 to 10 hours.

3. Just before serving, in a large nonstick skillet cook and stir mushrooms in hot oil over medium-high heat for 8 to 10 minutes or until golden. Remove chicken from cooker. Remove chicken from bones; discard bones. Stir chicken and mushrooms into mixture in cooker. Serve ragoût over hot cooked noodles. If desired, sprinkle each serving with parsley. **Makes 8 servings.**

PER SERVING: 234 cal., 4 g fat (1 g sat. fat), 57 mg chol., 163 mg sodium, 33 g carb., 7 g fiber, 20 g pro.

[*make it a meal*

Balsamic roasted Brussels sprouts
Maple, Apple, and Date Fruit Crisp,
recipe page 281]

Serving these sandwiches open-faced saves about 100 calories per serving, and it's no great sacrifice to eat with a knife and fork—maybe even a little more refined.

turkey reubens

PREP: 15 minutes   **SLOW COOK:** 7 hours (low) or 3½ hours (high) + 30 minutes   **BROIL:** 2 minutes

2   stalks celery, cut crosswise into thirds
1   medium onion, cut into wedges
1   cup water
½   teaspoon caraway seeds, crushed
¼   teaspoon celery seeds
¼   teaspoon salt
¼   teaspoon ground black pepper
2   to 2½ pounds bone-in turkey breast halves
6   cups shredded fresh cabbage
2   cups purchased coarsely shredded carrots
6   slices rye bread
6   ¾-ounce slices reduced-fat Swiss cheese
½   cup bottled reduced-calorie Thousand Island salad dressing
Celery seeds (optional)

1. Place a disposable slow cooker liner in a 3½- or 4-quart ceramic slow cooker liner. Place the celery and onion in disposable liner; add the water. In a small bowl combine caraway seeds, ¼ teaspoon celery seeds, the salt, and pepper. Sprinkle evenly over turkey. Place turkey on the celery and onions. Using a twist tie close the disposable liner. Place the ceramic liner in the refrigerator overnight.

2. Place the ceramic liner in the slow cooker. Remove the twist tie from the disposable liner. Cover and cook on low-heat setting for 7 to 8 hours or on high-heat setting for 3½ to 4 hours. If using low-heat setting, turn to high-heat setting. Add cabbage and carrots to cooker; cover and cook for 30 minutes more.

3. Preheat broiler. Using tongs, remove cabbage and carrots from cooker; set aside. Transfer turkey to a cutting board; remove and discard skin. Thinly slice or shred turkey. Discard celery and onion from cooker. Place bread slices on a large baking sheet. Broil 3 to 4 inches from the heat for 1 to 2 minutes or until tops are lightly toasted. Turn bread slices over and top each with a slice of cheese. Broil 1 to 2 minutes more or until cheese is melted.

4. Place ¾ cup turkey and ¾ cup cabbage on each cheese-topped bread slice. Top each sandwich with about 1 tablespoon of the salad dressing. If desired, sprinkle with additional celery seeds. **Makes 6 servings.**

PER SERVING: 341 cal., 8 g fat (3 g sat. fat), 86 mg chol., 591 mg sodium, 28 g carb., 4 g fiber, 41 g pro.

[**make it a meal**

Baked sweet potato fries
Gingered Pears, recipe page 289]

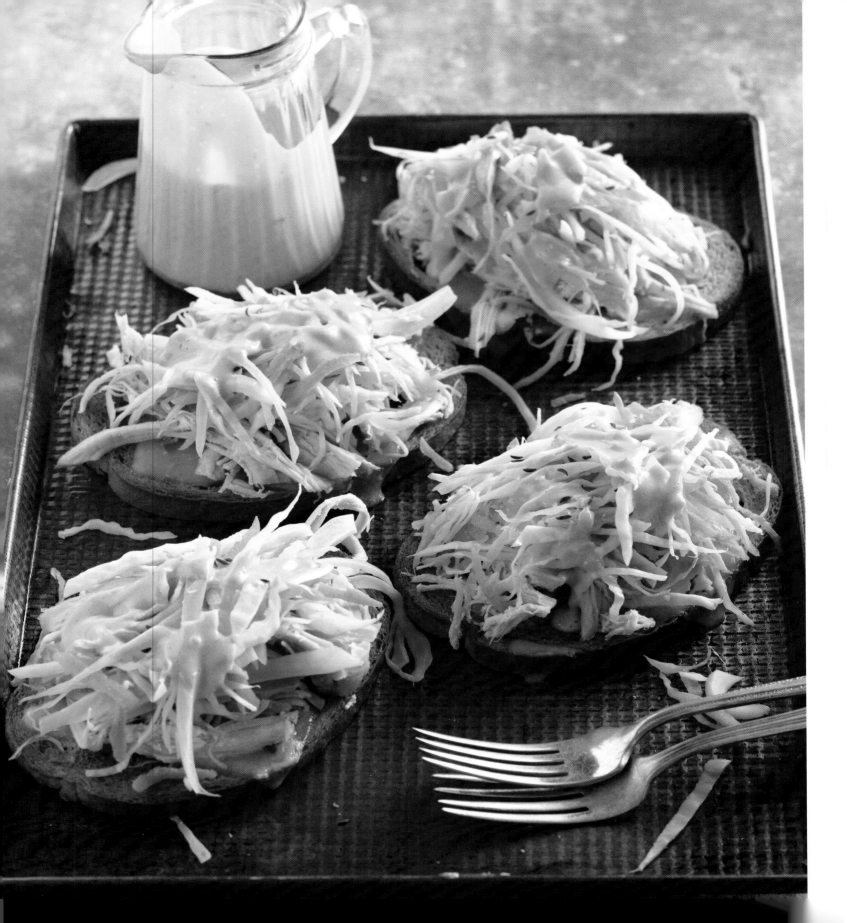

Tomatoes, Italian seasoning, cheese tortellini, and baby spinach turn leftovers from the Thanksgiving bird into a warming, welcome change-of-pace soup.

turkey tortellini soup

PREP: 25 minutes **SLOW COOK:** 6 hours (low) or 3 hours (high) + 30 minutes

4 cups reduced-sodium chicken broth

4 cups water

4 cups coarsely chopped roasted turkey breast (1 pound)

1 14.5-ounce can no-salt-added diced tomatoes, undrained

1 tablespoon dried Italian seasoning, crushed

1 9-ounce package refrigerated cheese tortellini

2 cups fresh baby spinach

6 tablespoons shredded Parmesan cheese (optional)

1. Place a disposable slow cooker liner in a 5- to 6-quart ceramic slow cooker liner. Add broth, the water, chopped turkey, tomatoes, and Italian seasoning. Using a twist tie close the disposable liner. Place the ceramic liner in the refrigerator overnight.

2. Place ceramic liner in the slow cooker. Remove the twist tie from the disposable liner. Cover and cook on low-heat setting for 6 to 8 hours or on high-heat setting for 3 to 4 hours. If using low-heat setting, turn to high-heat setting. Stir in tortellini. Cover and cook for 30 minutes more or until tortellini is tender. Stir in spinach. If desired, sprinkle each serving with 1 tablespoon cheese. **Makes 6 servings.**

PER SERVING: 240 cal., 3 g fat (2 g sat. fat), 63 mg chol., 656 mg sodium, 25 g carb., 3 g fiber, 28 g pro.

make it a meal

Crusty multigrain bread
Chocolate-Filled Lemon Meringues,
recipe page 288

● HIGH FIBER   ● VEGETARIAN   ● GLUTEN FREE

This version of the Mexican soup called posole relies on black beans and sweet potatoes for protein and bulk. Hominy is dried and rehydrated corn. A staple of posole, it adds a delightful chewiness to the soup.

southwestern sweet potato stew

PREP: 15 minutes   **SLOW COOK:** 10 hours (low)

2 **cups lower-sodium vegetable broth**
2 **cups water**
1½ **pounds sweet potatoes, peeled, and cut into 2-inch pieces**
1 **medium onion, chopped (½ cup)**
2 **cloves garlic, minced**
1½ **teaspoons dried oregano, crushed**
1 **teaspoon chili powder**
½ **teaspoon ground cumin**
¼ **teaspoon salt**
1 **15-ounce can golden hominy, rinsed and drained**
1 **15-ounce can no-salt-added black beans, rinsed and drained**
1 **poblano chile pepper, roasted,* seeds removed and cut into thin strips (see tip, page 62) (optional)**
Snipped fresh cilantro
Lime wedges

1. Place a disposable slow cooker liner in a 3½- or 4-quart ceramic slow cooker liner. Place vegetable broth, the water, sweet potatoes, onion, garlic, oregano, chili powder, cumin, and salt in liner. Stir in hominy, beans, and poblano pepper (if using). Using a twist tie close the disposable liner. Place the ceramic liner in the refrigerator overnight.

2. Place ceramic liner in the slow cooker. Remove the twist tie from the disposable liner. Cover and cook on low-heat setting for 10 to 12 hours.

3. Use a potato masher to coarsely mash the sweet potatoes. Sprinkle individual servings with snipped cilantro. Serve with lime wedges. **Makes 6 servings.**

PER SERVING: 202 cal., 1 g fat (0 g sat. fat), 0 mg chol., 491 mg sodium, 42 g carb., 8 g fiber, 7 g pro.

*tip: To roast a poblano chile pepper, preheat oven to 425°F. Cut pepper in half lengthwise; remove stem, seeds, and membranes. Place pepper halves, cut sides down, on a foil-lined baking sheet. Bake for 15 to 20 minutes or until pepper is charred and tender. Bring foil around pepper and fold edges to enclose. Let stand 15 minutes or until cool enough to handle. Use a sharp knife to loosen edges and pull off the skin in strips. Discard skin.

tip: Both sweet potatoes and pumpkin are high on the list as dietary sources for beta-carotene, which has been linked to the prevention of heart disease and cancer.

make it a meal

Sauteed greens with garlic
Broccoli slaw
Sparkling watermelon-mint tea

cook smart *Of the 1,440 minutes in a day, spend at least 30 of them being active.*

● GLUTEN FREE

Most chowders get body and richness from heavy cream—or at the very least from whole milk. Fat-free evaporated milk stands in for those high-fat ingredients in this very low-fat soup.

clam chowder

PREP: 35 minutes   **SLOW COOK:** 7 hours (low) or 3½ hours (high) + 30 minutes

3   stalks celery, chopped (1½ cups)
1½ cups chopped onions (3 medium)
1½ cups chopped red-skin potatoes
2   medium carrots, chopped (1 cup)
1¼ cups water
1   8-ounce bottle clam juice
1   cup reduced-sodium chicken broth or low-sodium vegetable broth
1½ teaspoons dried thyme, crushed
½   teaspoon coarsely ground black pepper
1   12-ounce can fat-free evaporated milk
3   tablespoons cornstarch
2   6.5-ounce cans chopped clams, drained
2   tablespoons dry sherry (optional)
1   teaspoon red wine vinegar
2   slices turkey bacon, cooked according to package directions and chopped
    Chopped green onion (optional)

1. Place a disposable slow cooker liner in a 3½- or 4-quart ceramic slow cooker liner. Add celery, onions, potatoes, carrots, the water, clam juice, broth, thyme, and pepper to liner. Using a twist tie close the disposable liner. Place the ceramic liner in the refrigerator overnight.

2. Place ceramic liner in the slow cooker. Remove the twist tie from the disposable liner. Cover and cook on low-heat setting for 7 hours or on high-heat setting for 3½ hours.

3. If using low-heat setting, turn to high-heat setting. In a medium bowl combine evaporated milk and cornstarch. Stir milk mixture, clams, and sherry (if using) into cooker. Cover and cook for 30 to 60 minutes more or until bubbly around edge. Stir in vinegar just before serving. Sprinkle each serving with bacon and, if desired, green onion. **Makes 6 servings.**

PER SERVING: 222 cal., 2 g fat (1 g sat. fat), 48 mg chol., 599 mg sodium, 27 g carb., 3 g fiber, 25 g pro.

[make it a meal]

Sauteed mushrooms with shallots and thyme
Watercress-baby romaine salad
Apples with blue cheese crumbles

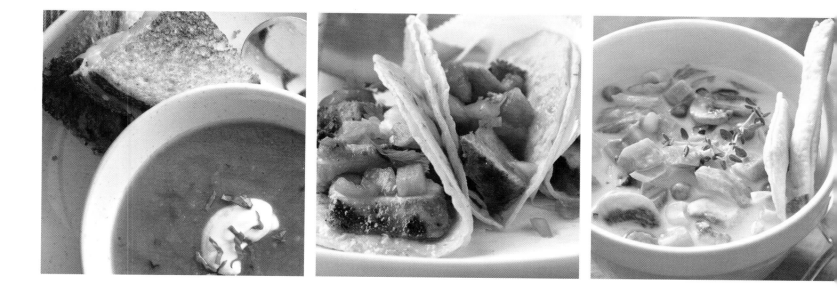

recipe makeovers

Your favorite foods—creamy pastas, nachos, gyros, curries, and fried chicken—slimmed down to work into your healthy-eating plan.

Grilling—a naturally lean cooking method—infuses the meat for these fresh-tasting tacos with great smoky flavor. Make these in summer, when watermelon is at its sweet and juicy peak.

pork tacos with spicy watermelon salsa

PREP: 10 minutes   **GRILL:** 10 minutes

1½   cups chopped seeded watermelon

1   to 2 fresh banana or Anaheim peppers, finely chopped (see tip, page 62)

¼   cup snipped fresh cilantro

1   recipe Southwestern Seasoning or 2 teaspoons purchased Southwestern smoky-blend chipotle seasoning

4   boneless s country-style ribs (about 1¼ pounds total)

24   extra-thin or 12 regular corn tortillas

1. For salsa, in a medium bowl combine watermelon, banana pepper, and cilantro; set aside.

2. Rub Southwestern Seasoning onto ribs to coat. Set ribs aside. Wrap tortillas in foil.

3. For a charcoal or gas grill, place ribs on the grill rack directly over medium heat. Cover and grill for 10 to 12 minutes or until an instant-read thermometer inserted in meat registers 145°F, turning once halfway through grilling. Place foil-wrapped tortillas on grill rack for the last 5 minutes of grilling; turn once.

4. Transfer ribs to a cutting board; let rest for 2 minutes. Slice meat. Serve with tortillas and watermelon salsa. **Makes 6 servings.**

southwestern seasoning: In a small bowl combine ½ teaspoon salt, ½ teaspoon sugar, ½ teaspoon garlic powder, and ½ teaspoon ground chipotle chile powder or chili powder.

PER SERVING: 294 cal., 12 g fat (2 g sat. fat), 69 mg chol., 265 mg sodium, 25 g carb., 4 g fiber, 21 g pro.

[make it a meal]

Lemon-Cilantro Slaw, recipe page 257
White rice with toasted garlic and herbs
Iced tea

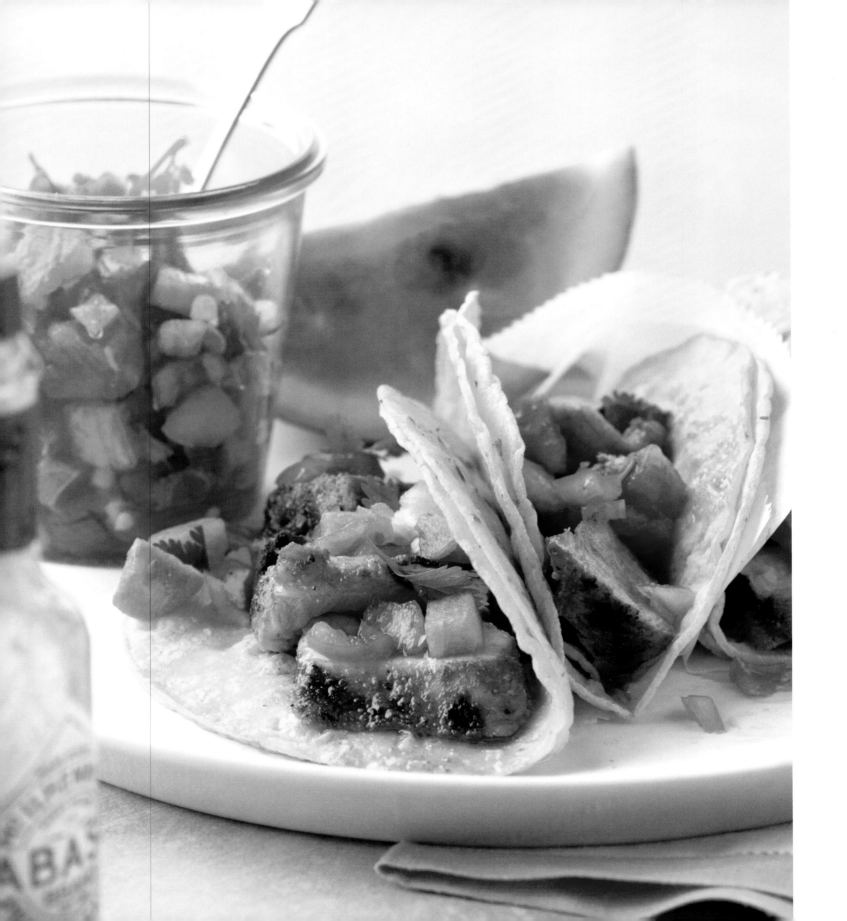

● HIGH FIBER

While traditional flautas are deep-fried to achieve their crispy goodness, these are pan-fried in just a little bit of heart-healthy canola oil—then topped with a fresh corn and tomato salad for a nutrient boost.

mole pork flautas with corn salad

PREP: 35 minutes   **COOK:** 8 minutes

1	cup fresh or frozen whole kernel corn
1	cup grape tomatoes, halved, or chopped tomatoes (2 medium)
¼	cup finely chopped red onion
2	tablespoons snipped fresh cilantro
2	tablespoons lime juice
2	tablespoons canola oil
8	ounces lean boneless pork
	Nonstick cooking spray
1	15-ounce can reduced-sodium black beans, rinsed and drained
¼	cup reduced-sodium chicken broth
2	tablespoons water
2	tablespoons bottled mole sauce
8	6- to 7-inch whole wheat or white low-carb flour tortillas

1. For the corn salad, thaw corn, if frozen; drain well. In a medium bowl combine fresh or thawed corn, tomatoes, red onion, cilantro, lime juice, and 2 teaspoons of the oil. Set aside.

2. Trim fat from meat. Cut meat into ½-inch pieces. Coat a large nonstick skillet with cooking spray; heat skillet over medium heat. Add meat; cook until brown. Add beans, broth, the water, and mole sauce. Cook and stir for 1 to 2 minutes or until heated through. Using the back of a wooden spoon, slightly mash beans.

3. To assemble flautas, spoon meat mixture along one side of each tortilla. Roll up tortilla; secure with wooden toothpicks. Lightly coat outsides of flautas with cooking spray.

4. Using paper towels, wipe out skillet used to cook meat mixture. In the skillet heat 2 teaspoons of the remaining oil over medium-high heat. Add four of the flautas. Cook for 4 to 6 minutes or until brown and crisp on all sides (remove toothpicks as needed). Remove from skillet and keep warm. Repeat with the remaining 2 teaspoons oil and the remaining four flautas. Serve flautas with corn salad. **Makes 4 servings.**

PER SERVING: 377 cal., 14 g fat (2 g sat. fat), 33 mg chol., 651 mg sodium, 54 g carb., 23 g fiber, 30 g pro.

make it a meal

Avocado dip with baked tortilla chips
Cut-up raw veggies
Almond-Tangerine Panna Cotta, recipe, page 290

Spaghetti alla carbonara made the old-fashioned way contains cream, eggs, and bacon. In this slimmed-down version, fat-free half-and-half, cholesterol-free egg product, and a little bit of pancetta provide richness and flavor.

spaghetti alla carbonara

START TO FINISH: 35 minutes

6 ounces dried multigrain spaghetti
3 ounces thinly sliced pancetta
1 medium yellow or red sweet pepper, seeded and cut into thin bite-size strips
½ cup chopped onion (1 medium)
4 cloves garlic, minced
⅓ cup dry white wine
¾ cup fat-free half-and-half
½ cup refrigerated or frozen egg product, thawed
3 ounces grated Pecorino Romano or Parmesan cheese
Freshly ground black pepper (optional)
Fresh Italian parsley sprigs

1. Cook spaghetti according to package directions; drain. Return to hot pan; cover and keep warm.

2. Meanwhile, remove and discard some of the fat from edges of pancetta. Coarsely chop pancetta. In a large nonstick skillet cook pancetta over medium heat until brown. Remove pancetta and drain on paper towels, reserving drippings in skillet. Add sweet pepper and onion to the reserved drippings. Cook over medium heat for 8 to 10 minutes or until very tender, stirring occasionally. Add garlic; cook and stir for 30 seconds.

3. Remove skillet from heat. Carefully add wine; return to heat. Cook for 2 to 4 minutes or until most of the wine is evaporated. Add half-and-half; bring just to boiling, stirring constantly. Add pancetta and cooked spaghetti; toss to coat. Remove from heat. Add egg and half of the cheese; quickly toss to coat.

4. Divide carbonara among serving plates. Sprinkle with the remaining cheese and, if desired, black pepper. Garnish with parsley. **Makes 4 servings.**

PER SERVING: 391 cal., 14 g fat (6 g sat. fat), 32 mg chol., 504 mg sodium, 40 g carb., 4 g fiber, 23 g pro.

[make it a meal]

Porcini Eggplant, recipe page 250
Brussels sprouts-apple salad
Frozen low-fat vanilla ice cream

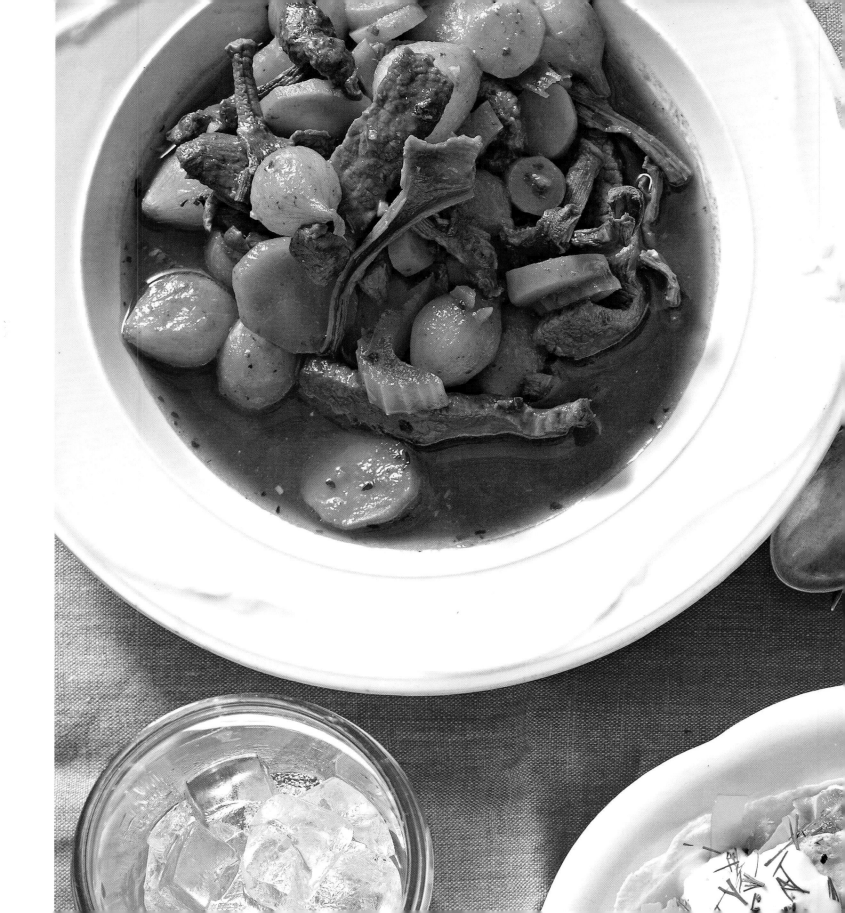

A bounty of vegetables and a cut of lean beef make this quick-to-fix take on Boeuf Bourguignon able to fit into both a healthy eating plan and a busy schedule.

weeknight boeuf bourguignon

PREP: 30 minutes   **COOK:** 10 minutes

12	ounces boneless beef sirloin steak
1	tablespoon olive oil
1	cup thinly sliced carrots (2 medium)
½	cup thinly sliced celery (1 stalk)
2	cloves garlic, minced
1	cup frozen small whole onions
1	ounce dried chanterelle mushrooms, rinsed and chopped
2¾	cups lower-sodium beef broth
¾	cup dry red wine
½	of a 6-ounce can tomato paste (⅓ cup)
1	teaspoon dried herbes de Provence, crushed
¼	teaspoon ground black pepper

1. Trim fat from meat. Cut meat into thin bite-size strips. In a 4-quart nonstick Dutch oven heat 2 teaspoons of the oil over medium-high heat. Add meat; cook until brown. Remove meat from Dutch oven. Add the remaining 1 teaspoon oil to Dutch oven; add carrots, celery, and garlic. Cook for 8 to 10 minutes or until vegetables are tender, stirring occasionally. Return meat to Dutch oven; add onions and dried mushrooms.

2. In a medium bowl whisk together broth, wine, tomato paste, herbes de Provence, and pepper until smooth. Stir broth mixture into meat and vegetables. Bring to boiling; reduce heat. Simmer, covered, for 10 minutes. **Makes 4 servings.**

PER SERVING: 265 cal., 8 g fat (2 g sat. fat), 52 mg chol., 525 mg sodium, 17 g carb., 3 g fiber, 22 g pro.

make it a meal

Cauliflower-parsnip mash
Mixed greens salad
Coconut-Almond Frozen Greek Yogurt with
Hot Chocolate Drizzle, recipe page 293

Rather than simply piling on the cheese—as many versions of their namesake sandwiches do—these burritos feature a cheese sauce made with fat-free milk and lower-fat cheeses.

philly cheesesteak burritos

FREEZE: 30 minutes   **PREP:** 40 minutes

1   **pound beef top round steak**
2   **teaspoons flour**
¼   **teaspoon dry mustard**
½   **cup fat-free milk**
1   **ounce reduced-fat Provolone cheese, torn into pieces (1 to 2 slices)**
2   **tablespoons grated Parmesan cheese**
1   **teaspoon olive oil**
1   **8-ounce package sliced fresh mushrooms, such as shiitake, button, or cremini**
1   **large onion, thinly sliced**
1   **medium red sweet pepper, cut into thin strips**
1   **medium yellow sweet pepper, cut into thin strips**
½   **to 1 teaspoon bottled hot pepper sauce**
4   **8- to 9-inch low-carb whole wheat flour tortillas, such as La Tortilla Factory Smart & Delicious brand**

1. Trim fat from meat. For easier slicing, partially freeze meat for 30 minutes. Thinly slice across the grain into bite-size strips.

2. Meanwhile, prepare cheese sauce. In a small saucepan combine flour and dry mustard. Gradually add milk, stirring with a whisk until blended. Cook and stir until mixture comes to boiling; reduce heat. Cook and stir for 1 minute or until slightly thickened. Gradually add cheeses, stirring until smooth. Remove from heat; cover and keep warm. The mixture will thicken as it cools.

3. In an extra-large skillet heat oil over medium-high heat. Add half of the meat; cook and stir about 3 minutes or until slightly pink in center. Remove with a slotted spoon. Repeat with remaining meat; remove. Add mushrooms, onion, half of the red pepper strips, and half of the yellow pepper strips to skillet; cook and stir about 4 minutes or just until vegetables are tender. Return all of the meat to skillet. Season mixture with hot pepper sauce.

4. To assemble, spoon about 1¼ cups of the meat mixture onto each tortilla. Top with about 2 tablespoons of the cheese sauce. Fold bottom edge of tortilla up and over filling. Fold in one opposite side; roll up from the bottom. If necessary, secure with toothpicks. Serve with remaining sweet pepper strips. **Makes 4 servings.**

PER SERVING: 329 cal., 11 g fat (3 g sat. fat), 65 mg chol., 488 mg sodium, 31 g carb., 14 g fiber, 39 g pro.

[make it a meal

Chopped romaine and light blue cheese dressing
Lemonade with ginger]

Extra-lean ground beef, reduced-fat or fat-free cheeses, and lots of fresh vegetables make these game-time favorites fit into a healthy eating plan any night of the week.

loaded nachos

PREP: 30 minutes   **BAKE:** 10 minutes at 375°F

8	**6-inch corn tortillas**
	Nonstick cooking spray
2	**teaspoons unsalted butter**
1	**tablespoon all-purpose flour**
¾	**cup fat-free milk**
½	**cup shredded part-skim mozzarella cheese (2 ounces)**
½	**cup shredded reduced-fat cheddar cheese (2 ounces)**
1	**ounce fat-free cream cheese, softened**
¼	**teaspoon paprika**
¼	**teaspoon ground turmeric**
8	**ounces extra-lean ground beef (95% lean)**
¼	**cup water**
1	**recipe Taco Seasoning**
1	**cup chopped tomato (1 large)**
½	**cup chopped green sweet pepper**
¼	**cup sliced green onions (2)**
1	**fresh jalapeño pepper, stemmed, seeded, and thinly sliced (see tip, page 62)**
½	**cup chunky mild salsa**
2	**tablespoons snipped fresh cilantro**

1. Preheat oven to 375°F. Cut each tortilla into eight wedges. Place tortilla wedges in a single layer on a large baking sheet. Coat wedges with cooking spray. Bake for 10 to 13 minutes or until wedges are crisp and golden brown on edges. Set aside.

2. For cheese sauce, in a saucepan melt butter over medium heat. Stir in flour until combined. Whisk in milk until smooth. Cook and stir until thickened and bubbly. Cook for 2 minutes more. Stir in mozzarella cheese, cheddar cheese, cream cheese, paprika, and turmeric. Cook and stir over medium heat until cheese is melted and mixture is smooth. Reduce heat to low, stirring occasionally.

3. Coat a large skillet with cooking spray; heat skillet over medium heat. Add meat; cook until brown. Drain off fat. Stir the water and Taco Seasoning into meat in skillet. Cook and stir for 3 to 5 minutes more or until most of the water has evaporated.

4. Arrange tortilla wedges on a serving plate. Top with taco meat, cheese sauce, tomato, sweet pepper, green onions, and, jalapeño. Serve with salsa and cilantro. **Makes 4 servings.**

taco seasoning: In a small bowl stir together 2 teaspoons paprika, 1 teaspoon ground cumin, ½ teaspoon black pepper, ½ teaspoon ground coriander, ⅛ to ¼ teaspoon ground chipotle chile pepper, and ⅛ teaspoon cayenne pepper.

PER SERVING: 291 cal., 11 g fat (6 g sat. fat), 61 mg chol., 356 mg sodium, 23 g carb., 3 g fiber, 24 g pro.

make it a meal

Mixed greens-herb salad
Chocolate-Sesame Cookies, recipe page 276
Water with crushed raspberries

Be sure to buy Indian red curry paste to make this classic dish—not Thai red curry paste, which would give it a completely different flavor!

simplified chicken tikka masala

PREP: 30 minutes   **MARINATE:** 2 hours   **BAKE:** 10 minutes at 400°F

1   **pound skinless, boneless chicken breast halves**
½   **cup plain fat-free yogurt**
1   **tablespoon grated fresh ginger or 1 teaspoon ground ginger**
3   **cloves garlic, minced, or ½ teaspoon garlic powder**
½   **teaspoon ground coriander**
½   **teaspoon paprika**
¼   **teaspoon ground cardamom**
¼   **teaspoon ground cumin Nonstick cooking spray**
1   **8-ounce can no-salt-added tomato sauce**
¼   **cup half-and-half or light cream**
1   **to 2 tablespoons red curry paste**
½   **teaspoon garam masala**
⅛   **teaspoon salt**
2   **tablespoons snipped fresh cilantro (optional)**
2   **cups hot cooked brown basmati rice or one 8.8-ounce pouch cooked brown rice, heated according to package directions**

1. Cut chicken breast halves into 3-inch pieces; pierce each piece in several places with a sharp knife. Cut any thicker chicken pieces in half horizontally. Place chicken in a resealable plastic bag set in a shallow dish. For marinade, in a small bowl combine yogurt, ginger, garlic, coriander, paprika, cardamom, and cumin. Pour marinade over chicken. Seal bag; turn to coat chicken. Marinate in the refrigerator for 2 to 4 hours, turning bag occasionally.

2. Preheat oven to 400°F. Drain chicken, discarding marinade. Coat a grill pan with cooking spray; heat pan over medium heat. Add chicken pieces; cook for 8 to 10 minutes or until light brown, turning once.

3. Transfer chicken to a 2-quart shallow baking dish or gratin dish. In a medium bowl combine tomato sauce, half-and-half, curry paste, garam masala, and salt. Pour over chicken, stirring to coat.

4. Bake, uncovered, about 10 minutes or until chicken is no longer pink (170°F), stirring once. If desired, sprinkle chicken with cilantro. Serve chicken and sauce over rice. **Makes 4 servings.**

PER SERVING: 312 cal., 6 g fat (2 g sat. fat), 79 mg chol., 507 mg sodium, 34 g carb., 4 g fiber, 30 g pro.

make it a meal

Sauteed spinach with garlic and feta
Roasted cauliflower and shallots
Fresh apricots

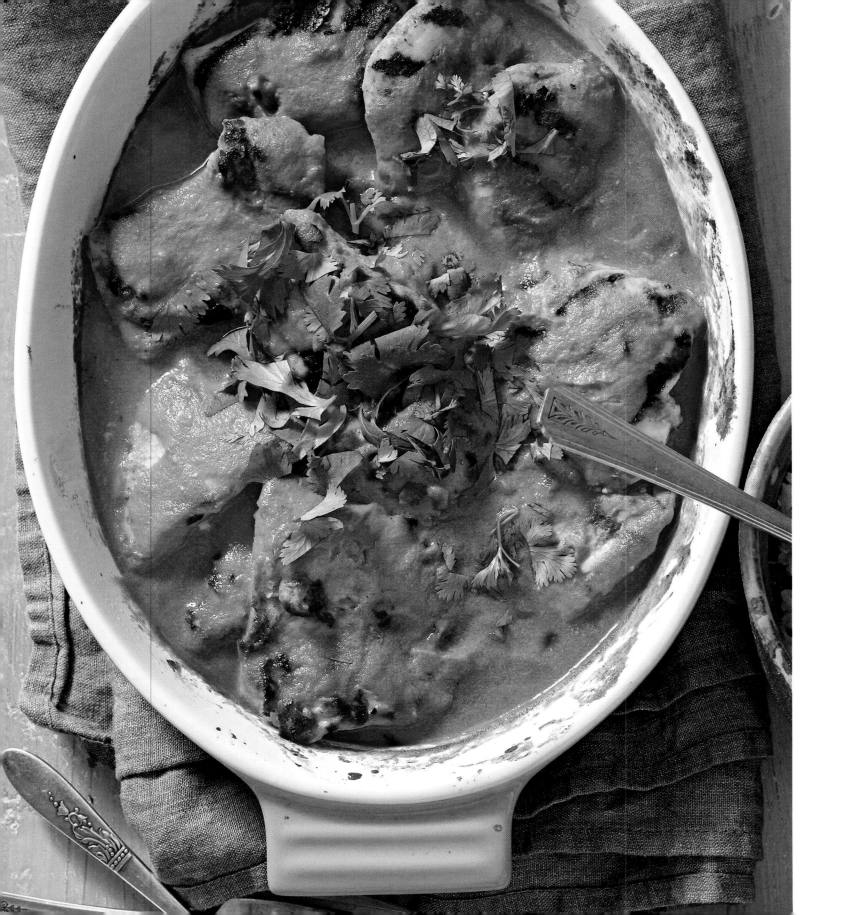

These are a little fussy to make—save them for a leisurely Saturday—but they are well worth the effort. A brightly flavored pico de gallo salsa is the crowning touch on the creamy corn and chicken filling.

chicken and green chile tamales

STAND: 30 minutes   **PREP:** 45 minutes   **COOK:** 30 minutes

16	**dried corn husks**
	Boiling water
2	**cups shredded cooked skinless, boneless chicken thighs**
1	**cup green salsa**
1½	**cups masa harina**
¼	**cup vegetable oil**
1	**teaspoon salt**
¼	**teaspoon baking powder**
1¼	**cups reduced-sodium chicken broth**
2	**cups chopped fresh tomatoes**
1	**cup chopped onion (1 large)**
¼	**cup snipped fresh cilantro**
½	**to 1 fresh jalapeño pepper, halved, seeded, and finely chopped (see tip, page 62)**
3	**tablespoons lime juice**
¼	**teaspoon ground black pepper**

1. In a large bowl combine corn husks and enough boiling water to cover. Weight down with a heavy pan lid or plate. Let stand for 30 minutes or until corn husks are soft. Drain; pat dry.

2. For filling, in a bowl combine chicken and salsa. For dough, in a mixing bowl beat masa harina, oil, ½ teaspoon of the salt, and baking powder with an electric mixer on medium speed until combined. Beat in enough broth to make a thick paste.

3. To assemble tamales, starting 1½ inches from the wide edge of a corn husk, spread 2 tablespoons dough into a 3×4-inch rectangle. Spoon 2 tablespoons filling down center of dough. Fold long edge of husk over filling so it overlaps dough slightly. Roll husk around outside of filled dough. Tie ends with strips of corn husk or 100-percent cotton kitchen string. Repeat with the remaining corn husks, dough, and filling.

4. To steam, stand tamales upright in a steamer basket set over at least 1½ inches of boiling water in a deep Dutch oven. Cover basket. Reduce heat to medium. Steam for 30 minutes or until tamales easily pull away from corn husks and dough is spongy. Remove from steamer; let stand 10 minutes.

5. In a bowl combine the tomatoes, onions, cilantro, jalapeño, lime juice, the remaining salt, and the black pepper. Serve over tamales. **Makes 8 servings.**

PER SERVING: 233 cal., 11 g fat (2 g sat. fat), 47 mg chol., 591 mg sodium, 24 g carb., 3 g fiber, 12 g pro.

[*make it a meal*

Toasted pistachios with lime peel and garlic
Avocado salad
Raspberry sorbet]

A corn flake coating baked to crispy perfection really does give these chicken cutlets a satisfying crunch comparable to traditional fried chicken.

oven-fried chicken with tomato gravy

START TO FINISH: 15 minutes   **BAKE:** 15 minutes at 425°F

Nonstick cooking spray

1 **6-ounce carton plain Greek yogurt**

2 **tablespoons honey**

2½ **cups corn flakes, coarsely crushed**

½ **cup fresh basil leaves, snipped**

4 **skinless, boneless chicken breast halves, cut crosswise into 8 pieces**

Salt

Ground black pepper

1 **14.5-ounce can fire-roasted tomatoes with garlic, undrained**

2 **teaspoons Worcestershire sauce**

1. Preheat oven to 425°F. Lightly coat a baking sheet with cooking spray; set aside.

2. In a shallow dish combine yogurt and honey. In another shallow dish combine corn flakes and ¼ cup of the basil. Arrange chicken pieces on a tray; cover with plastic wrap. Pound lightly with the flat side of a meat mallet to make pieces of uniform thickness. Sprinkle chicken with salt and pepper and dip in yogurt mixture then in corn flake mixture. Place on prepared baking sheet.

3. Bake for 15 to 18 minutes or until chicken is crisp and golden on outside and no longer pink.

4. Meanwhile, for tomato gravy, in a small saucepan combine undrained tomatoes, Worcestershire sauce, and the remaining ¼ cup basil. Cook and stir over medium-low heat until heated through. Serve with chicken. **Makes 4 servings.**

PER SERVING: 301 cal., 6 g fat (3 g sat. fat), 80 mg chol., 634 mg sodium, 32 g carb., 3 g fiber, 30 g pro.

make it a meal

Asparagus and Wild Mushrooms, recipe page 242
Roasted red potatoes
Cherry frozen yogurt

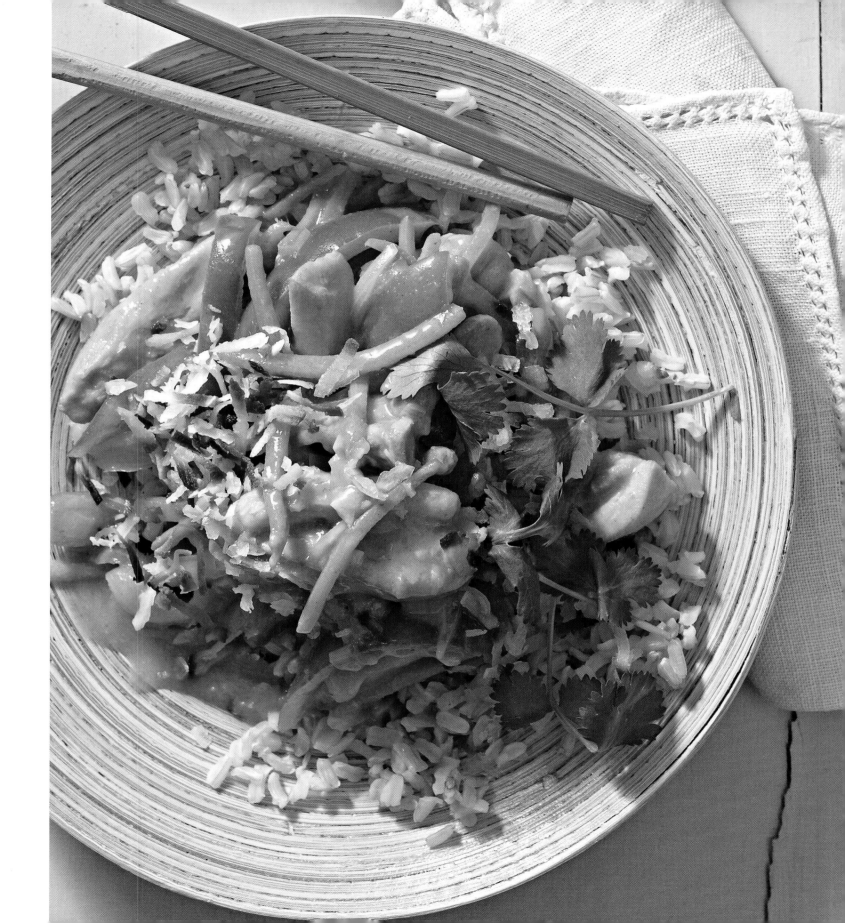

Curries may be packed with nutrient-rich vegetables, but regular coconut milk can contribute unwanted calories and fat. Here, just enough light coconut milk coats the chicken and vegetables.

thai green chicken curry

START TO FINISH: 35 minutes

1	cup canned unsweetened light coconut milk
¼	cup reduced-sodium chicken broth
2	to 3 tablespoons green curry paste
2	teaspoons cornstarch
2	teaspoons finely chopped fresh lemon grass or 1 teaspoon finely shredded lemon peel
	Nonstick cooking spray
1	medium green sweet pepper, seeded and cut into thin bite-size strips
1	medium onion, halved and thinly sliced
¾	cup packaged julienned or coarsely shredded fresh carrots
3	cloves garlic, minced
12	ounces skinless, boneless chicken thighs
2	teaspoons canola oil
2	cups hot cooked brown basmati rice or regular brown rice
¼	cup flaked coconut, toasted (see tip, page 64)
	Fresh cilantro

1. For sauce, in a medium bowl whisk together coconut milk, broth, curry paste, cornstarch, and lemon peel (if using); set aside.

2. Coat a wok or large nonstick skillet with cooking spray; heat wok over medium-high heat. Add sweet pepper and onion; cook and stir for 3 minutes. Add carrots, garlic, and lemon grass (if using); cook and stir about 2 minutes more or until vegetables are crisp-tender. Remove vegetables from wok.

3. Trim fat from chicken and cut into thin bite-size strips. Add oil to wok; add chicken. Cook and stir over medium-high heat for 3 to 5 minutes or until chicken is no longer pink. Push from center of wok.

4. Stir sauce; add to center of wok. Cook and stir until slightly thickened and bubbly. Return vegetables to wok; stir all ingredients together to coat with sauce. Cook and stir for 2 minutes or until heated through.

5. Serve chicken curry over rice. Sprinkle with coconut and cilantro. **Makes 4 servings.**

PER SERVING: 344 cal., 13 g fat (5 g sat. fat), 81 mg chol., 445 mg sodium, 37 g carb., 4 g fiber, 21 g pro.

[**make it a meal**

Tom Yum Soup or other brothy soup
Cucumber salad
Sliced mango]

Traditional "chicken and fries" means skin-on, oven roasted chicken and deep-fried potatoes. Skinning the chicken and oven-baking the fries helps this classic French dish fit into a weight-loss plan.

poulet frites

PREP: 30 minutes   **BAKE:** 35 minutes at 400°F

4	bone-in chicken thighs (about 1¼ pounds total), skinned
4	chicken drumsticks (about 1 pound total), skinned
½	teaspoon salt
½	teaspoon ground black pepper
1	tablespoon Dijon-style mustard Nonstick cooking spray
3	medium shallots, quartered
½	cup dry white wine
½	cup reduced-sodium chicken broth
4	sprigs fresh thyme
8	ounces russet potatoes, peeled
8	ounces sweet potatoes, peeled
4	teaspoons olive oil or canola oil
1	tablespoon snipped fresh chives
2	teaspoons snipped fresh thyme

1. Arrange oven racks toward top of oven. Preheat oven to 400°F. Sprinkle chicken with ¼ teaspoon of the salt and ¼ teaspoon of the pepper; spread with mustard. Coat an extra-large oven going skillet with cooking spray; heat skillet over medium-high heat. Add chicken pieces, meaty sides down. Cook for 3 to 5 minutes or until brown. Remove from heat. Turn chicken pieces. Add shallots, wine, broth, and thyme sprigs. Place skillet on center oven rack. Bake, uncovered, for 10 minutes.

2. Coat a 15×10×1-inch baking pan with cooking spray. For fries, cut potatoes lengthwise into ⅜-inch-thick strips. Place russet potatoes and sweet potatoes in separate bowls. Add 2 teaspoons of the oil to each bowl; toss to coat. Transfer russet potatoes to the baking pan; place pan on top oven rack. Bake chicken and potatoes, uncovered, for 5 minutes. Add sweet potatoes to pan with russet potatoes. Bake chicken and potatoes, uncovered, 20 minutes more or until chicken is no longer pink (180°F) and potatoes are just tender, turning potatoes once.

3. Remove chicken and shallots from skillet, reserving cooking juices. Transfer fries to a bowl. Add chives, thyme, the remaining ¼ teaspoon salt, and the remaining ¼ teaspoon pepper; toss to coat.

4. Bring cooking juices to boiling over medium heat. Cook, uncovered, for 3 to 5 minutes or until juices are slightly reduced. Remove thyme sprigs. Spoon cooking juices over chicken and shallots. Serve with fries. **Makes 4 servings.**

PER SERVING: 375 cal., 11 g fat (2 g sat. fat), 157 mg chol., 664 mg sodium, 25 g carb., 3 g fiber, 35 g pro.

make it a meal

Roasted red pepper dip with veggies
Mixed greens salad
Maple, Apple, and Date Fruit Crisp, recipe page 281

To substitute dry herbs for the fresh, use ½ teaspoon dried thyme leaves, crushed, and ¼ teaspoon dried oregano, crushed. Add dried herbs with the chicken broth.

chicken pot pie stew *pictured on page 184*

PREP: 25 minutes   **BAKE:** 6 minutes at 400°F   **COOK:** 25 minutes

4	teaspoons canola oil
1	pound skinless, boneless chicken thighs, cut into ¾-inch pieces
1	cup chopped celery (2 stalks)
1	cup chopped carrots (2 medium)
½	cup chopped onion (1 medium)
2	cloves garlic, minced
2½	cups reduced-sodium chicken broth
2	cups fresh mushrooms, sliced
1	cup fresh sweet corn kernels or frozen whole kernel corn, thawed
½	cup frozen peas, thawed
1	12-ounce can evaporated fat-free milk
¼	cup all-purpose flour
1	teaspoon snipped fresh thyme
½	teaspoon snipped fresh oregano
¼	teaspoon salt
¼	teaspoon ground black pepper
1	recipe Piecrust Crackers (use about ¼ of the recipe)

1. In a 4- to 5-quart nonstick Dutch oven heat 2 teaspoons of the oil over medium heat. Add chicken. Cook and stir about 4 to 5 minutes until chicken pieces are browned on all sides. Remove from Dutch oven and transfer to a bowl; set aside.

2. In the same Dutch oven heat the remaining oil over medium heat. Add celery, carrots, onion, and garlic. Cook and stir for 8 to 10 minutes or until vegetables are just tender.

3. Add chicken broth to pot; bring to boiling. Add chicken, mushrooms, corn, and peas. Return to boiling; reduce heat. Simmer, uncovered, about 8 minutes or until chicken is done and vegetables are just tender.

4. In a small bowl whisk together evaporated milk and flour; add to stew. Cook and stir until stew thickens and bubbles. Cook and stir for 2 minutes. Stir in fresh thyme, fresh oregano, salt, and pepper. Ladle into six bowls and serve with 3 Piecrust Crackers. **Makes 6 servings.**

PER SERVING: 295 cal., 9 g fat (2 g sat. fat), 72 mg chol., 557 mg sodium, 30 g carb., 3 g fiber, 24 g pro.

piecrust crackers: Preheat oven to 400°F. Let half of a 15-ounce package rolled refrigerated unbaked piecrust (1 crust) stand according to package directions. Unroll piecrust onto a lightly floured surface. In a small bowl whisk 1 tablespoon refrigerated or frozen egg product, thawed, and ¼ teaspoon water together. Lightly brush mixture over piecrust. Sprinkle piecrust with 1 teaspoon fresh thyme leaves. Using a 1¼-inch floured cutter or knife, cut piecrust into desired shapes. Place piecrust shapes on a baking sheet. Bake for 6 to 8 minutes or until golden brown. Cool completely on the baking sheet. To store extra piecrust crackers, place them in an airtight container and freeze for up to 1 month. Serve with soup, salad, or mix into your favorite snack mix. **Makes about 72 piecrust crackers.**

make it a meal

Yogurt dip with sweet peppers

Wilted spinach and olives

Blood orange sorbet

Any dish with the word "Alfredo" in it implies that it's off limits for anyone on a weight-loss journey, but this dish is different. A few ingredient swaps, and it's not only allowed but encouraged!

chicken alfredo

START TO FINISH: 35 minutes

4 ounces dried whole grain linguine
5 cups bite-size strips zucchini and/or yellow summer squash
1 pound skinless, boneless chicken breast halves, cut into bite-size strips
1 small onion, cut into thin wedges
2 cloves garlic, minced
1 tablespoon butter
1 8-ounce carton light sour cream
2 tablespoons all-purpose flour
⅔ cup fat-free milk
½ teaspoon salt
⅛ teaspoon ground black pepper
¼ cup finely shredded Parmesan cheese (1 ounce)
2 tablespoons snipped fresh parsley
¼ cup finely shredded Parmesan cheese (1 ounce)

1. In a Dutch oven cook linguine according to package directions, adding the zucchini strips for the last 2 minutes of cooking. Drain well. Return to hot Dutch oven; cover and keep warm.

2. Meanwhile, in a large nonstick skillet cook chicken, onion, and garlic in melted butter over medium heat for 8 minutes or until chicken is cooked through and onion is tender, stirring occasionally.

3. In a medium bowl stir together sour cream and flour until well mixed. Stir in milk, salt, and pepper. Add sour cream mixture to chicken in skillet. Cook and stir over medium heat just until bubbly; cook and stir for 2 minutes. Add ¼ cup Parmesan cheese, stirring until melted.

4. Serve the chicken over the noodles and zucchini. Sprinkle with parsley and ¼ cup Parmesan cheese. **Makes 6 servings.**

PER SERVING: 272 cal., 10 g fat (6 g sat. fat), 57 mg chol., 477 mg sodium, 25 g carb., 3 g fiber, 21 g pro.

tip: Visually learning proper portions of energy dense foods like pasta, butter, and salad dressing helps one get back to reality. Enlist the help of your measuring cups and/or spoons when dishing up at home.

[make it a meal

Sauteed broccoli with garlic and almonds
Sauteed nectarines with pistachios
Green tea with lemon]

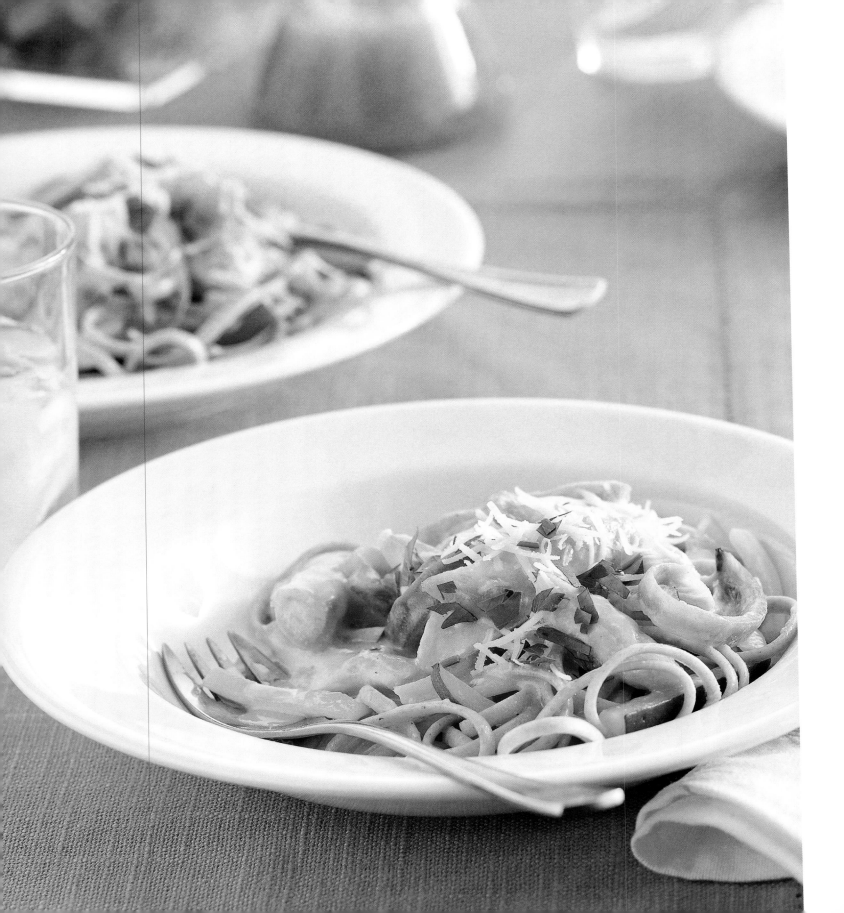

The meatballs can be made ahead, then cooled and refrigerated or frozen. Just reheat in the microwave until warm and proceed with Step 3.

turkey meatball grinder

PREP: 25 minutes   **BAKE:** 15 minutes at 400°F   **BROIL:** 2 minutes

Nonstick cooking spray

1   **14.5-ounce can no-salt-added diced tomatoes**

2   **tablespoons no-salt-added tomato paste**

1   **tablespoon balsamic vinegar**

2   **cloves garlic, halved**

1   **teaspoon Italian seasoning, crushed**

¼   **teaspoon crushed red pepper**

¼   **teaspoon salt**

1   **egg, lightly beaten**

⅔   **cup soft whole grain or whole wheat bread crumbs**

12   **ounces uncooked ground turkey breast**

1   **medium red sweet pepper, cut into thin strips**

1   **small sweet onion, cut into thin wedges**

2   **teaspoons olive oil**

4   **whole grain or whole wheat hot dog buns, toasted**

1   **ounce thinly sliced mozzarella cheese**

1. Preheat oven to 400°F. Coat a 15×10×1-inch baking pan with nonstick cooking spray; set aside. In a blender or food processor combine undrained diced tomatoes, tomato paste, vinegar, garlic, Italian seasoning, crushed red pepper, and salt. Cover and blend or process until smooth.

2. In a large bowl combine the egg, ¼ cup of the sauce, and bread crumbs. Add turkey and mix until combined. Form meat into twelve 2-inch meatballs. Place meatballs in prepared baking pan. Bake about 15 minutes or until no longer pink (165°F).

3. Meanwhile, in a large skillet cook sweet pepper and onion in hot oil over medium heat about 8 minutes or until very tender, stirring occasionally. Stir in remaining sauce. Heat through. Add meatballs and stir gently to coat with sauce.

4. Increase oven temperature to broil. Broil split buns 4 to 5 inches from the heat for 1 minute. Line buns with cheese slices. Broil about 1 minute more or until cheese is melted and bread is toasted.

5. Place three meatballs in each bun. Top with sauce.
Makes 4 servings.

PER SERVING: 364 cal., 8 g fat (2 g sat. fat), 98 mg chol., 600 mg sodium, 43 g carb., 8 g fiber, 31 g pro.

make it a meal

Baked potato fries
Spinach salad with light Italian vinaigrette
Carrot Cake Parfaits, recipe page 285

A garlicky cucumber-yogurt sauce gives these lean turkey gyros the great flavor of the high-fat lamb-and-beef gyros you get at Greek or Middle Eastern restaurants—with none of the guilt.

grilled turkey gyros

PREP: 25 minutes   **GRILL:** 6 minutes

12	ounces uncooked ground turkey breast
¼	cup finely chopped onion
1	egg, lightly beaten
1	tablespoon fine dry bread crumbs
1	teaspoon ground coriander
½	teaspoon ground cumin
⅛	teaspoon salt
⅛	teaspoon ground black pepper
2	cloves garlic, minced
1	tablespoon olive oil
4	whole wheat pita bread rounds
1	cup thinly sliced cucumber
1	cup diced tomatoes (2 medium)
2	tablespoons snipped fresh Italian parsley
1	recipe Cucumber-Yogurt Sauce

1. For patties, in a large bowl combine turkey breast, onion, egg, bread crumbs, coriander, cumin, salt, pepper, and garlic. Shape meat into twelve ½-inch-thick patties. Brush all sides of the patties with olive oil; set aside. Wrap pita bread rounds in foil.

2. For a charcoal or gas grill, place patties and foil-wrapped pita bread on the greased rack of a covered grill directly over medium heat. Grill for 6 minutes or until an instant-read thermometer inserted into patties registers 165°F and pitas are heated through, turning once halfway through grilling.

3. Divide cucumber slices among pita bread rounds. Top each with three patties, ¼ cup of the tomatoes, and parsley. Drizzle with Cucumber-Yogurt Sauce. Fold pitas around fillings; secure with toothpicks. **Makes 4 servings.**

cucumber-yogurt sauce: In a small bowl combine ⅓ cup yogurt, ¼ cup shredded seeded cucumber, 1 tablespoon tahini (sesame seed paste), 2 cloves minced garlic, and ⅛ teaspoon salt. Cover and chill for at least 20 minutes.

PER SERVING: 332 cal., 9 g fat (1 g sat. fat), 95 mg chol., 560 mg sodium, 37 g carb., 6 g fiber, 31 g pro.

make it a meal

Carrot slaw
Chopped endive with light Greek vinaigrette
Low-fat vanilla ice cream

Spicy, heavily smoked—and high fat—andouille sausage is an element in authentic jambalaya, but a spicy, lower fat turkey sausage does the flavoring trick quite nicely in this slimmed-down version.

catfish and turkey sausage jambalaya

PREP: 30 minutes   **COOK:** 10 minutes   **STAND:** 5 minutes

8	ounces fresh or frozen skinless catfish fillets
4	ounces uncooked turkey hot Italian sausage links, cut into ½-inch pieces
1	teaspoon olive oil or cooking oil
½	cup chopped onion (1 medium)
½	cup chopped green sweet pepper
½	cup stalk chopped celery (1 stalk)
3	cloves garlic, minced
1	14.5-ounce can no-salt-added diced tomatoes, drained
1	14-ounce can reduced-sodium chicken broth
1½	cups instant brown rice
1½	teaspoons paprika
1	teaspoon dried oregano, crushed, or 1 tablespoon snipped fresh oregano
½	teaspoon dried thyme, crushed, or 1½ teaspoons snipped fresh thyme
⅛	to ¼ teaspoon cayenne pepper
	Fresh oregano (optional)

1. Thaw fish, if frozen. Rinse fish; pat dry with paper towels. Cut fish into ¾-inch chunks. Set aside.

2. In a large saucepan cook sausage pieces in hot oil over medium heat for 3 to 4 minutes or until browned. Add onion, sweet pepper, celery, and garlic; cook for 10 minutes or until vegetables are tender and sausage is no longer pink, stirring occasionally.

3. Stir in tomatoes, chicken broth, uncooked rice, paprika, dried oregano and dried thyme (if using), and cayenne pepper. Bring to boiling; reduce heat to medium-low. Cover and simmer for 5 minutes. Stir in catfish pieces, fresh oregano and fresh thyme (if using); cook about 5 minutes more or until liquid is nearly absorbed and rice is tender. Remove from heat. Cover and let stand for 5 minutes. Using a slotted spoon, spoon jambalaya into shallow bowls. If desired, garnish with fresh oregano.

Makes 4 servings.

PER SERVING: 263 cal., 9 g fat (2 g sat. fat), 44 mg chol., 548 mg sodium, 29 g carb., 4 g fiber, 18 g pro.

make it a meal

Corn bread
Sauteed greens
Amazing Apple Tart, recipe page 275

● HIGH FIBER ● VEGETARIAN

These elegant seafood enchiladas have a rich, creamy sauce just like similar recipes, but—thanks to reduced-fat cream cheese and sour cream, and fat-free milk—not even close to the calorie count.

seafood enchiladas

PREP: 40 minutes   **BAKE:** 35 minutes at 350°F

1¼ **pounds fresh or frozen medium shrimp**

8 **ounces fresh or frozen halibut, cod, tilapia, or sea bass**

¾ **cup chopped red sweet pepper (1 medium)**

2 **fresh poblano chile peppers, stemmed, seeded, and chopped (see tip, page 62)**

½ **cup chopped onion (1 medium)**

2 **teaspoons canola oil**

2 **cloves garlic, minced**

8 **low-carb whole wheat flour tortillas**

4 **ounces reduced-fat cream cheese (Neufchâtel), softened**

1 **8-ounce carton light sour cream**

2 **tablespoons all-purpose flour**

¼ **teaspoon salt**

¼ **teaspoon ground black pepper**

¾ **cup fat-free milk**

½ **cup thinly sliced green onions (4)**

1. Thaw shrimp and halibut, if frozen. Peel and devein shrimp. Rinse shrimp and halibut; pat dry with paper towels. Preheat oven to 350°F. Grease a 3-quart rectangular baking dish. Cook shrimp in boiling water for 1 to 3 minutes or until shrimp are opaque. Rinse with cold water; drain and chop.

2. Measure thickness of fish. Place a steamer insert in a large skillet. Add water to skillet to just below the steamer insert; bring to boiling. Place fish in the steamer insert. Cover; steam over medium heat 4 to 6 minutes per ½-inch thickness or until fish flakes easily with a fork. Flake fish into bite-size pieces.

3. In a nonstick skillet cook sweet pepper, chile peppers, and onion in hot oil over medium heat for 5 to 10 minutes or until vegetables are tender. Stir in garlic; cook for 1 minute. Remove from heat. Stir in shrimp and halibut.

4. Stack tortillas; wrap in foil. Bake 10 minutes or until heated through. For sauce, in a mixing bowl beat cream cheese with an electric mixer on medium speed until smooth. Beat in sour cream, flour, ¼ teaspoon salt, and black pepper. Beat in milk. Add ½ cup sauce to shrimp mixture; stir. Divide among tortillas; roll up and place seam sides down in baking dish. Pour remaining sauce over tortillas.

5. Bake, covered, for 35 minutes or until heated through. Sprinkle with green onions. **Makes 8 servings.**

PER SERVING: 283 cal., 11 g fat (4 g sat. fat), 139 mg chol., 540 mg sodium, 22 g carb., 9 g fiber, 24 g pro.

make it a meal

Red leaf lettuce salad
Roasted asparagus with shaved Parmesan
Citrus granita

Waistline-watching chowder lovers, take note. There's no need to deny yourselves a bowl of the creamy stuff. This recipe—made with turkey bacon and fat-free dairy products—denies you nothing.

new england clam chowder

START TO FINISH: 45 minutes

2	10-ounce cans whole baby clams, undrained
	Water
	Nonstick cooking spray
2	slices turkey bacon, halved
½	cup chopped onion (1 medium)
½	cup thinly sliced celery (1 stalk)
2	medium potatoes, cut into ½-inch pieces
2	cups small cauliflower florets (about 1-inch pieces)
¼	teaspoon dried thyme, crushed
⅛	teaspoon ground black pepper
2½	cups fat-free milk
½	cup fat-free half-and-half
2	tablespoons all-purpose flour
¾	cup coarsely shredded carrots

1. Drain clams, reserving liquid. Chop half of the clams; set chopped and whole clams aside. Add enough water to the reserved clam liquid to measure 1½ cups total liquid; set aside.

2. Coat a large saucepan with cooking spray; heat saucepan over medium heat. Add bacon, onion, and celery to saucepan. Cook for 5 to 8 minutes or until onion is tender and bacon is cooked through, stirring occasionally. Remove bacon from pan; drain on paper towels. Chop bacon and set aside.

3. Stir potatoes, cauliflower, thyme, pepper, and the reserved 1½ cups clam liquid into onion mixture. Bring to boiling; reduce heat. Simmer, covered, for 10 to 12 minutes or until potatoes are tender. Remove from heat; cool slightly. Transfer half of the potato mixture (about 2 cups) to a blender or food processor. Cover and blend or process until smooth. Return to the saucepan.

4. In a medium bowl whisk together milk, half-and-half, and flour until smooth. Add all at once to the saucepan. Cook and stir just until boiling. Stir in chopped and whole clams and carrots. Return to boiling; reduce heat. Cook for 1 minute. Serve chowder with chopped bacon. **Makes 6 servings.**

PER SERVING: 208 cal., 3 g fat (1 g sat. fat), 77 mg chol., 642 mg sodium, 25 g carb., 3 g fiber, 22 g pro.

make it a meal

Multigrain rolls
Wilted escarole with apples
Pomegranate tea

● HIGH FIBER

There are few combinations more comforting than grilled cheese and tomato soup. Rest easy knowing this rendition has all the great taste of what you're used to, with less sugar and more fiber.

roasted tomato soup and grilled cheese sandwiches

PREP: 40 minutes   **ROAST:** 30 minutes at 350°F

3½   **pounds roma tomatoes, halved**
½   **cup chopped onion (1 medium)**
¼   **cup finely chopped celery**
¼   **cup shredded carrot**
1   **clove garlic, minced**
2   **teaspoons olive oil**
1   **cup unsalted chicken stock or reduced-sodium chicken broth**
1   **tablespoon snipped fresh thyme**
1   **teaspoon snipped fresh rosemary**
1   **tablespoon snipped fresh basil**
¼   **teaspoon salt**
¼   **teaspoon ground black pepper**
2   **tablespoons plain fat-free Greek yogurt**
     Plain fat-free Greek yogurt
     Snipped fresh basil
1   **recipe Grilled Cheese Sandwiches**

1. Preheat oven to 350°F. Arrange tomatoes, cut sides down, in two shallow baking pans. Roast for 30 minutes. Remove from oven; let stand until cool enough to handle. Using your fingers, lift skins from tomatoes and discard skins.

2. In a saucepan cook onion, celery, carrot, and garlic in hot oil for 4 minutes or until onion is tender. Add tomatoes and liquid from pans, the chicken stock, thyme, and rosemary. Bring to boiling; reduce heat. Simmer, covered, for 5 minutes. Cool slightly.

3. Transfer half of the tomato mixture to a food processor. Cover and process until smooth. Repeat with the remaining tomato mixture. Return all to the saucepan. Stir in the 1 tablespoon basil, the salt, and pepper. Stir in the 2 tablespoons yogurt.

4. Ladle soup into bowls. Top with additional yogurt and fresh basil. Serve with Grilled Cheese Sandwiches. **Makes 4 servings.**

grilled cheese sandwiches: Coat one side of each of 4 slices reduced-calorie whole wheat bread with nonstick cooking spray. Lay bread, coated sides down, on waxed paper. Sprinkle 2 slices with ¼ cup shredded reduced-fat cheddar cheese and ¼ cup shredded American cheese. Top with the remaining bread, coated sides up. Grill sandwiches in a hot large skillet over medium heat for 6 minutes or until bread is golden brown and cheese is melted, turning once halfway through cooking time.

PER SERVING: 213 cal., 8 g fat (3 g sat. fat), 12 mg chol., 466 mg sodium, 29 g carb., 8 g fiber, 12 g pro.

make it a meal

Cauliflower, bacon, golden raisin salad
Sliced apples

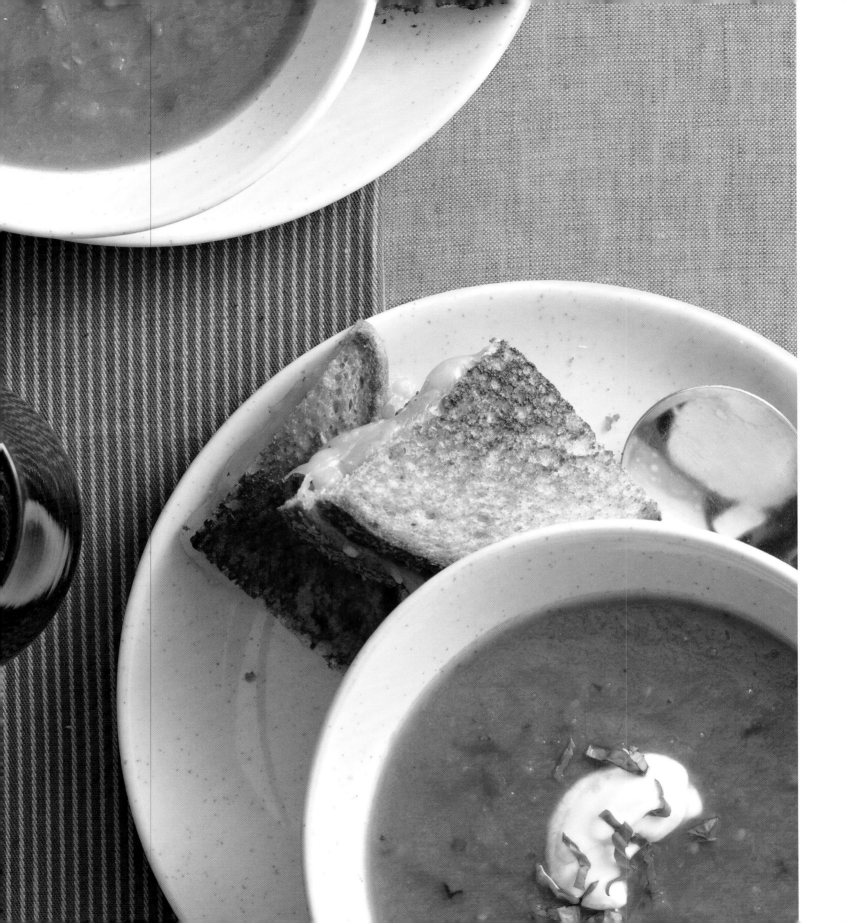

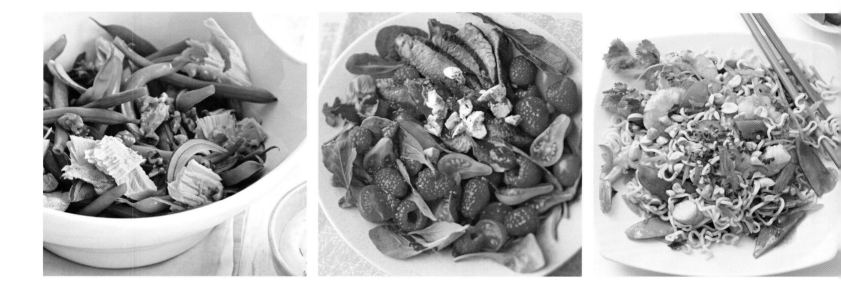

fresh & fast

Keep cool with these main-dish salads. Vibrant in color and flavor and loaded with fresh vegetables and fruits, they're feel-good food.

Fresh apricots are in season from May through August. If you can't find them, canned apricots in light syrup make a perfectly acceptable substitute.

citrus pork and arugula salad

START TO FINISH: 30 minutes

1	1-pound natural pork tenderloin
¼	teaspoon salt
¼	teaspoon black pepper
1	tablespoon canola oil
½	teaspoon finely shredded orange peel
⅓	cup orange juice
1	tablespoon rice vinegar or white wine vinegar
2	teaspoons reduced-sodium soy sauce
2	teaspoons honey
1	teaspoon toasted sesame oil
½	teaspoon grated fresh ginger or ⅛ teaspoon ground ginger
6	cups baby arugula
2	medium fresh apricots, halved, seeded, and quartered, or ½ cup canned unpeeled apricot halves in light syrup, drained and quartered
1	small avocado, peeled, seeded, and sliced or chopped
¼	cup dried apricots, sliced

1. Trim fat from pork. Cut pork crosswise into ¼-inch slices. Sprinkle with the salt and pepper.

2. In an extra-large skillet cook pork, half at a time, in hot oil over medium-high heat for 2 to 3 minutes or until meat is just slightly pink in center, turning once. Remove from skillet and set aside.

3. For dressing, in a screw-top jar combine orange peel and juice, vinegar, soy sauce, honey, sesame oil, and ginger. Cover and shake well to combine.

4. Place arugula on a serving platter. Top with pork slices, apricots, avocado slices, and dried apricots. Drizzle with the dressing. **Makes 4 servings.**

PER SERVING: 272 cal., 11 g fat (2 g sat. fat), 74 mg chol., 314 mg sodium, 19 g carb., 3 g fiber, 26 g pro.

tip: Enjoy creamy, rich avocado in place of mayonnaise on sandwiches or in salads for a fraction of the fat, plus added fiber and vitamins.

[make it a meal

Cold soba noodle salad
Muligrain flat bread]

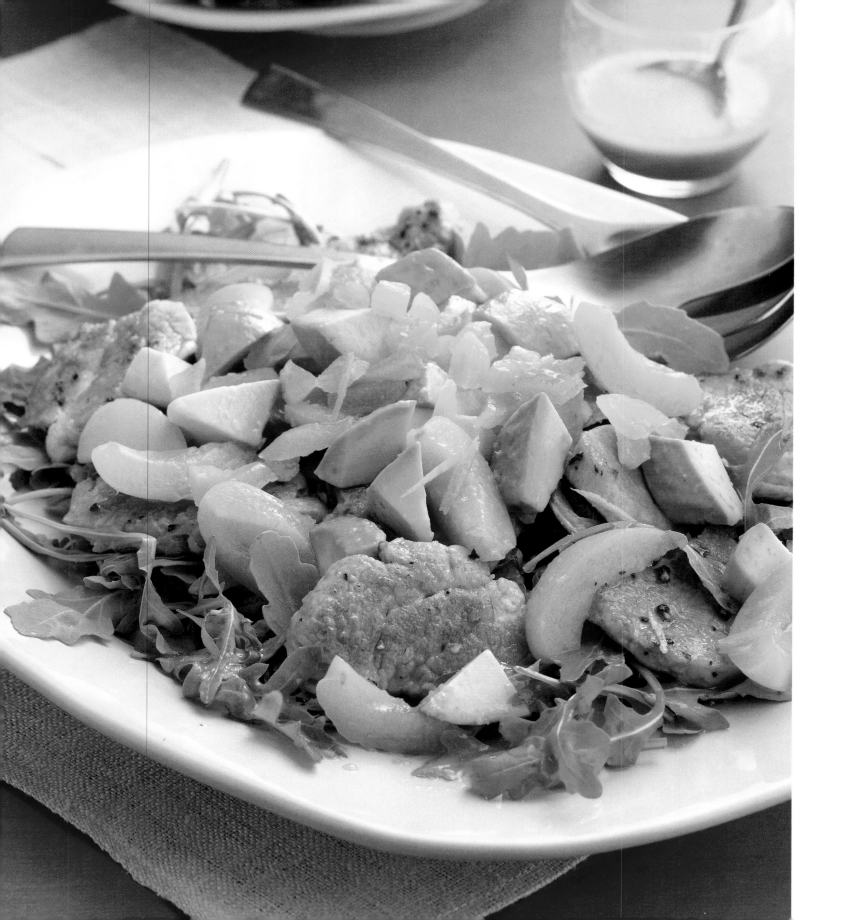

Dressing can contribute lots of calories to a main-dish salad. This fresh homemade dressing calls for only 1 tablespoon of oil and gets its intense flavor from sweet-tart raspberries and chipotle chiles.

beef and arugula with raspberry-chipotle dressing

PREP: 15 minutes   **GRILL:** 8 minutes   **STAND:** 5 minutes

1   **pound lean boneless beef sirloin steak, cut 1 inch thick**
¼   **teaspoon salt**
¼   **teaspoon ground black pepper**
6   **cups arugula leaves**
2   **cups halved red and/or yellow cherry tomatoes**
2   **cups fresh raspberries**
2   **tablespoons soft goat cheese (chèvre)**
1   **recipe Raspberry-Chipotle Dressing**

1. Sprinkle steak with salt and pepper. For a gas or charcoal grill, place steak on the grill rack directly over medium heat. Cover and grill to desired doneness, turning once halfway through grilling. Allow 8 to 12 minutes for medium-rare and 12 to 15 minutes for medium. Let steak stand for 5 minutes. Thinly slice steak.

2. To serve, place arugula on a serving platter. Arrange cherry tomatoes, steak, and raspberries on arugula. Dot with goat cheese. Drizzle with Raspberry-Chipotle Dressing. **Makes 4 servings.**

raspberry-chipotle dressing: Mash ½ cup fresh raspberries. In a screw-top jar combine mashed raspberries, 2 tablespoons white wine vinegar, 1 tablespoon canola oil, 2 teaspoons honey, and 1 teaspoon chopped canned chipotle chile peppers in adobo sauce (see tip, page 62). Cover and shake to combine.

PER SERVING: 249 cal., 10 g fat (3 g sat. fat), 61 mg chol., 246 mg sodium, 17 g carb., 7 g fiber, 23 g pro.

make it a meal

Greek yogurt with sliced fruit
Baked pita wedges
Raspberry Semifreddo with Pistachios and
Raspberry Swirl, recipe page 292

Picadillo, a favorite in many Spanish speaking countries, is an intensely flavorful combination of ground meat or poultry, tomatoes, spices, salty olives—and the sweetness of dried fruit.

picadillo-style chicken taco salad

START TO FINISH: 30 minutes

12	ounces uncooked ground chicken
⅓	cup chopped onion (1 small)
2	teaspoons ground coriander
2	teaspoons ground cumin
½	teaspoon salt
1	14.5-ounce can no-salt-added diced tomatoes, undrained
⅔	cup finely chopped peeled potato (1 small)
¼	cup snipped pitted dried plums (prunes)
¼	cup chopped pimiento-stuffed green olives
2	corn tostada shells
6	cups shredded romaine lettuce
¼	cup shredded reduced-fat Monterey Jack cheese (1 ounce)
	Sliced green onion (optional)
	Snipped fresh cilantro (optional)

1. In a large skillet cook chicken and chopped onion over medium heat until chicken is no longer pink, using a wooden spoon to break up chicken as it cooks. Drain off fat. Add coriander, cumin, and salt to chicken mixture in skillet; cook and stir for 1 to 2 minutes. Add tomatoes, potato, dried plums, and olives. Bring to boiling; reduce heat. Cover and simmer about 10 minutes or until potatoes are tender. Uncover; cook about 3 minutes more or until most of the liquid has evaporated.

2. Meanwhile, heat tostada shells according to package directions until crisp. Arrange shredded romaine on a serving platter. Spoon chicken mixture over romaine. Sprinkle cheese over all. Coarsely crush the tostada shells; sprinkle over salad. If desired, garnish with green onion and/or cilantro. **Makes 4 servings.**

PER SERVING: 272 cal., 12 g fat (4 g sat. fat), 78 mg chol., 596 mg sodium, 25 g carb., 5 g fiber, 20 g pro.

[
make it a meal
Guacamole with veggies
Rice with tomatoes and cilantro
Fresh apricots
]

cook smart *Restaurant portions have increased in the last 20 years. So be aware—these larger portions encourage overeating. Save some of your order for tomorrow's lunch.*

To cut even more fat out of this super-fast-to-fix salad, use turkey pepperoni in place of the regular pepperoni. Just a little bit of the spicy stuff adds lots of flavor.

italian pasta-spinach salad

PREP: 20 minutes

1	**cup dried whole grain rotini pasta**
6	**cups fresh baby spinach**
24	**slices pepperoni, chopped**
8	**tablespoons chopped roasted red sweet pepper**
8	**tablespoons bottled reduced-fat Italian salad dressing**
12	**ounces grilled chicken breast, sliced**
4	**tablespoons finely shredded Parmesan cheese (optional)**

1. Cook pasta according to package directions; drain and cool.

2. Meanwhile, divide spinach between individual serving bowls. In a medium bowl combine pepperoni, sweet pepper, and salad dressing. Stir in cooked pasta; spoon on top of spinach. Top with some of the chicken and sprinkle with Parmesan cheese, if desired. **Makes 4 servings.**

PER SERVING: 395 cal., 13 g fat (4 g sat. fat), 89 mg chol., 541 mg sodium, 36 g carb., 6 g fiber, 37 g pro.

[**make it a meal**

Cantaloupe with feta and black pepper
Crisp-cooked green beans and olives
Carrot Cake Parfaits, recipe page 285]

If you happen to have leftover roast or grilled chicken breast in the refrigerator, by all means use that in place of the refrigerated chicken breast strips. Just cut it up into bite-size pieces.

almond chicken salad

START TO FINISH: 15 minutes

12	ounces refrigerated grilled chicken breast strips, cut up
1	11-ounce can mandarin orange sections, drained
1	6-ounce package fresh baby spinach
1	cup seedless red grapes, halved
¼	cup sliced almonds
½	cup orange juice
2	tablespoons balsamic vinegar
1	tablespoon toasted sesame oil
¼	teaspoon ground black pepper

1. In a very large bowl combine chicken, orange sections, spinach, grapes, and almonds.

2. For dressing, in a screw-top jar combine orange juice, vinegar, oil, and pepper; cover and shake well. Pour dressing over salad; toss gently to coat. **Makes 4 servings.**

PER SERVING: 249 cal., 8 g fat (1 g sat. fat), 55 mg chol., 429 mg sodium, 25 g carb., 3 g fiber, 22 g pro.

tip: Skip bottled salad dressing. Making your own is an easy way to save calories, sodium, and room in your fridge.

make it a meal

Multi-seed crackers
Hummus and veggies
Amazing Apple Tart, recipe page 275

This recipe makes very efficient use of your broiler: The chicken and the ingredients for the corn salad are "roasted" at the same time—in the same pan, even—while you make a quick dressing for everything.

bbq chicken and roasted corn salad

PREP: 25 minutes   **BROIL:** 6 minutes

1   to 1¼ pounds skinless, boneless chicken breast halves
2   teaspoons ground ancho chile pepper or chili powder
1   teaspoon dried oregano, crushed
1   teaspoon dried thyme, crushed
¼   teaspoon salt
¼   teaspoon black pepper
1   15-ounce can no-salt-added black beans, rinsed and drained
1   cup frozen whole kernel corn, thawed
1   tablespoon canola oil
2   tablespoons bottled light ranch salad dressing
2   tablespoons low-sodium barbecue sauce
1   tablespoon white wine vinegar
4   cups chopped romaine lettuce
1   cup cherry tomatoes, halved
1   ounce queso fresco, crumbled, or Monterey Jack cheese, shredded (¼ cup)

1. Place each chicken breast half between two pieces of plastic wrap. Using the flat side of a meat mallet, pound chicken to about ½-inch thickness. Remove plastic wrap.

2. Preheat broiler. In a small bowl stir together ground chile pepper, oregano, thyme, salt, and black pepper. Sprinkle half the spice mixture over chicken pieces; rub in with your fingers.

3. In a medium bowl combine beans, corn, oil, and the remaining half of the spice mixture. Stir to combine.

4. Line a 15×10×1-inch baking pan with foil. Place chicken on one side of the pan. Add bean mixture to the other side of the pan. Broil 4 to 5 inches from the heat for 6 to 8 minutes or until chicken is tender and an instant-read thermometer inserted in chicken registers 165°F, turning chicken and stirring bean mixture once halfway through broiling.

5. Meanwhile, in a small bowl combine salad dressing, barbecue sauce, and vinegar; set aside.

6. To assemble, divide romaine among four serving plates. Slice chicken. Top romaine with bean mixture, chicken, and tomatoes, dividing evenly. Sprinkle with queso fresco and serve with salad dressing mixture. **Makes 4 servings.**

PER SERVING: 345 cal., 11 g fat (2 g sat. fat), 80 mg chol., 435 mg sodium, 30 g carb., 8 g fiber, 33 g pro.

[
make it a meal

Baked fat bread crisps
Bibb and blueberry salad
Iced tea with lemon
]

Even low-fat or no-fat Greek yogurt has a rich, creamy consistency that makes it a great base for salad dressings. It really clings to the meat or poultry and vegetables with which it's tossed.

curried chicken salad with melon

START TO FINISH: 20 minutes

½   cup plain low-fat Greek yogurt
1   teaspoon curry powder
½   teaspoon finely shredded lemon peel
1   teaspoon lemon juice
½   teaspoon salt
¼   teaspoon dry mustard
2   cups chopped cooked chicken breast
½   cup chopped celery (1 stalk)
¼   cup chopped walnuts, toasted (see tip, page 64)
¼   cup snipped fresh cilantro
¼   cup finely chopped onion
8   thin slices cantaloupe (2 cups)
8   thin slices honeydew melon (2 cups)
1   cup fresh blueberries

1. In a medium bowl combine yogurt, curry powder, lemon peel, lemon juice, salt, and mustard. Add chicken, celery, walnuts, cilantro, and onion. Stir to combine.

2. To serve, arrange 2 cantaloupe slices, 2 honeydew slices, and ¼ cup blueberries on each of four serving plates. Divide chicken salad evenly among the plates. **Makes 4 servings.**

PER SERVING: 266 cal., 9 g fat (2 g sat. fat), 61 mg chol., 379 mg sodium, 22 g carb., 3 g fiber, 27 g pro.

tip: In the habit of ending your dinner with a sweet? Sip a favorite tea—warm or cold—or chew a stick of sugar free gum to quench the craving and save unwanted calories.

make it a meal

Shaved fennel-red onion salad
Bibb with Gorgonzola
Iced tea with mint

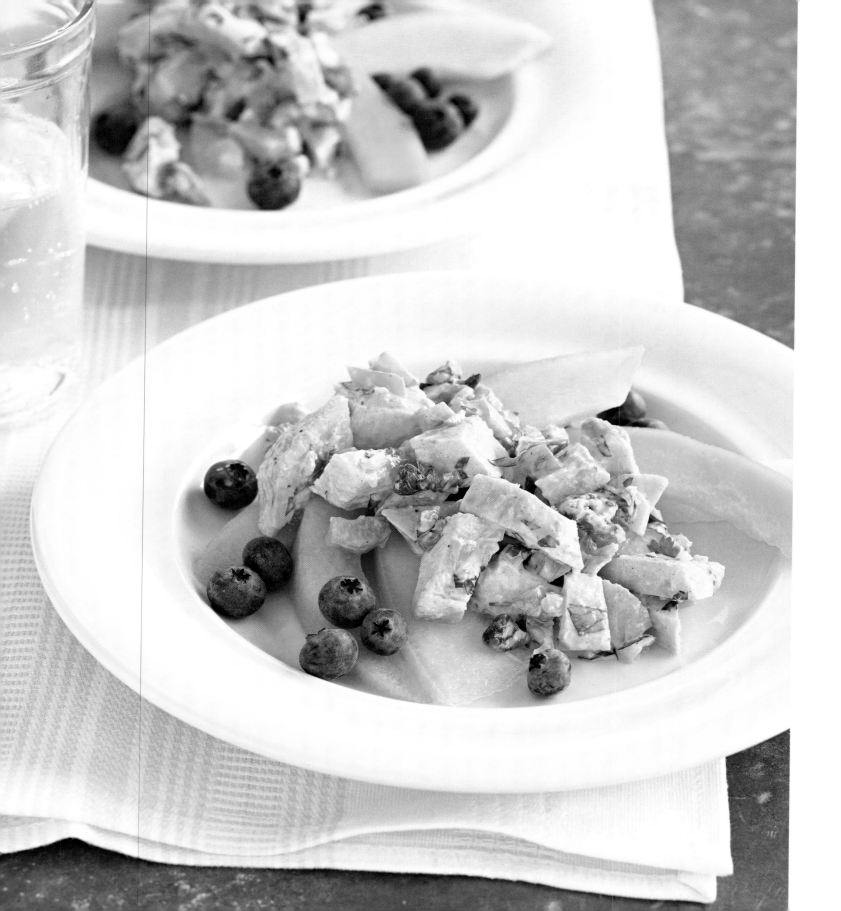

Walnuts add flavor, crunch—and a whole host of other good things to this salad. They're high in protein—which helps you feel satisfied and full—and are a good source of omega-3 fatty acids as well.

spinach salad with chicken and herb-toasted walnuts

START TO FINISH: 30 minutes

½   **cup walnuts, coarsely chopped**
1   **teaspoon walnut oil or olive oil**
2   **teaspoons snipped fresh thyme or ½ teaspoon dried thyme, crushed**
¼   **teaspoon salt**
¼   **cup balsamic vinegar glaze**
2   **tablespoons pure maple syrup**
1   **teaspoon Dijon-style mustard**
⅛   **teaspoon salt**
6   **cups fresh baby spinach leaves**
2   **cups coarsely shredded, cooked chicken breast**
2   **medium blood or cara cara oranges, peeled and sectioned**
1   **cup julienned jicama**
¼   **cup crumbled reduced-fat blue cheese**

1. Place walnuts in a small nonstick skillet. Drizzle with the 1 teaspoon walnut oil and sprinkle with thyme and the ¼ teaspoon salt. Toss to coat. Heat over medium heat for 3 to 4 minutes or until walnuts are lightly toasted, stirring frequently. Remove from heat and let cool.

2. For vinaigrette, in a small screw-top jar combine balsamic vinegar glaze, maple syrup, mustard, and the ⅛ teaspoon salt. Cover and shake well.

3. Divide spinach among four serving plates. Top evenly with chicken, orange sections, jicama, blue cheese, and toasted walnuts. Drizzle evenly with the vinaigrette. **Makes 4 servings.**

PER SERVING: 349 cal., 14 g fat (3 g sat. fat), 63 mg chol., 461 mg sodium, 26 g carb., 6 g fiber, 29 g pro.

[*make it a meal*

Carrot hummus with rice crackers
Peach, blueberry, and ginger salad
Zucchini Cupcakes with Greek Yogurt Frosting,
recipe page 274]

Old-school chef's salads—loaded with cheese and heavy dressing—were not necessarily the healthiest choice. This chopped version goes easy on the cheese and gets dressed with a light vinaigrette.

chopped chef's salad

PREP: 30 minutes

- 8 **cups chopped romaine and/or iceberg lettuce**
- 6 **ounces cooked turkey breast, chopped**
- 1 **medium cucumber, seeded and chopped**
- 1 **large tomato, chopped**
- 2 **hard-cooked eggs, chopped**
- ⅓ **cup shredded reduced-fat sharp cheddar cheese**
- 2 **tablespoons white wine vinegar**
- 2 **tablespoons olive oil**
- 1 **tablespoon snipped fresh basil, thyme, and/or oregano, or 1 teaspoon dried Italian seasoning, crushed**
- ½ **teaspoon Dijon-style mustard**
- ¼ **teaspoon ground black pepper**

1. In a large serving bowl layer lettuce, turkey, cucumber, tomato, eggs, and cheese.

2. In a small screw-top jar combine vinegar, olive oil, basil, mustard, and pepper. Cover and shake well. Drizzle over salad and toss to coat. **Makes 4 servings.**

PER SERVING: 221 cal., 12 g fat (3 g sat. fat), 147 mg chol., 148 mg sodium, 8 g carb., 3 g fiber, 21 g pro.

make it a meal

Sliced avocado with lime and smoked paprika
Mango-black bean salad
Seltzer water with cucumber

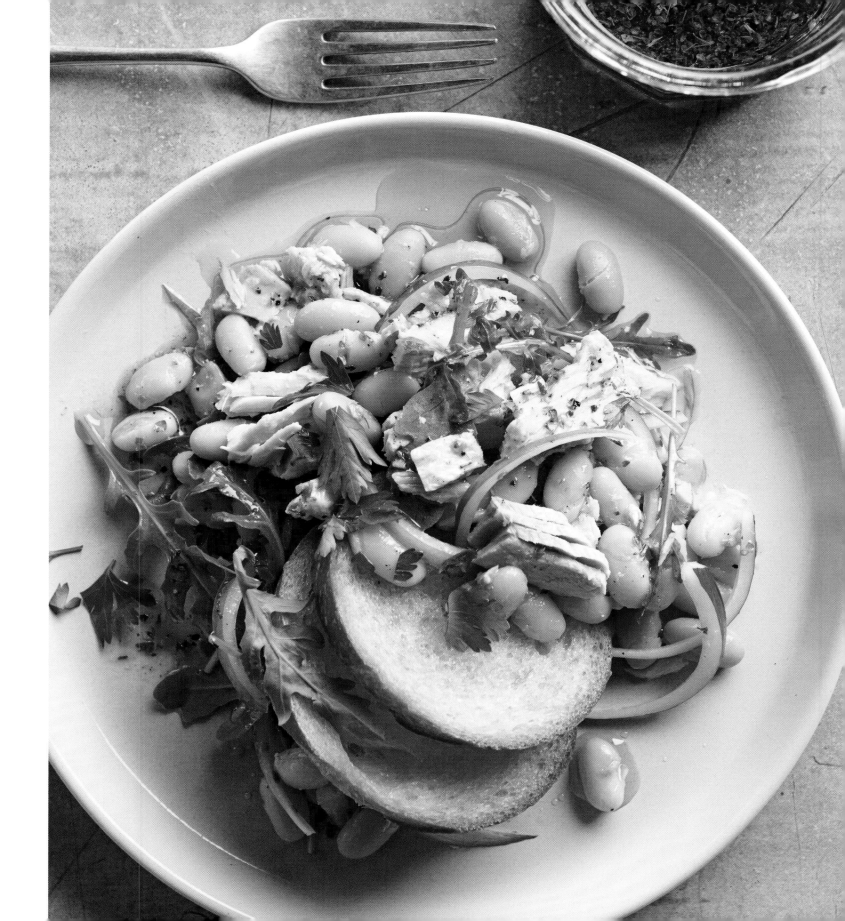

For the most elegant rendition of this Mediterranean-style salad, use albacore tuna. Its firm texture holds together in larger, more toothsome chunks than the other types of canned tuna.

white bean tuna salad

START TO FINISH: 20 minutes

1	15-ounce can cannellini beans, rinsed and drained
2	5-ounce cans tuna packed in water, drained
2	cups lightly packed arugula or spinach
½	of a small red onion, thinly sliced
¼	cup fresh Italian parsley, chopped
¼	cup red wine vinegar
3	tablespoons extra-virgin olive oil
½	teaspoon dried leaf oregano, crushed
¼	teaspoon salt
¼	teaspoon ground black pepper
½	of a lemon

1. In a very large bowl combine beans, tuna, arugula, red onion, and parsley.

2. For dressing, in a screw-top jar combine vinegar, oil, oregano, salt, and pepper. Shake well to combine.

3. Pour dressing over tuna mixture; toss gently to combine. Squeeze juice from half of a lemon over salad. **Makes 4 servings.**

PER SERVING: 274 cal., 13 g fat (2 g sat. fat), 30 mg chol., 644 mg sodium, 15 g carb., 5 g fiber, 22 g pro.

tip: Love your legumes! Their unique combination of protein, fiber, and slow-digesting carbs is super satisfying and can help keep appetite under control.

make it a meal

Quinoa pilaf
Melon with feta

This salad is so simple to make you could easily put it together for lunch—even on a very busy day. Make it in mid- to late summer, when nectarines are in season. Look for fragrant fruit that is firm, not mushy.

tuna-nectarine salad with bread toasts

START TO FINISH: 25 minutes

½ cup plain fat-free Greek yogurt
3 tablespoons low-fat buttermilk
2 tablespoons mayonnaise
¼ teaspoon garlic powder
2 tablespoons snipped fresh chives
1 11-ounce pouch chunk light tuna in water, drained
4 ripe, yet firm, nectarines or peaches, pitted and diced
¼ cup chopped pecans, toasted (see tip, page 64)
2 whole wheat sandwich thins, split, toasted, and quartered

1. For the dressing, in a medium bowl whisk together yogurt, buttermilk, mayonnaise, and garlic powder until smooth. Stir in chives.

2. Add tuna and nectarines to the yogurt dressing; toss gently to combine. Spoon tuna salad onto four serving plates; sprinkle with pecans. Serve with bread toasts. **Makes 4 servings.**

PER SERVING: 319 cal., 12 g fat (2 g sat. fat), 27 mg chol., 441 mg sodium, 28 g carb., 6 g fiber, 28 g pro.

[make it a meal

Radishes with pesto
Sauteed kale with garlic and lemon
Vanilla Tres Leches Cake, recipe page 268
]

For the tenderest texture in this hearty salad, buy the thinnest fresh green beans you can find—and then be careful not to overcook them.

green bean and tuna salad

PREP: 15 minutes   **COOK:** 6 minutes

1 **pound fresh green beans, trimmed**
2 **6-ounce cans chunk white tuna (water pack), drained and broken into chunks**
½ **cup slivered red onion**
¼ **cup chopped walnuts, toasted (see tip, page 64)**
⅓ **cup light sour cream**
2 **teaspoons Dijon-style mustard or coarse brown mustard**
2 **teaspoons balsamic vinegar**
2 **teaspoons cider vinegar**
1 **teaspoon snipped fresh dillweed**
¼ **teaspoon ground black pepper**

1. Leave beans whole or cut into 1-inch pieces. In a medium saucepan cook beans, covered, in a small amount of boiling water for 6 to 8 minutes or until crisp-tender; drain. Rinse beans with cold water; drain again. Transfer to a bowl.

2. Add tuna, red onion, and walnuts to beans. Toss gently to combine. For dressing, in a small bowl whisk together sour cream, mustard, balsamic and cider vinegars, dillweed, and pepper. Drizzle dressing over bean mixture. **Makes 4 servings.**

PER SERVING: 226 cal., 9 g fat (2 g sat. fat), 41 mg chol., 400 mg sodium, 12 g carb., 4 g fiber, 24 g pro.

make it a meal

Multi-seed crackers
Lemon-dill spread
Low-fat chocolate chip cookie bites

A combination of maple syrup, vinegar, onion, honey mustard, and olive oil does double duty as both a glaze for the fish and as a dressing for the vegetables and greens in this unusual salad.

maple mahi mahi salad

START TO FINISH: 30 minutes

½ cup frozen shelled sweet soybeans (edamame)

8 ounces fresh or frozen skinless mahi mahi fillets

2 tablespoons pure maple syrup

1 tablespoon balsamic vinegar

1 tablespoon finely chopped onion

1 tablespoon honey mustard

2 teaspoons olive oil

⅛ teaspoon salt

⅛ teaspoon ground black pepper

4 cups coarsely shredded napa cabbage

½ cup fresh snow peas pods, trimmed and halved crosswise

2 tablespoons snipped dried cherries

2 tablespoons sliced almonds, toasted (see tip, page 64)

1. Cook edamame according to package directions; drain. Set aside to cool.

2. Preheat broiler. Thaw fish, if frozen. Rinse fish; pat dry with paper towels. Cut fish into two portions. Measure thickness of fish; set aside.

3. For dressing, in a small bowl whisk together maple syrup, vinegar, onion, honey mustard, oil, salt, and pepper.

4. Remove 2 tablespoons of the dressing and brush on all sides of the fish pieces.

5. Place fish on the unheated greased rack of a broiler pan. Broil 4 inches from heat until fish flakes easily when tested with a fork. Allow 4 to 6 minutes per ½-inch thickness of fish.

6. Meanwhile, in a large bowl combine napa cabbage, snow pea pods, and cooked edamame. Pour the remaining dressing over cabbage mixture; toss to coat. To serve, divide cabbage between two serving plates. Sprinkle with cherries and almonds and top with fish. **Makes 2 servings.**

PER SERVING: 359 cal., 11 g fat (1 g sat. fat), 83 mg chol., 313 mg sodium, 37 g carb., 6 g fiber, 30 g pro.

[make it a meal]

Asian pear salad
Gluten-free rice pasta
Chai masala tea

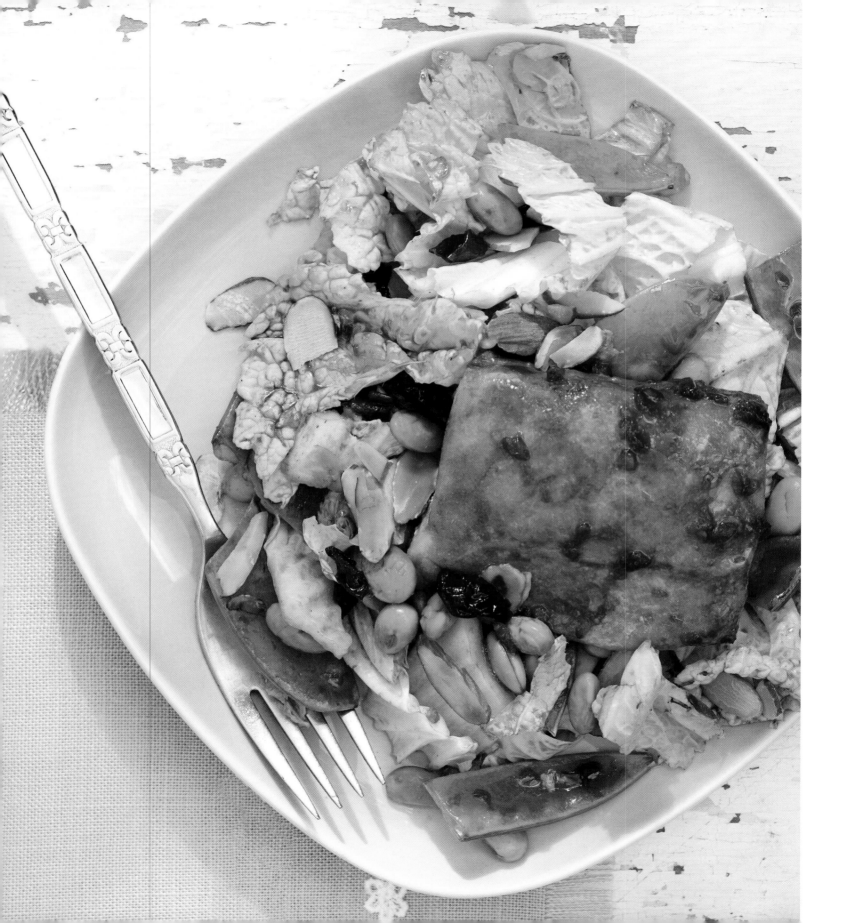

FRESH & FAST

To get the best browning on the scallops, be sure they are completely dry before you add them to the pan with the hot oil. It will keep the oil from spattering as well.

sesame scallop salad

START TO FINISH: 30 minutes

4	fresh or frozen sea scallops or peeled and deveined large shrimp
2	ounces dried multigrain spaghetti
3	cups shredded napa cabbage and/ or shredded romaine lettuce
½	cup coarsely shredded carrot
¼	cup quartered and thinly sliced red onion
2	tablespoons rice vinegar or white wine vinegar
1	tablespoon reduced-sodium soy sauce
2	teaspoons canola oil
1½	teaspoons honey
¼	teaspoon crushed red pepper
2	teaspoons canola oil
1	teaspoon sesame seeds, toasted (see tip, page 64)

1. Thaw scallops, if frozen. Rinse and pat dry with paper towels. Cut scallops in half and set aside.

2. Cook spaghetti according to package directions; drain. Rinse with cold water; drain again. In a medium bowl toss together spaghetti, cabbage, carrot, and onion. Transfer to a serving bowl.

3. For dressing, in a small bowl whisk together vinegar, soy sauce, 2 teaspoons oil, the honey, and crushed red pepper. Set aside.

4. In a medium skillet heat the 2 teaspoons oil over medium heat. Add scallops; cook for 3 to 4 minutes or until opaque, turning once to brown evenly. Place scallops over the cabbage mixture. Drizzle the salad with dressing and sprinkle with sesame seeds. Gently toss to coat. **Makes 2 servings.**

PER SERVING: 355 cal., 12 g fat (1 g sat. fat), 37 mg chol., 514 mg sodium, 35 g carb., 5 g fiber, 27 g pro.

make it a meal

Sweet pepper salad
Miso-Ginger Kale, recipe page 263
Sparkling water with lemon

To remove the orange sections, cut with a paring knife along the membrane on either side of each section toward the center of the fruit. The segment will slip out. Work over a bowl to catch the juice.

asparagus and shrimp salad

START TO FINISH: 30 minutes

12	ounces fresh or frozen medium shrimp in shells
½	teaspoon finely shredded orange peel
2	tablespoons orange juice
1	pound fresh asparagus, trimmed
3	oranges
	Orange juice (optional)
1	tablespoon olive oil or salad oil
1	tablespoon white wine vinegar
1	clove garlic, minced
1	teaspoon chopped fresh tarragon
¼	teaspoon ground black pepper
⅛	teaspoon salt
6	cups torn mixed salad greens
¼	cup sliced green onions (2)

1. Thaw shrimp, if frozen. Peel and devein shrimp, leaving tails intact, if desired. Rinse shrimp; pat dry with paper towels. In a large saucepan bring 4 cups water to boiling. Add shrimp; reduce heat. Simmer, uncovered, for 1 to 3 minutes or until shrimp are opaque. Drain in a colander. Rinse with cold water; drain again. Transfer shrimp to a bowl. Add orange peel and the 2 tablespoons orange juice; toss gently to coat.

2. In a medium saucepan cook asparagus, covered, in a small amount of boiling water for 4 to 6 minutes or until crisp-tender. Drain; rinse with cold water and drain again.

3. Peel oranges. Working over a bowl, cut oranges into sections; reserve ⅓ cup of the juice. (If necessary, add additional orange juice to make ⅓ cup.) For dressing, in a small bowl whisk together the ⅓ cup orange juice, the oil, vinegar, garlic, tarragon, pepper, and salt.

4. In a large bowl combine shrimp, asparagus, orange sections, greens, and green onions. Pour dressing over salad; toss gently to coat. **Makes 4 servings.**

PER SERVING: 174 cal., 5 g fat (1 g sat. fat), 107 mg chol., 504 mg sodium, 17 g carb., 5 g fiber, 16 g pro.

make it a meal

Spicy almonds
Quinoa pilaf
Whole strawberries

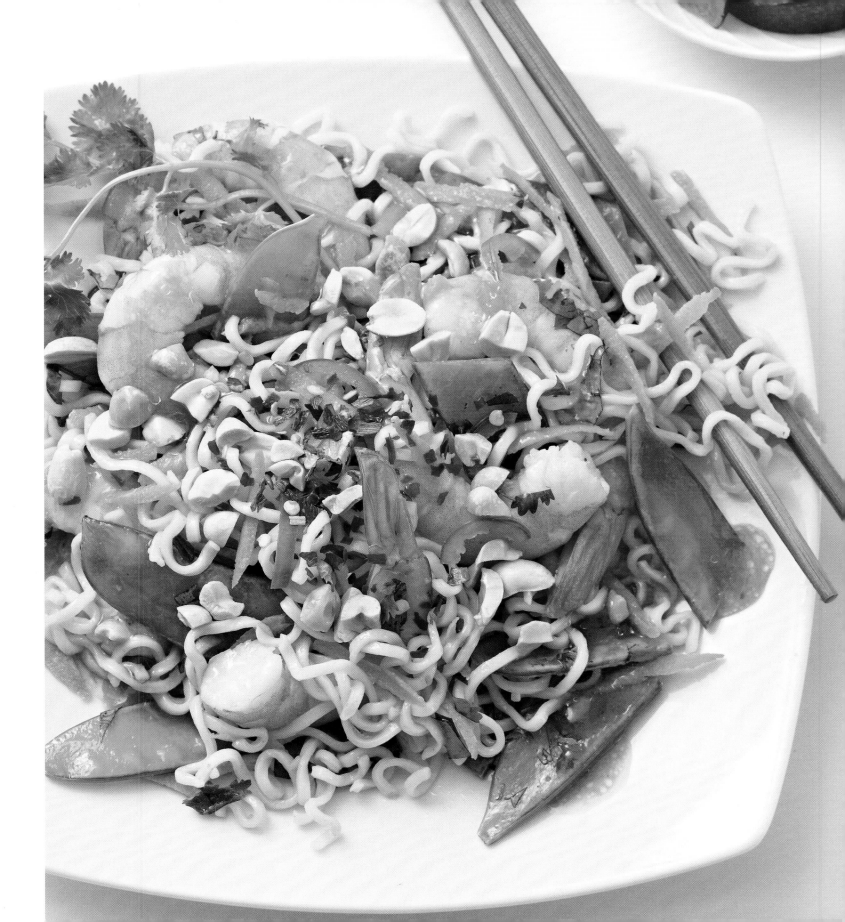

This salad goes together in just 15 minutes, making it faster to prepare a meal and eat at home than to grab something out—and much more likely to have it fall within the guidelines of your weight-loss plan.

shrimp and rice noodle salad

START TO FINISH: 15 minutes

6 ounces dried rice noodles

12 ounces peeled and deveined cooked small shrimp

1 cup fresh snow pea pods, trimmed and halved diagonally

1 cup coarsely shredded carrots

3 tablespoons coarsely snipped fresh cilantro

½ cup light Asian salad dressing

1 small fresh serrano pepper, thinly sliced (see tip, page 62)

¼ cup unsalted dry-roasted peanuts, coarsely chopped
   Crushed red pepper

4 medium plums, sliced

1. Cook rice noodles according to package directions; drain and cool. Set aside.

2. Meanwhile, in a small bowl combine shrimp, snow pea pods, carrots, cilantro, salad dressing, and serrano pepper. Toss with cooked noodles.

3. Transfer salad to a serving plate. Sprinkle with peanuts and crushed red pepper. Serve with plum slices. **Makes 4 servings.**

PER SERVING: 392 cal., 11 g fat (2 g sat. fat), 107 mg chol., 801 mg sodium, 57 g carb., 4 g fiber, 16 g pro.

[make it a meal]

Ginger-sesame bok choy
Sauteed mushrooms and asparagus
Chocolate-Filled Lemon Meringues,
recipe page 288

Cutting the shrimp in half horizontally means you get more pieces of shrimp in the salad—it makes a little bit of shrimp go a long way. To make it easier, cut the tails off of the shrimp before you cut it in half.

teriyaki shrimp and edamame salad

START TO FINISH: 25 minutes

½ cup frozen shelled sweet soybeans (edamame)

2 ounces dried radiatore or rotini pasta

3 cups packaged fresh baby spinach

2 cups shredded romaine lettuce

¾ cup coarsely shredded carrots

¾ cup fresh pea pods, trimmed, strings removed, and halved

1 small red or yellow sweet pepper, cut into thin strips

¼ cup thinly sliced green onions (2)

6 ounces cooked medium shrimp, halved horizontally

3 tablespoons rice vinegar or cider vinegar

1 tablespoon canola oil

1 tablespoon reduced-sodium soy sauce

4 cloves garlic, minced

1 teaspoon toasted sesame oil

1 teaspoon grated fresh ginger

⅛ teaspoon crushed red pepper

1. Cook soybeans according to package directions; drain. Cook pasta according to package directions; drain and rinse with cold water. Set aside.

2. Divide spinach and romaine among four shallow bowls. Top each with carrots, pea pods, sweet pepper, sweet soybeans, and green onions. In a medium bowl combine shrimp and cooked pasta; set aside.

3. For dressing, in a screw-top jar combine vinegar, canola oil, soy sauce, garlic, toasted sesame oil, ginger, and crushed red pepper. Cover and shake well. Pour half of the dressing over the shrimp and pasta; toss to coat.

4. Top vegetables in bowls with shrimp and pasta. Drizzle salads with remaining dressing. **Makes 4 servings.**

PER SERVING: 181 cal., 7 g fat (1 g sat. fat), 90 mg chol., 593 mg sodium, 15 g carb., 4 g fiber, 15 g pro.

[make it a meal]

Sweet and spicy almonds
Grilled pineapple
Lemon sorbet

Leftovers of this bean-and-grain salad studded with crunchy vegetables make a great totable lunch.

cucumber-radish barley salad

PREP: 15 minutes   **COOK:** 10 minutes

1½   **cups water**
¾   **cup uncooked quick-cooking barley**
1   **14.5- to 15-ounce can no-salt-added garbanzo beans (chickpeas), rinsed and drained**
2   **cups chopped peeled cucumber (1 medium)**
1   **cup thinly sliced radishes**
½   **cup sliced green onions (4)**
3   **tablespoons cider vinegar**
2   **tablespoons olive oil**
2   **tablespoons apple juice or orange juice**
2   **tablespoons snipped fresh oregano**
½   **teaspoon ground black pepper**
¼   **teaspoon salt**
4   **cups torn fresh spinach**
2   **ounces feta cheese, crumbled**

1. In a medium saucepan bring the water to boiling. Add barley; reduce heat. Simmer, covered, for 10 to 12 minutes or until barley is tender and water is absorbed. Transfer barley to a colander and rinse with cold water; drain well.

2. In a large bowl combine barley, garbanzo beans, cucumber, radishes, and green onions; set aside.

3. For dressing, in a small bowl stir together the vinegar, olive oil, apple juice, oregano, pepper, and salt. Add to barley mixture; toss to coat.

4. To serve, arrange spinach on a platter. Spoon barley and vegetables over spinach and sprinkle with feta cheese. **Makes 5 servings.**

PER SERVING: 251 cal., 9 g fat (2 g sat. fat), 10 mg chol., 283 mg sodium, 34 g carb., 7 g fiber, 10 g pro.

tip: When food takes more time to chew it slows you down and you will most likely eat less. This colorful salad of barley, cucumbers, radishes, and spinach is a delicious example.

make it a meal

Lentil-walnut spread with veggies
Kale-apple salad
Coconut-Almond Frozen Greek Yogurt with
Hot Chocolate Drizzle, recipe page 293

FRESH & FAST

If you can't find queso fresco—a slightly tangy, crumbly Mexican cheese—feta makes a good substitute.

mexican edamame and couscous salad

START TO FINISH: 30 minutes

¼ cup cider vinegar

3 tablespoons snipped fresh cilantro

3 tablespoons olive oil

1 to 2 teaspoons chopped canned chipotle chile pepper in adobo sauce (see tip, page 62)

1 clove garlic, minced

¼ teaspoon salt

¼ teaspoon ground black pepper

2 cups cooked Israeli (large pearl) couscous, whole grain small pasta, or whole grain penne pasta

8 cups coarsely shredded romaine lettuce

10 grape tomatoes, halved

1 medium yellow sweet pepper, cut into bite-size pieces

½ cup frozen shelled sweet soybeans (edamame), cooked according to package directions

½ cup canned no-salt-added black beans, rinsed and drained

1 lime, cut into thin wedges

2 tablespoons crumbled queso fresco

1. For dressing, in a screw-top jar combine vinegar, cilantro, oil, chile pepper, garlic, salt, and black pepper. Cover and shake well. Toss couscous with 1 tablespoon dressing.

2. Cover a large serving platter with romaine. In a small bowl combine tomatoes and sweet pepper. Arrange tomatoes-pepper, couscous, edamame, black beans, and lime wedges on romaine on the platter. To serve, drizzle with the remaining dressing and sprinkle with queso fresco. **Makes 4 servings.**

PER SERVING: 290 cal., 12 g fat (2 g sat. fat), 3 mg chol., 184 mg sodium, 37 g carb., 7 g fiber, 10 g pro.

[make it a meal

Chili-lime cashews
Salsa and baked tortilla chips
Watermelon slices]

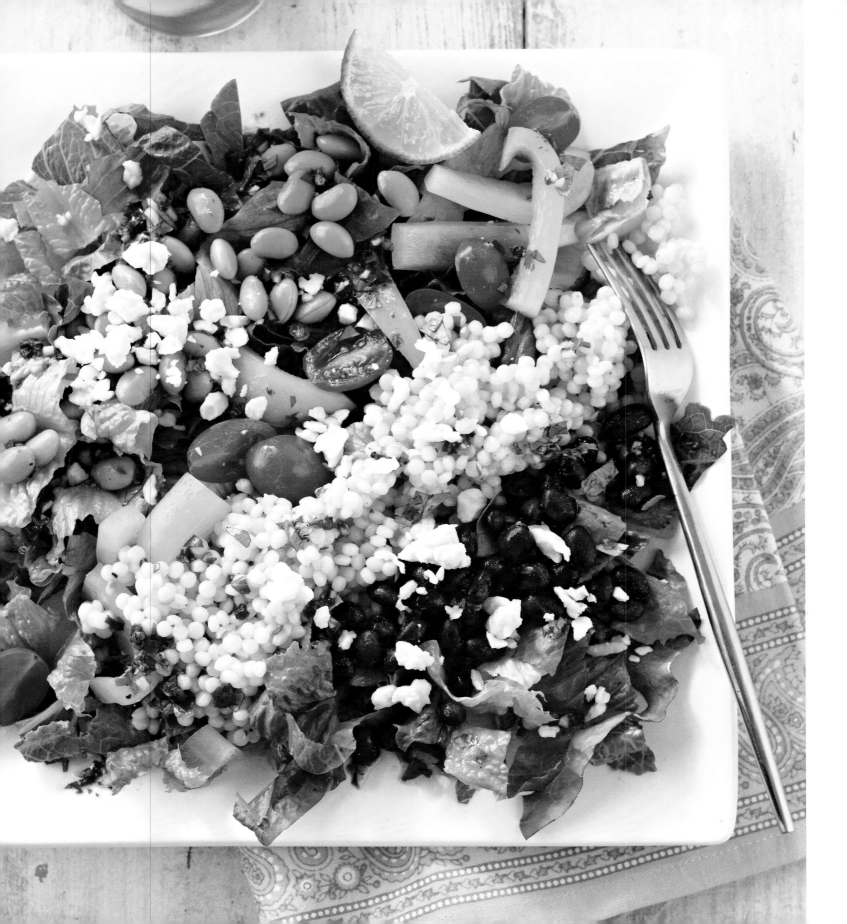

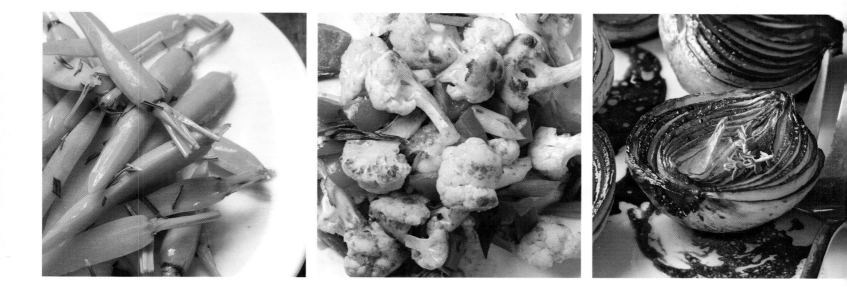

CHAPTER 10

100-calorie
side dishes

The entrée may be the main event, but sides make the meal. Bring interest to the table with these salads, grains, and vegetable dishes.

Tarragon has a licoricey, slightly sweet flavor similar to basil. It pairs well with chicken, fish, and vegetables. It can be an acquired taste—if you're not a tarragon fan, fresh basil works just as well here.

asparagus and wild mushrooms

PREP: 20 minutes   **ROAST:** 15 minutes at 400°F

3   cups halved cremini, shiitake, and/or button mushrooms
2   tablespoons white wine
2   teaspoons snipped fresh tarragon
1   pound fresh asparagus spears
1   tablespoon olive oil
¼   teaspoon salt
¼   teaspoon ground black pepper
    Snipped fresh tarragon (optional)

1. Preheat oven to 400°F. In a medium bowl toss together mushrooms, wine, and 2 teaspoons tarragon; set aside.

2. Snap off and discard woody bases from asparagus. Place asparagus in a 15×10×1-inch baking pan. Drizzle with oil and sprinkle with the salt and pepper. Toss to coat.

3. Roast, uncovered, for 5 minutes. Add mushrooms to the pan; toss gently. Return to oven; roast for 10 minutes or until asparagus is crisp-tender. If desired, sprinkle with additional fresh tarragon. **Makes 4 servings.**

PER SERVING: 64 cal., 4 g fat (1 g sat. fat), 0 mg chol., 151 mg sodium, 5 g carb., 2 g fiber, 4 g pro.

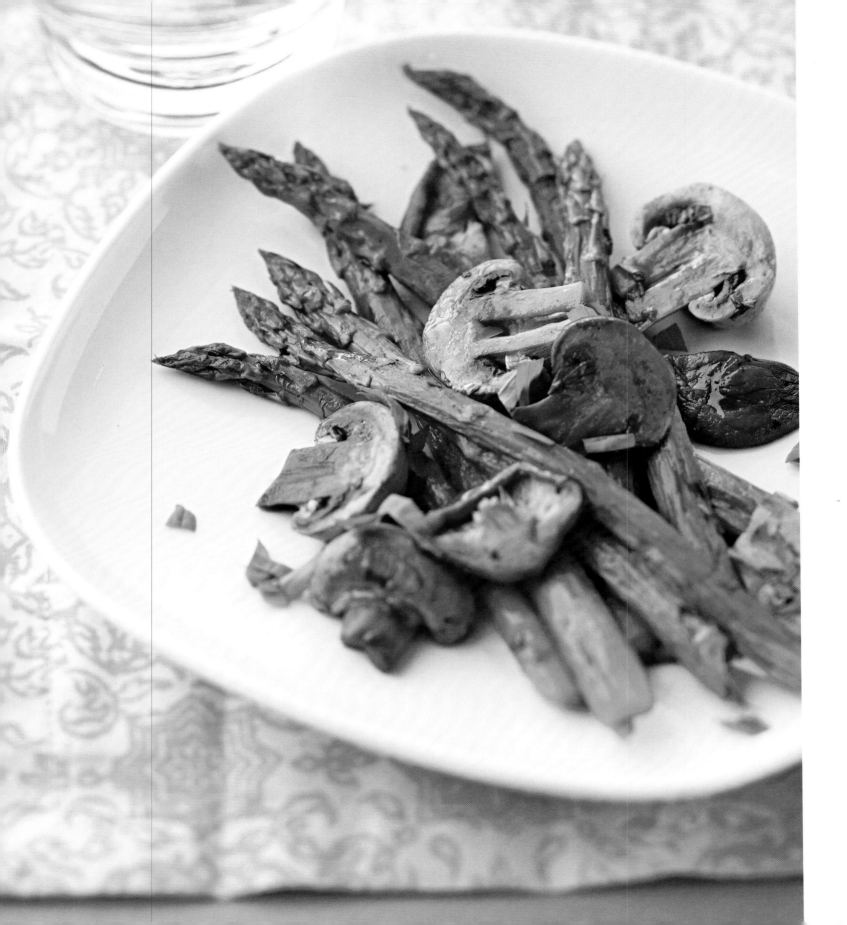

The oils of citrus fruit are contained in the peel. When the lemons are seared in the hot butter, the oils are released into it. The lemon-infused butter then flavors this nutrient-packed trio of green vegetables.

broccoli with peas and seared lemons

START TO FINISH: 30 minutes

2	**pounds broccoli, trimmed**
8	**ounces Swiss chard, trimmed and cut into 2- to 3-inch lengths**
1	**cup frozen peas**
2	**tablespoons butter**
1	**lemon, thinly sliced**
¼	**cup chicken broth**
¼	**teaspoon crushed red pepper**
¼	**cup snipped fresh chives**
½	**teaspoon coarse salt**

1. In a Dutch oven cook broccoli in salted boiling water for 2 minutes. Add Swiss chard and peas; cover and simmer for 4 minutes or until bright green; drain.

2. Meanwhile, melt butter in a large skillet over medium to medium-high heat. Add lemon slices; cook about 3 minutes per side or until lemons are soft and browned and butter is browned. (Don't move lemons around too much to ensure a nice sear.)

3. Return broccoli, chard, and peas to the Dutch oven. Add the broth and crushed red pepper; toss gently to coat. Transfer the broccoli mixture to a serving platter. Top with the lemons, chives, and salt. **Makes 12 servings.**

PER SERVING: 48 cal., 2 g fat (1 g sat. fat), 5 mg chol., 200 mg sodium, 6 g carb., 2 g fiber, 2 g pro.

Just a splash of bourbon infuses the carrots with warm, spicy, bold flavor. If you don't use the bourbon, the carrots still benefit from a bath in honey, rosemary, and fresh chives.

honey-bourbon carrots

START TO FINISH: 30 minutes

12   **small carrots, peeled and halved lengthwise (1 to 1¼ pounds total)**

1   **tablespoon snipped fresh chives or 1 teaspoon snipped fresh rosemary**

1   **tablespoon tub-style vegetable oil spread**

1   **tablespoon bourbon, vegetable broth, or water**

1   **tablespoon honey**

⅛   **teaspoon salt**

1. In a large skillet cook carrots, covered, in a small amount of boiling water for 6 to 8 minutes or until crisp-tender. Remove carrots from skillet and drain any remaining water. Set aside.

2. In the same skillet combine chives, vegetable oil spread, bourbon, honey, and salt. Add carrots; cook and stir over medium heat for 1 minute or until carrots are heated through. **Makes 4 servings.**

PER SERVING: 92 cal., 3 g fat (1 g sat. fat), 0 mg chol., 170 mg sodium, 15 g carb., 3 g fiber, 1 g pro.

Cauliflower takes particularly well to high-heat roasting or stir frying, which caramelizes its natural sugars and gives it a deliciously crisp exterior. Here, the cauliflower browns in just a little bit of oil but finishes cooking in broth for a side that is low in calories and fat but big on flavor.

spiced cauliflower

START TO FINISH: 20 minutes

½   teaspoon dry mustard
¼   teaspoon salt
¼   teaspoon ground turmeric
¼   teaspoon ground cumin
⅛   teaspoon ground coriander
⅛   teaspoon cayenne pepper
1   tablespoon vegetable oil
4   cups cauliflower florets
1   medium red or green sweet pepper, cut into 1-inch pieces
4   green onions, bias-sliced into 1-inch pieces
¼   cup reduced-sodium chicken broth

1. In a small bowl combine mustard, salt, turmeric, cumin, coriander, and cayenne pepper. Set aside.

2. In a wok or extra-large skillet heat oil over medium-high heat. (Add more oil if necessary during cooking.) Add cauliflower; cook and stir for 6 minutes. Add sweet pepper and green onions; cook and stir for 1 minute. Reduce heat to medium; add mustard mixture. Cook and stir for 30 seconds. Carefully stir in broth. Cook for 1 minute or until vegetables are heated through. **Makes 4 servings.**

PER SERVING: 72 cal., 4 g fat (0 g sat. fat), 0 mg chol., 215 mg sodium, 8 g carb., 3 g fiber, 3 g pro.

● VEGETARIAN   ● GLUTEN FREE

A small bit of butter is all you need to give this brightly colored combination of vegetables great taste. Serve it with a simple grilled steak.

tricolor summer squash

PREP: 25 minutes   **COOK:** 8 minutes

1¼	cups coarsely chopped yellow summer squash
1¼	cups coarsely chopped zucchini
1	cup frozen shelled sweet soybeans (edamame)
¾	cup coarsely chopped red sweet pepper
¾	cup thinly sliced red onion
2	cloves garlic, minced
1	tablespoon butter
1	tablespoon champagne vinegar or white wine vinegar
1½	teaspoons snipped fresh oregano
1	teaspoon snipped fresh thyme
¼	teaspoon salt
¼	teaspoon ground black pepper

1. In a large skillet cook yellow squash, zucchini, soybeans, sweet pepper, red onion, and garlic in melted butter over medium heat for 8 minutes or until vegetables are crisp-tender.

2. Stir in vinegar, oregano, thyme, salt, and black pepper.
Makes 6 servings.

PER SERVING: 61 cal., 3 g fat (1 g sat. fat), 5 mg chol., 119 mg sodium, 6 g carb., 2 g fiber, 3 g pro.

When it's too hot to turn on the oven—for anything—grill some lean meat, fish, or chicken and make this marinated vegetable salad as a side dish.

herbed dijon-marinated veggies

PREP: 20 minutes   **MARINATE:** 30 minutes

3   **tablespoons dry white wine, such as Pinot Grigio or Sauvignon Blanc**
2   **tablespoons snipped fresh basil**
1   **tablespoon snipped fresh Italian parsley**
1   **tablespoon olive oil**
2   **teaspoons snipped fresh thyme or oregano or ½ teaspoon dried thyme or oregano, crushed**
2   **teaspoons Dijon-style mustard**
1   **clove garlic, minced**
¼   **teaspoon salt**
1½   **cups fresh small cremini mushrooms**
1   **cup grape tomatoes or cherry tomatoes**
1   **cup yellow and/or orange sweet pepper strips**
1   **small zucchini, quartered lengthwise and cut into 1-inch pieces (about 1 cup)**

1. In a large bowl whisk together wine, basil, parsley, oil, thyme, mustard, garlic, and salt. Add mushrooms, tomatoes, sweet pepper, and zucchini; toss gently to coat. Cover and marinate vegetables at room temperature for 30 to 60 minutes, stirring occasionally.

2. Using a slotted spoon, transfer vegetables to a serving bowl. **Makes 6 servings.**

PER SERVING: 52 cal., 3 g fat (0 g sat. fat), 0 mg chol., 143 mg sodium, 5 g carb., 1 g fiber, 2 g pro.

If you've ever wondered what to do with eggplant, roast it. It takes on a beautiful golden-brown color, crispy exterior and creamy interior.

porcini eggplant

PREP: 15 minutes   **ROAST:** 15 minutes at 425°F   **STAND:** 15 minutes   **COOK:** 5 minutes

1 **pound eggplant, peeled and cut into 1-inch cubes**
2 **tablespoons olive oil**
¼ **teaspoon salt**
¼ **teaspoon ground black pepper**
½ **ounce dried porcini mushrooms**
⅓ **cup balsamic vinegar**
1 **teaspoon snipped fresh thyme**
½ **cup grape tomatoes, quartered**
1 **tablespoon snipped fresh basil**

1. Preheat oven to 425°F. Arrange eggplant in a 15×10×1-inch baking pan. Drizzle with olive oil and sprinkle with the salt and pepper; toss to coat. Roast for 15 to 20 minutes or until tender and browned, stirring once or twice.

2. Meanwhile, place mushrooms in a small bowl. And 1 cup boiling water to bowl. Let stand for 15 minutes; drain water. Chop mushrooms.

3. In a small saucepan heat balsamic vinegar over medium heat until boiling; reduce heat. Simmer, uncovered, about 5 minutes or until reduced by half. Stir in mushrooms and thyme. Drizzle roasted eggplant with reduced balsamic vinegar.

4. In a small bowl combine grape tomatoes and basil. Sprinkle over the eggplant and mushrooms. **Makes 6 servings.**

PER SERVING: 77 cal., 5 g fat (1 g sat. fat), 0 mg chol., 103 mg sodium, 8 g carb., 3 g fiber, 1 g pro.

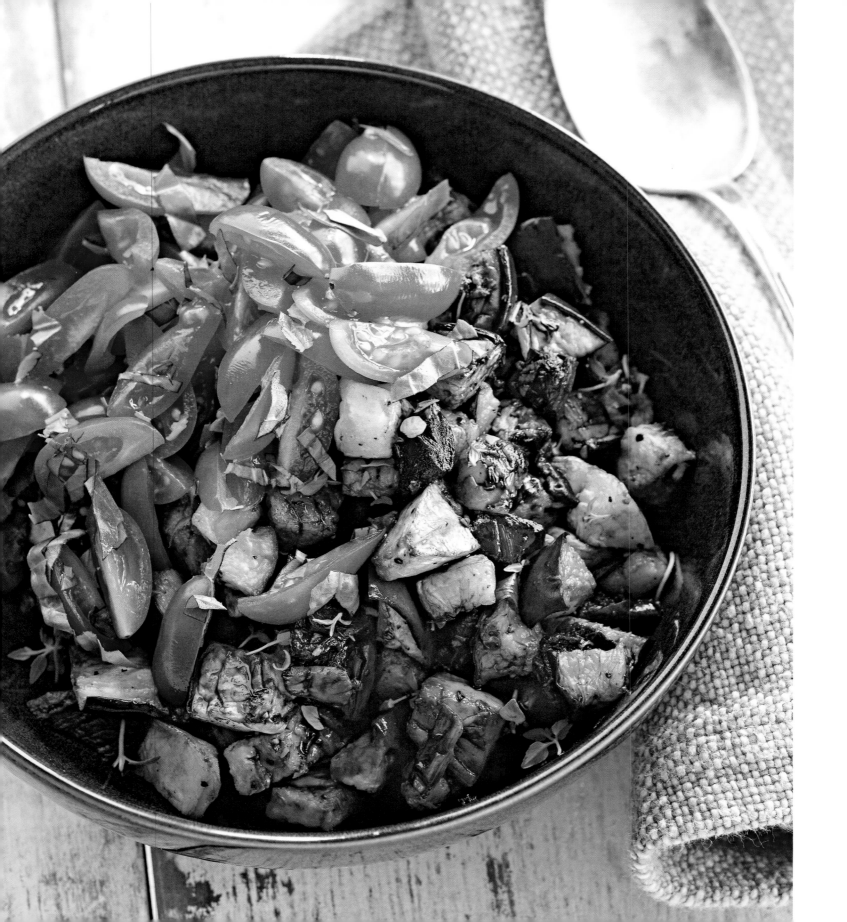

Be careful. Don't trim too much of the stem from each sprout—just a very thin slice to get rid of the dried out or less-than-fresh layer. You want to keep each tiny head intact.

soy and chile-glazed brussels sprouts with shiitake mushrooms

START TO FINISH: 40 minutes

1	pound Brussels sprouts
4	green onions
1	teaspoon finely shredded orange peel
2	tablespoons orange juice
1	tablespoon soy sauce
1½	teaspoons honey
½	red serrano chile pepper, seeded and finely chopped (see tip, page 62), or ¼ teaspoon crushed red pepper
1	to 2 cloves garlic, minced
1½	tablespoons vegetable oil
4	ounces fresh shiitake mushrooms, stemmed and thinly sliced

1. Trim Brussels sprouts;* cut lengthwise into quarters. Finely chop one of the green onions; cut the remaining three green onions diagonally into 1-inch pieces. In a small bowl stir together orange peel, orange juice, soy sauce, honey, serrano pepper, and garlic. Set aside.

2. Working in a well-ventilated area, in a large skillet heat oil over medium-high heat. Add Brussels sprouts, mushrooms, and green onions. Cook and stir for 8 to 10 minutes or until sprouts are blackened in places and are nearly tender.

3. Pour orange juice mixture over sprout mixture; toss to coat. Cook and stir for 3 to 4 minutes more or until sprouts are tender. **Makes 5 servings.**

PER SERVING: 99 cal., 5 g fat (1 g sat. fat), 0 mg chol., 233 mg sodium, 14 g carb., 4 g fiber, 4 g pro.

*tip: To trim Brussels sprouts, cut off the stems just at the spot where the leaves start to grow. Remove dark green outer leaves until the tender, light green leaves are uniformly exposed.

Use a pair of clean kitchen scissors to cut up the stewed tomatoes right in the can. It's tidier and you can preserve the liquid, which you'll need to add to the skillet when cooking the vegetables..

tomato and pepper sweet potatoes

START TO FINISH: 35 minutes

2	cups bite-size sweet potato chunks (about 12 ounces)
1	medium onion, thinly sliced
1½	teaspoons olive oil
1	medium green sweet pepper, thinly sliced
1	14.5-ounce can Italian-style stewed tomatoes, undrained and cut up
¼	teaspoon packed brown sugar (optional)
⅛	teaspoon salt
⅛	teaspoon ground black pepper
2	tablespoons fresh small Italian parsley leaves (optional)

1. In a medium saucepan cook sweet potatoes in enough boiling water to cover for 10 to 12 minutes or until tender. Drain well.

2. Meanwhile, in a large nonstick skillet cook onion in hot oil over medium-high heat for 5 minutes. Add sweet pepper and cook for 3 minutes. Add tomatoes, brown sugar (if using), salt, and black pepper. Bring to boiling; reduce heat. Simmer, uncovered, for 5 minutes or until most of the liquid evaporates.

3. Stir sweet potatoes into tomato mixture. If desired, sprinkle with parsley leaves. **Makes 6 servings.**

PER SERVING: 80 cal., 1 g fat (0 g sat. fat), 0 mg chol., 221 mg sodium, 16 g carb., 3 g fiber, 2 g pro.

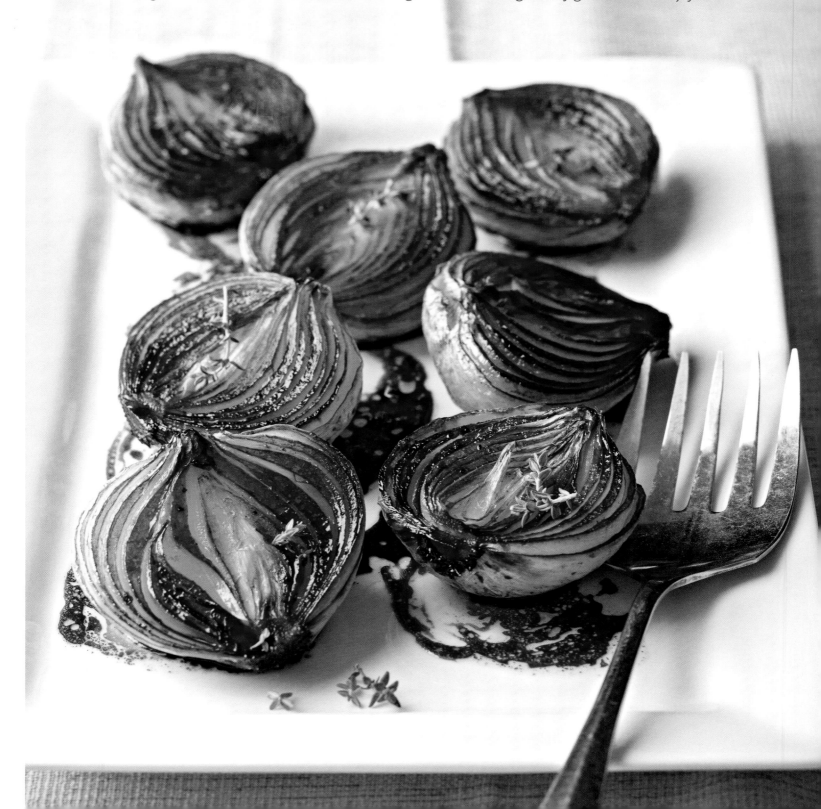

Change your onion paradigm. This recipe turns the humble allium from a mere flavoring agent into the starring attraction—sweet, oven-roasted onions that are delicious with roast or grilled pork or beef.

caramelized balsamic onions

PREP: 20 minutes   **BAKE:** 50 minutes at 425°F

2 tablespoons butter, melted
1 tablespoon olive oil
⅓ cup balsamic vinegar
2 tablespoons dry white wine, reduced-sodium chicken broth, or water
1 tablespoon sugar
¼ teaspoon salt
⅛ teaspoon freshly ground black pepper
4 medium yellow onions (about 1½ pounds total)
Fresh thyme leaves (optional)

1. Preheat oven to 425°F. In a 3-quart rectangular baking dish combine butter and olive oil. Whisk in vinegar, wine, sugar, salt, and pepper. Set aside.

2. Peel off papery outer layers of onions; do not cut off either end. Cut onions in half from stem through root end. Place onions in dish, cut sides up. Cover loosely with foil and bake for 30 minutes.

3. Remove foil. Using tongs, carefully turn onions over to cut sides down. Bake, uncovered, for 20 to 25 minutes longer or until onions are tender and balsamic mixture is thickened and caramelized. Serve cut sides up. If desired, sprinkle with fresh thyme. **Makes 8 servings.**

PER SERVING: 81 cal., 5 g fat (2 g sat. fat), 8 mg chol., 103 mg sodium, 9 g carb., 1 g fiber, 1 g pro.

Limiting the amount of water in which you cook vegetables helps retain nutrients. While boiling leaches out vitamins (and they're ultimately poured down the drain), steaming or microwaving preserves them.

lemony green beans and arugula

START TO FINISH: 25 minutes

4 cups fresh green beans, trimmed (12 ounces)
4 cloves garlic, minced
1 tablespoon olive oil
½ teaspoon finely shredded lemon peel
¼ teaspoon salt
¼ teaspoon ground black pepper
2 cups arugula
4 lemon wedges

1. Place a steamer basket in a large saucepan or Dutch oven with a tight-fitting lid. Add water to just below the basket. Bring water to boiling over medium-high heat. Place green beans in the steamer basket. Cover and steam for 8 to 10 minutes or until beans are crisp-tender. Remove steamer basket with beans.

2. In a large nonstick skillet cook garlic in hot oil over medium heat for 30 seconds, stirring constantly. Add lemon peel, salt, and black pepper; stir to combine. Add arugula and green beans. Cook for 1 to 2 minutes or until arugula is wilted and green beans are coated, tossing occasionally. Serve with lemon wedges. **Makes 4 servings.**

PER SERVING: 62 cal., 4 g fat (1 g sat. fat), 0 mg chol., 153 mg sodium, 7 g carb., 2 g fiber, 2 g pro.

This crunchy slaw has to be made ahead—at least 2 hours and up to 24 hours—so it can be ready and waiting in the refrigerator when you're ready to serve.

lemon-cilantro slaw

PREP: 20 minutes   **CHILL:** 2 hours

2   tablespoons lemon juice
1   tablespoon olive oil
½   teaspoon sugar
½   teaspoon Dijon-style mustard
⅛   teaspoon ground black pepper
4   cups packaged shredded cabbage
    with carrot (coleslaw mix)
½   cup coarsely shredded carrot
2   tablespoons snipped fresh
    cilantro
2   tablespoons chopped green onion

1. In a large bowl whisk together lemon juice, oil, sugar, mustard, and black pepper. Add coleslaw mix, carrot, cilantro, and green onion; toss gently to coat. Cover and chill for 2 to 24 hours before serving. **Makes 4 servings.**

PER SERVING: 59 cal., 3 g fat (0 g sat. fat), 0 mg chol., 43 mg sodium, 6 g carb., 2 g fiber, 1 g pro.

● VEGETARIAN ● GLUTEN FREE

Sweet corn and tomatoes—the edible essence of summer—are barely cooked in just a little bit of butter to enhance their juiciness and sweetness.

summer corn and tomatoes

PREP: 15 minutes   **COOK:** 5 minutes

4   ears of fresh sweet corn or 2 cups frozen whole kernel corn, thawed
1   tablespoon butter
½   cup sliced green onions
2   cloves garlic, minced
2   cups grape tomatoes or cherry tomatoes, halved
1   tablespoon red wine vinegar
¼   teaspoon salt
¼   teaspoon ground black pepper

1. If using fresh corn, cut corn from cobs; set aside. In a large skillet heat butter over medium heat. Add green onions and garlic; cook and stir about 1 minute or until onions and garlic are slightly softened. Add corn and tomatoes; cook and stir for 4 to 5 minutes or until vegetables are crisp-tender. Drizzle with vinegar and sprinkle with the salt and pepper. **Makes 6 servings.**

PER SERVING: 81 cal., 2 g fat (1 g sat. fat), 5 mg chol., 120 mg sodium, 15 g carb., 2 g fiber, 2 g pro.

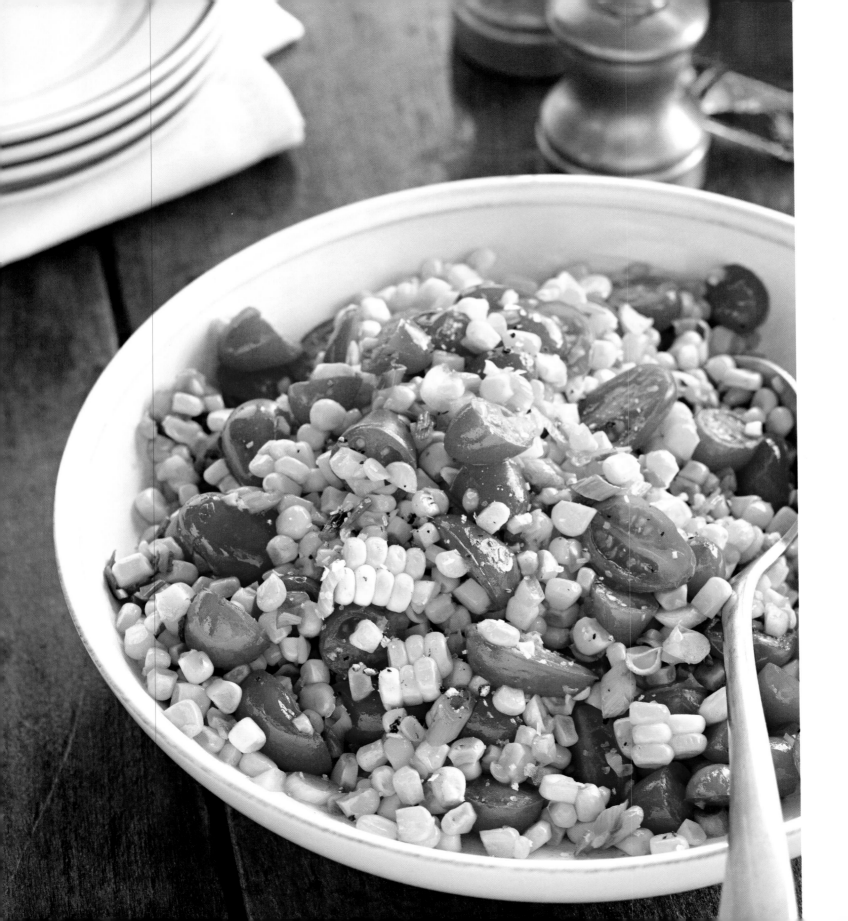

Although bacon should be a rare treat when you're trying to lose weight (and even then, it should be turkey bacon or one of the lower-fat pork varieties), a little bit goes a long way as a condiment to add flavor. Center-cut bacon, for instance, has 25 to 30 percent less fat than regular pork bacon.

sauteed cabbage with bacon

START TO FINISH: 20 minutes

2 slices turkey bacon or lower-fat, lower-sodium bacon, chopped
4 cups thinly sliced green cabbage
1 medium red sweet pepper, cut into bite-size strips
1 onion, halved and thinly sliced
2 tablespoons water
2 tablespoons light mayonnaise
1 tablespoon coarse ground mustard
1 tablespoon cider vinegar
¼ teaspoon caraway seeds, crushed
⅛ teaspoon celery seeds

1. In a large nonstick skillet cook bacon over medium heat for 5 minutes or until cooked through, stirring occasionally. Remove bacon from skillet; set aside. Add cabbage, sweet pepper, onion, and the water to skillet. Cover and cook over medium heat for 5 minutes or just until vegetables are tender, stirring occasionally.

2. In a small bowl combine mayonnaise, mustard, vinegar, caraway seeds, and celery seeds. Add to cabbage mixture in skillet. Toss until well coated. Sprinkle with cooked bacon and serve warm. **Makes 4 servings.**

PER SERVING: 82 cal., 4 g fat (1 g sat. fat), 10 mg chol., 255 mg sodium, 8 g carb., 3 g fiber, 2 g pro.

Remove the tough, fibrous stems from the shiitake mushrooms before slicing the tender caps. You can discard the stems—or save them to help flavor your next pot of homemade broth. Shiitake mushroom stems can be frozen in a tightly sealed bag or container almost indefinitely.

shiitake and bok choy

START TO FINISH: 25 minutes

1	tablespoon toasted sesame oil
2	cups sliced zucchini
1½	cups sliced shiitake mushrooms
2	cloves garlic, minced
4	cups halved, trimmed baby bok choy (about 1 pound)
1	tablespoon oyster sauce
2	teaspoons reduced-sodium soy sauce
¼	teaspoon ground black pepper
1	tablespoon sesame seeds, toasted (see tip, page 64)

1. In an extra-large skillet heat sesame oil over medium-high heat. Add zucchini, mushrooms, and garlic; cook and stir about 4 minutes or just until vegetables are tender. Carefully add baby bok choy; cook for 2 minutes. Add oyster sauce, soy sauce, and pepper; cook and stir for 1 minute. Sprinkle with sesame seeds. **Makes 4 servings.**

PER SERVING: 97 cal., 5 g fat (1 g sat. fat), 172 mg chol., 254 mg sodium, 13 g carb., 3 g fiber, 3 g pro.

cook smart *Make a little work out of snacking to slow down your eating. Crack shelled nuts, peel an orange, or pop edamame out of the pod and into your mouth.*

If you can't find miso at your supermarket, look for it an Asian market. To remove the tough stems on the kale, simply hold each stem at the top with one hand and strip the leaf off with the other hand.

miso-ginger kale

PREP: 25 minutes   **COOK:** 10 minutes

2   **8-ounce bunches fresh kale**
2   **tablespoons rice vinegar**
2   **tablespoons canola oil**
½   **teaspoon finely shredded lime peel**
1   **tablespoon lime juice**
2   **teaspoons miso (soybean paste)**
1   **teaspoon grated fresh ginger**
1   **clove garlic, minced**
2   **tablespoons dry-roasted cashews or peanuts, chopped (optional)**

1. Rinse and dry kale. Trim and discard tough stems. Stack leaves, then cut crosswise into ½-inch strips.

2. Place a steamer basket in a Dutch oven with a tight-fitting lid. Add water to just below the basket. Bring water to boiling over medium-high heat. Place kale in the steamer basket. Cover and steam about 10 minutes or just until tender, tossing leaves once or twice. Remove steamer basket with kale and transfer kale to a bowl.

3. For dressing, in a small bowl combine vinegar, oil, lime peel, lime juice, miso paste, ginger, and garlic; whisk to combine. Drizzle dressing over kale. Sprinkle with chopped nuts.
Makes 6 servings.

PER SERVING: 86 cal., 5 g fat (0 g sat. fat), 0 mg chol., 103 mg sodium, 9 g carb., 2 g fiber, 3 g pro.

tip: Kale has stormed the fresh veggie scene and for good reason—it's mild and delicious. One cup of raw kale has only 33 calories and more than a day's worth of vitamin A and C.

If the main dish takes a bit of effort, keep the sides as simple as possible—and vice versa. It doesn't get much easier than this 15-minute fruit and spinach salad. Make it in the summer with a peach—and with an apple in the fall.

peach and spinach salad with feta

START TO FINISH: 15 minutes

6   cups packaged fresh baby spinach
1   recipe Honey-Mustard Vinaigrette
1   medium peach, pitted, or 1 apple,
      cored and thinly sliced
3   tablespoons crumbled
      reduced-fat feta cheese
1   tablespoon pine nuts, toasted
      (see tip, page 64)

1. In a large bowl toss spinach with Honey-Mustard Vinaigrette. Divide spinach among four salad plates. Top with peach slices, feta cheese, and pine nuts. **Makes 4 servings.**

honey-mustard vinaigrette: In a screw-top jar combine 2 tablespoons white wine vinegar, 1 tablespoon olive oil, 1 tablespoon finely chopped shallot, 2 teaspoons water, 1 teaspoon honey mustard, and ⅛ teaspoon salt. Cover and shake well. Makes ¼ cup.

PER SERVING: 99 cal., 5 g fat (1 g sat. fat), 2 mg chol., 234 mg sodium, 8 g carb., 3 g fiber, 4 g pro.

tip: Whole fruits—with the peel—provide antioxidants and fiber to your diet.

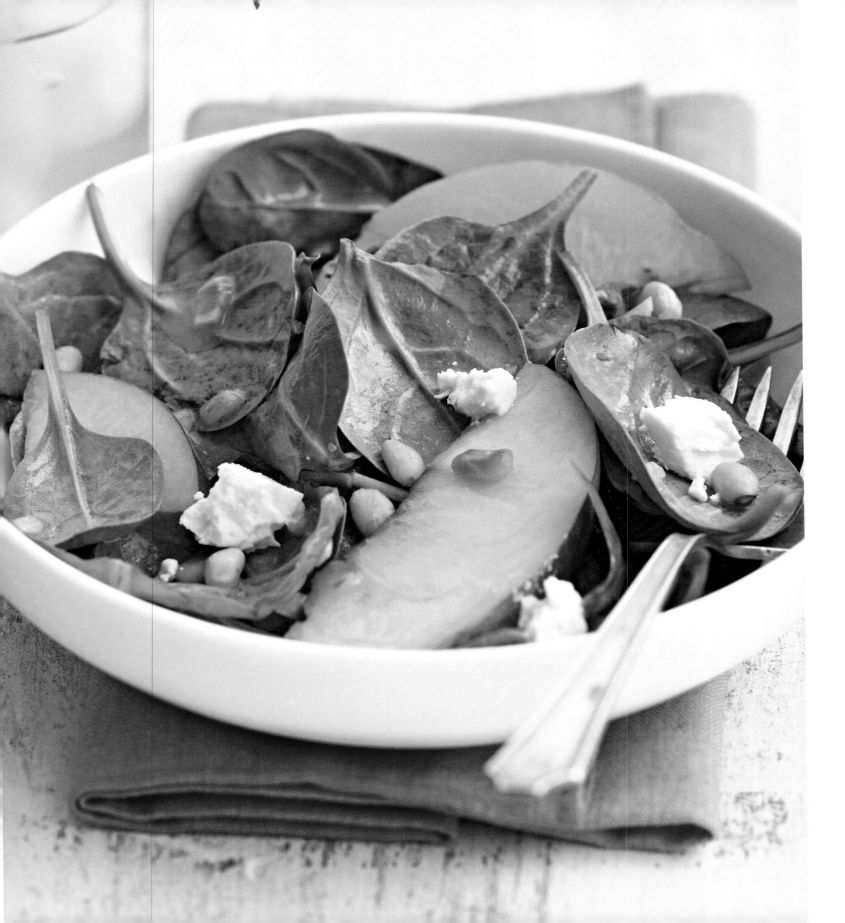

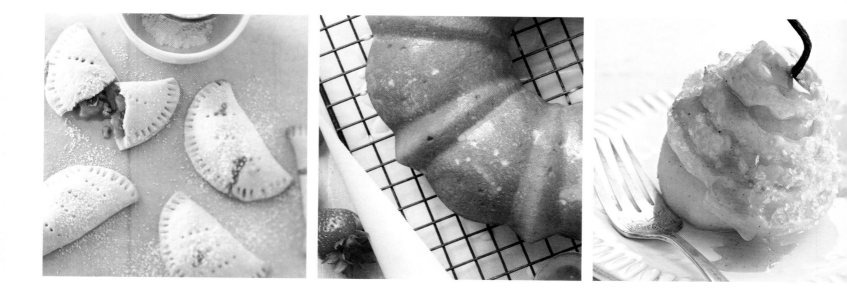

sweets under
200 calories

Following a healthy diet doesn't mean there's no dessert. These treats will satisfy your sweet tooth without sabotaging your plan.

"Tres leches" means "three milks" in Spanish. The three milks in this cake include evaporated fat-free milk, evaporated fat-free sweetened condensed milk, and a small amount of whipping cream or fat-free milk.

vanilla tres leches cake

STAND: 30 minutes   **PREP:** 15 minutes   **BAKE:** 30 minutes at 325°F   **COOL:** 15 minutes

3	**eggs or ¾ cup refrigerated or frozen egg product, thawed**
1	**cup evaporated fat-free milk**
½	**cup butter, softened**
	Nonstick cooking spray for baking
1½	**cups all-purpose flour**
¾	**cup brown rice flour or all-purpose flour**
1	**teaspoon baking powder**
¼	**teaspoon salt**
¾	**cup sugar**
½	**vanilla bean**
1	**tablespoon vanilla**
2	**tablespoons fat-free sweetened condensed milk**
2	**tablespoons whipping cream or fat-free milk**
	Fresh berries (optional)

1. Allow eggs, milk, and butter to stand at room temperature for 30 minutes. Preheat oven to 325°F. Coat a 10-inch fluted tube pan with cooking spray for baking; set aside. In a medium bowl stir together flours, baking powder, and salt; set aside.

2. In a large mixing bowl beat butter with an electric mixer on medium speed for 30 seconds. Add sugar and beat on medium speed about 5 minutes or until very light and fluffy. Using a small sharp knife, split the vanilla bean half in half lengthwise and use the knife to scrape the seeds into the butter mixture. Add 1½ teaspoons of the vanilla. Add eggs, 1 egg or ¼ cup at a time, beating well after each addition.

3. Alternately add flour mixture and ¾ cup of the evaporated milk to butter mixture, beating on low speed after each addition just until combined. Pour batter into the prepared pan, spreading evenly. Bake for 30 to 35 minutes or until a wooden skewer inserted in the center comes out clean. (Cake will appear shallow in the pan.) Cool in the pan on a wire rack for 15 minutes. Invert cake onto a wire rack.

4. Meanwhile, in a small bowl combine remaining ¼ cup evaporated milk, the sweetened condensed milk, whipping cream, and remaining 1½ teaspoons vanilla extract. Using a long skewer, poke holes all over the top of the hot cake. Using small spoonfuls, evenly spoon the condensed milk mixture over the hot cake, allowing the milk mixture to soak into the cake before adding more. Cool cake completely. **Makes 16 servings.**

PER SERVING: 200 cal., 8 g fat (4 g sat. fat), 53 mg chol., 156 mg sodium, 28 g carb., 1 g fiber, 4 g pro.

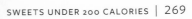

Rather than relying on a fat such as butter for moistness and a tender texture, this cake calls for shredded apple. The natural sweetness of the dates means there's less refined sugar in it as well.

apple-date cake

PREP: 30 minutes   **BAKE:** 25 minutes at 350°F

Nonstick cooking spray
⅔ cup fat-free milk
⅔ cup chopped pitted dates
¼ teaspoon salt
¾ cup coarsely shredded peeled cooking apple
1 teaspoon vanilla
1 egg, lightly beaten
2 tablespoons vegetable oil
½ cup chopped pecans
¼ cup packed brown sugar
1 tablespoon butter, softened
1 teaspoon all-purpose flour
1 teaspoon ground cinnamon
1½ cups all-purpose flour
1 teaspoon baking powder
½ teaspoon baking soda

1. Preheat oven to 350°F. Lightly coat an 8×8×2-inch baking pan with cooking spray. Set aside.

2. In a small saucepan combine milk, dates, and salt; heat until steaming. Remove from heat. Stir in apple and vanilla; cool. Add egg and oil; stir until combined. Set aside.

3. In a small bowl stir together pecans, brown sugar, butter, the 1 teaspoon flour, and the cinnamon; set aside.

4. In a medium bowl whisk together the 1½ cups flour, the baking powder, and baking soda. Add milk mixture all at once to flour mixture. Stir just until combined. Spoon batter into the prepared baking pan. Sprinkle evenly with pecan mixture.

5. Bake about 25 minutes or until a knife inserted near the center comes out clean. Cool slightly. Serve warm. **Makes 12 servings.**

PER SERVING: 179 cal., 7 g fat (1 g sat. fat), 18 mg chol., 153 mg sodium, 27 g carb., 2 g fiber, 3 g pro.

White whole wheat flour has the same fiber and protein content as regular whole wheat flour. It is simply a *whole* flour—meaning it includes the bran, germ, and endosperm—made from a variety of white wheat.

upside-down pineapple-ginger carrot cake

PREP: 25 minutes   **BAKE:** 35 minutes at 350°F   **COOL:** 30 minutes

Nonstick cooking spray
2 **tablespoons butter, melted**
3 **tablespoons packed brown sugar**
4 **thin slices fresh pineapple**
1 **tablespoon finely chopped crystallized ginger**
1 **cup white whole wheat flour**
¾ **cup granulated sugar**
1½ **teaspoons apple pie spice**
½ **teaspoon baking powder**
½ **teaspoon baking soda**
⅛ **teaspoon salt**
1 **cup finely shredded carrots (2 medium)**
⅓ **cup canola oil**
¼ **cup fat-free milk**
3 **egg whites**
Powdered sugar (optional)

1. Preheat oven to 350°F. Lightly coat an 8×8×2-inch baking pan with cooking spray. Drizzle bottom of pan with melted butter; sprinkle with brown sugar. Arrange pineapple slices in pan; sprinkle with crystallized ginger.

2. In a large bowl stir together flour, granulated sugar, apple pie spice, baking powder, baking soda, and salt. Add carrots, oil, and milk, stirring until moistened. In a medium mixing bowl beat egg whites with an electric mixer on medium speed until stiff peaks form (tips stand straight). Fold beaten egg whites into carrot mixture. Pour batter into pan, evenly spreading over pineapple slices.

3. Bake for 35 to 40 minutes or until a wooden toothpick inserted near the center comes out clean. Cool in pan on a wire rack for 5 minutes. Loosen sides of cake; invert onto a serving platter. Cool for 30 minutes. If desired, sprinkle lightly with powdered sugar. Serve warm. **Makes 9 servings.**

PER SERVING: 192 cal., 8 g fat (2 g sat. fat), 5 mg chol., 130 mg sodium, 29 g carb., 1 g fiber, 3 g pro.

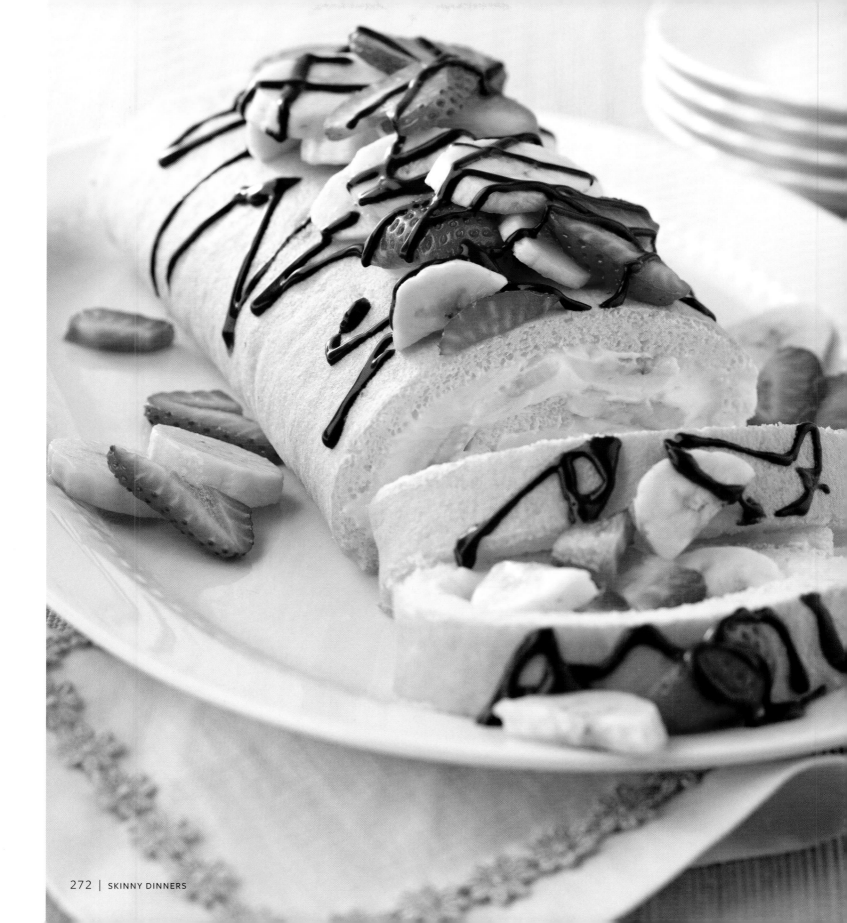

This airy jelly roll features all of the fun and flavors of a banana split—a cold and creamy filling, bananas, strawberries, and chocolate—in a whisper-light, low-fat cake. Cooling the cake rolled up in a towel on a wire rack helps it hold its shape after it's filled..

banana split cake roll

PREP: 25 minutes   **STAND:** 30 minutes   **BAKE:** 12 minutes at 350°F   **COOL:** 1 hour   **CHILL:** 2 hours

5 **egg whites**
3 **egg yolks**
  Nonstick cooking spray
½ **cup sifted cake flour**
1 **teaspoon baking powder**
¼ **teaspoon salt**
2 **teaspoons vanilla**
½ **cup sugar**
1½ **cups fat-free milk**
1 **4-serving-size package fat-free, sugar-free, reduced-calorie vanilla instant pudding**
1 **cup frozen sugar-free whipped dessert topping, thawed**
2 **bananas**
½ **cup sliced fresh strawberries**
2 **tablespoons sugar-free chocolate-flavor syrup**

1. For the cake, place egg whites in a large mixing bowl and place egg yolks in a medium mixing bowl; let stand at room temperature for 30 minutes. Meanwhile, coat a 15x10x1-inch baking pan with cooking spray. Line bottom of pan with parchment paper. Coat parchment paper with cooking spray; set aside. In a small bowl stir together cake flour, baking powder, and salt; set aside.

2. Preheat oven to 350°F. Add vanilla to egg yolks; beat with an electric mixer on high speed for 5 minutes or until thick and lemon color. Gradually beat in ¼ cup of the sugar, beating on high speed until sugar is almost dissolved. Sprinkle flour mixture over egg yolk mixture; gently fold in just until combined. Thoroughly wash beaters. Beat egg whites with an electric mixer on medium speed until soft peaks form (tips curl). Gradually add the remaining ¼ cup sugar, beating until stiff peaks form (tips stand straight). Fold ½ cup of the beaten egg whites into the egg yolk mixture to lighten. Fold in the remaining egg whites. Spread batter evenly in prepared pan.

3. Bake for 12 minutes or until cake springs back when lightly touched. Immediately loosen edges of cake from pan; turn cake out onto a clean dish towel. Remove parchment paper. Starting from a short side, roll towel and cake into a spiral. Cool on a wire rack.

4. For filling, in a medium bowl whisk together milk and pudding mix just until thickened. Fold in whipped topping. Cover and chill for at least 1 hour.

5. Unroll cooled cake; remove towel. Spread filling to within 1 inch of edges. Thinly slice one of the bananas; arrange slices over the filling. Roll up cake. Cover and chill for at least 2 hours or up to 8 hours. To serve, thinly slice the remaining banana. Top cake roll with banana and strawberry slices. Drizzle with chocolate syrup. Cut into 10 slices. **Makes 10 servings.**

PER SERVING: 155 cal., 2 g fat (1 g sat. fat), 56 mg chol., 286 mg sodium, 29 g carb., 1 g fiber, 5 g pro.

The moistness and tenderness in these cupcakes does not come primarily from fat—there is only ¼ cup of canola oil in the whole batch—but from applesauce and shredded zucchini.

zucchini cupcakes with greek yogurt frosting

PREP: 20 minutes   **BAKE:** 20 minutes at 350°F   **COOL:** 1 hour

Nonstick cooking spray
1 cup whole wheat flour
¼ cup granulated sugar
¼ cup packed brown sugar
1 teaspoon ground cinnamon
½ teaspoon baking powder
½ teaspoon salt
¼ teaspoon baking soda
2 eggs
¼ cup fat-free milk
1 cup cooked quinoa*
1 cup shredded zucchini
½ cup unsweetened applesauce
¼ cup canola oil
1 teaspoon vanilla
1 recipe Greek Yogurt Frosting
½ to 1 teaspoon finely shredded lemon peel

1. Preheat oven to 350°F. Lightly coat twelve 2½-inch muffin cups with cooking spray.

2. In a large bowl stir together flour, granulated sugar, brown sugar, cinnamon, baking powder, salt, and baking soda; set aside.

3. In a medium bowl beat together eggs and milk. Add quinoa, zucchini, applesauce, oil, and vanilla; stir until well mixed. Add quinoa mixture to flour mixture, gently stirring to combine. Spoon batter into prepared muffin cups, filling each about three-fourths full.

4. Bake about 20 minutes or until a toothpick inserted in centers comes out clean. Cool in muffin cups on a wire rack for 5 minutes. Loosen edges; remove from muffin cups. Cool on wire rack about 1 hour or until completely cool. Frost with Greek Yogurt Frosting; sprinkle with lemon peel. **Makes 12 servings.**

greek yogurt frosting: In a small bowl whisk together one 6-ounce carton plain fat-free Greek yogurt, 2 tablespoons light agave nectar or 3 tablespoons powdered sugar, and 1 teaspoon vanilla.

PER SERVING: 167 cal., 6 g fat (1 g sat. fat), 32 mg chol., 161 mg sodium, 24 g carb., 2 g fiber, 5 g pro.

*tip: For 1 cup cooked quinoa, rinse ⅓ cup quinoa. Place in a small saucepan with ⅔ cup water. Cook according to package directions. Cool. Measure out 1 cup. Use any remaining cooked quinoa in salads.

The "amazing" aspect of this apple tart is how a rich, beautiful sauce forms during baking and is collected in the custard cup at the center of the tart.

amazing apple tart

PREP: 30 minutes **BAKE:** 12 minutes at 400°F/25 minutes at 350°F **COOL:** 30 minutes

¼ cup apple juice or apple cider
3 tablespoons packed brown sugar
2 teaspoons butter or tub-style vegetable oil spread
¼ teaspoon ground cinnamon
   Dash salt
½ teaspoon vanilla
   Nonstick cooking spray
4 small apples, such as Jonathan, Winesap, or Empire, cored and halved lengthwise (about 1 pound total)
1 recipe Biscuit Pastry

1. Preheat oven to 400°F. For sauce, in a small saucepan combine apple juice, brown sugar, butter, cinnamon, and salt. Bring to boiling; reduce heat. Simmer, uncovered, for 2 minutes. Remove from heat. Stir in vanilla.

2. Place a 6-ounce custard cup upside down in the center of a 9-inch pie plate. Lightly coat cup with cooking spray. Using the tines of a fork, score the uncut sides of apple halves and place, cut sides up, around custard cup. Drizzle apples with sauce.

3. Prepare Biscuit Pastry. On a floured surface, roll into a 10-inch circle. Place pastry over apples and custard cup. Tuck dough between apples and pie plate. Bake for 12 minutes.

4. Reduce oven temperature to 350ºF. Bake for 25 to 30 minutes more or until pastry is golden and apples are tender. Cool on a wire rack for 30 minutes. Invert onto a 10- to 12-inch serving plate. To serve, cut into eight wedges and spoon sauce from custard cup over the apple and pastry wedges. **Makes 8 servings.**

biscuit pastry: In a bowl stir together ¾ cup flour, 1¼ teaspoons baking powder, 1 teaspoon granulated sugar, and ⅛ teaspoon salt. Using a pastry blender, cut in 3 tablespoons butter until mixture resembles coarse crumbs. Using a fork, stir in 3 tablespoons fat-free milk. Knead gently until dough forms a ball.

PER SERVING: 147 cal., 6 g fat (3 g sat. fat), 14 mg chol., 143 mg sodium, 24 g carb., 2 g fiber, 2 g pro.

While no one will buy the argument that these cookies are like medicine, the generous dose of sesame they contain—in the form of both sesame paste and sesame seeds—is actually a very good thing. Studies have shown that sesame seed oil has properties that lower blood pressure and may fight cancer.

chocolate-sesame cookies

PREP: 30 minutes   **CHILL:** 30 minutes   **BAKE:** 9 minutes at 350°F

8	ounces semisweet chocolate, coarsely chopped
2	tablespoons butter
3	tablespoons tahini (sesame seed paste)
⅔	cup all-purpose flour
½	teaspoon baking powder
½	teaspoon salt
2	eggs
¾	cup packed brown sugar
1	teaspoon vanilla
½	cup sesame seeds, toasted (see tip, page 64)

1. In a small saucepan cook and stir chocolate and butter over low heat until melted. Remove from heat; stir in tahini. Set aside.

2. In a small bowl stir together flour, baking powder, and salt; set aside. In a large mixing bowl beat eggs with an electric mixer on medium speed until frothy. Add brown sugar and vanilla; beat until combined. Beat in chocolate mixture. Beat in flour mixture until combined. Cover and chill for 30 minutes or until dough is easy to handle.

3. Preheat oven to 350°F. Place sesame seeds in a small bowl. Shape dough into 1-inch balls. Roll balls in sesame seeds to coat. Place balls 2 inches apart on an ungreased cookie sheet.

4. Bake for 9 to 11 minutes or until cookies are puffed and bottoms are set. Transfer cookies to a wire rack; cool. **Makes 42 servings.**

PER SERVING: 73 cal., 4 g fat (2 g sat. fat), 10 mg chol., 42 mg sodium, 9 g carb., 1 g fiber, 1 g pro.

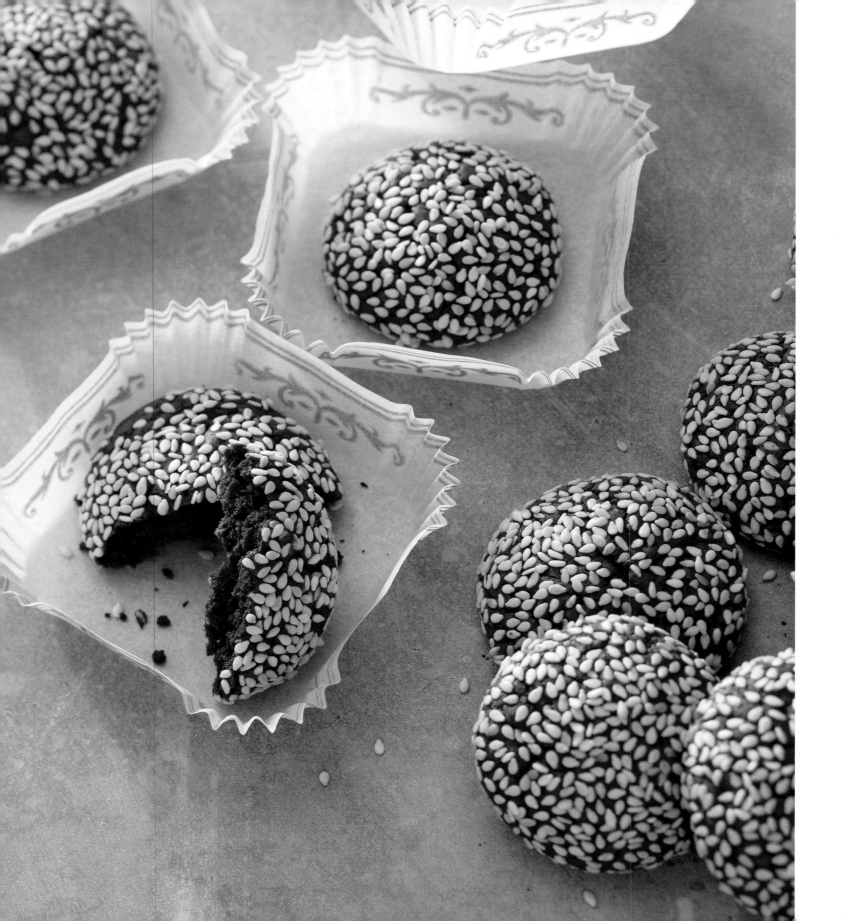

cook smart *Nuts—like pistachios—are the perfect snack. They are portable and their protein and fiber content leaves you feeling satisfied.*

In traditional baklava, every layer is brushed with melted butter. In this lightened up version, every third sheet is brushed with butter for flavor—and the rest are sprayed with cooking spray.

salted caramel pistachio-apricot baklava

PREP: 45 minutes   **BAKE:** 45 minutes at 325°F

SWEETS UNDER 200 CALORIES

1½   cups boiling water
1   cup finely chopped dried apricots
1½   cups shelled lightly salted
      pistachio nuts, finely chopped
2   tablespoons packed brown sugar
2   teaspoons finely shredded
      lemon peel
      Butter-flavor nonstick cooking
      spray
½   of a 16-ounce package frozen
      phyllo dough (14×9-inch
      rectangles), thawed
3   tablespoons butter, melted
⅔   cup packed brown sugar
⅛   teaspoon ground nutmeg
1   teaspoon kosher salt

1. Preheat oven to 325°F. In a medium bowl combine the boiling water and apricots. Let stand for 5 minutes. Strain apricots through a fine-mesh sieve, reserving the liquid and gently pressing on apricots with the back of a large spoon to press out as much liquid as possible. In a large bowl stir together drained apricots, the pistachios, 2 tablespoons brown sugar, and the lemon peel. Set aside.

2. Coat the bottom of a 13×9x2-inch baking pan with cooking spray. Unroll phyllo dough (keep phyllo covered with plastic wrap until needed.) Layer 5 or 6 phyllo sheets in the prepared baking pan, lightly coating the tops of the sheets with cooking spray except for every third sheet, which should be brushed with melted butter. Sprinkle with about one-third of the nut mixture. Repeat layering phyllo sheets and sprinkling with nut mixture two more times, coating the top of each phyllo sheet with cooking spray or melted butter.

3. Layer the remaining phyllo sheets on top of filling, coating each sheet with cooking spray or butter. Brush the final sheet with butter. Using a sharp knife, cut stacked layers into 24 diamond- or rectangular-shaped pieces.

4. Bake for 45 minutes or until golden brown. Cool slightly in pan on a wire rack.

5. Meanwhile, measure the drained apricot soaking liquid. Discard enough of the liquid or add water to the liquid to make ⅔ cup total liquid. In a small saucepan stir together the ⅔ cup apricot soaking liquid, ⅔ cup brown sugar, and the nutmeg. Bring to boiling; reduce heat. Simmer, uncovered, for 10 minutes or until reduced to about ⅓ cup. Pour the syrup evenly over slightly cooled baklava in the pan. Sprinkle top evenly with kosher salt. Re-cut diamonds or rectangles to serve. **Makes 24 servings.**

PER SERVING: 127 cal., 6 g fat (1 g sat. fat), 4 mg chol., 176 mg sodium, 18 g carb., 1 g fiber, 3 g pro.

CHAPTER 11

SWEETS UNDER 200 CALORIES | 279

The flavors of the famous New Orleans dessert that is traditionally flambéed table side have been captured in these diminutive pies.

bananas foster mini pies

PREP: 30 minutes   **CHILL:** 1 hour   **BAKE:** 15 minutes at 400°F

⅓	cup butter, softened
1	tablespoon granulated sugar
¼	teaspoon salt
1	egg
2	tablespoons cold water
1½	cups all-purpose flour
1	medium banana, chopped (about ¾ cup)
¼	cup sugar-free caramel-flavor ice cream topping
¼	cup chopped pecans, toasted (see tip, page 64)
1	tablespoon bourbon
¼	teaspoon ground cinnamon
1	tablespoon butter, melted
2	teaspoons powdered sugar

1. Line a baking sheet with parchment paper; set aside. In a large mixing bowl beat the ⅓ cup butter with an electric mixer on medium to high speed for 30 seconds. Add granulated sugar and salt. Beat for 3 minutes on medium speed. Add egg and the water; beat until combined. Beat in as much of the flour as you can. Stir in any remaining flour. Shape dough into a disk. Wrap in plastic wrap; chill 1 hour or until easy to handle.

2. Preheat oven to 400°F. For filling, in a bowl combine banana, ice cream topping, pecans, bourbon, and cinnamon.

3. On a lightly floured surface, roll dough to ⅛-inch thickness. Using a 4-inch round cutter, cut the dough into rounds, rerolling scraps as necessary. Place about 1 tablespoon of the filling in the center of each round. Brush edges of pastry circles with a little water. Fold each circle in half over filling; press edges to seal. Place pies on prepared baking sheet. Brush pies with the 1 tablespoon melted butter.

4. Bake for 15 minutes or until lightly browned. Sift powdered sugar over pies. Serve warm. **Makes 12 servings.**

PER SERVING: 165 cal., 8 g fat (4 g sat. fat), 32 mg chol., 118 mg sodium, 20 g carb., 1 g fiber, 3 g pro.

Good apple choices for this autumnal crisp include Granny Smith, McIntosh, Gala, Cortland, Braeburn, Jonathan, and Fuji. Use a single variety or a mix of varieties.

maple, apple, and date fruit crisp

PREP: 25 minutes   **BAKE:** 35 minutes at 375°F

1   tablespoon all-purpose flour
½   teaspoon apple pie spice
6   cups sliced, peeled cooking
     apples (6 medium)
½   cup snipped pitted whole dates
¼   cup maple syrup
¾   cup whole grain cereal flakes with
     multigrain clusters and crunchy
     pecans
1½ tablespoons butter, melted
     Vanilla low-fat yogurt (optional)

1. Preheat oven to 375°F. In a large bowl stir together flour and apple pie spice. Add apples and dates; toss gently to coat. Drizzle with maple syrup; toss gently to coat. Transfer to an ungreased 2-quart square baking dish.

2. In a small bowl toss together cereal and melted butter. Sprinkle over apple mixture. Bake, uncovered*, for 35 to 40 minutes or until apples are tender. Serve warm, with yogurt if desired. **Makes 6 servings.**

PER SERVING: 199 cal., 4 g fat (2 g sat. fat), 8 mg chol., 55 mg sodium, 42 g carb., 5 g fiber, 2 g pro.

*tip: If necessary to prevent overbrowning, cover top loosely with foil for the last 10 to 15 minutes of baking.

Vanilla bean paste is a fairly new product that offers intense vanilla flavor—and the beautiful speckled seeds—without having to deal with vanilla bean. Use the same amount of paste as you would use extract.

pastry-wrapped pears with vanilla-cardamom sauce

PREP: 30 minutes **BAKE:** 25 minutes at 375°F **COOL:** 20 minutes

1	cup pear nectar
¼	teaspoon ground cardamom
4	small red or green pears (6 to 8 ounces each)
1	tablespoon coarse sugar
1	tablespoon finely chopped crystallized ginger
½	of a sheet frozen puff pastry, thawed
2	tablespoons cold water
1	teaspoon cornstarch
½	of a vanilla bean, split lengthwise, or 1 teaspoon vanilla

1. In a large saucepan combine pear nectar and cardamom. Bring to boiling. Meanwhile, if desired, peel pears. Cut thin slices from bottoms of pears so they stand upright. Using a melon baller or small spoon, remove cores, starting from the bottom of each pear and leaving stems intact.

2. Add pears to nectar mixture in saucepan. Reduce heat; simmer, covered, for 5 to 7 minutes or just until pears are tender. Remove pears with a slotted spoon, reserving cooking liquid. Set pears aside to cool. In a small bowl stir together sugar and crystallized ginger; set aside.

3. Preheat oven to 375°F. On a lightly floured surface, roll pastry into a 12×4-inch rectangle. Using a fluted pastry wheel or pizza cutter, cut rectangle into eight 12×½-inch strips. Place the end of one pastry strip at the top of one of the pears. Working down from the top, wrap pastry strip around the pear in a spiral fashion. Add a second strip, pressing onto the end of the first strip. Press end of the last strip firmly onto the pear to secure. Repeat with the remaining pears and pastry strips. (Strips will spiral about three-fourths of the way down the pear.)

4. Place pastry-wrapped pears upright on a baking sheet. Brush pastry with a little water and sprinkle lightly with sugar-ginger mixture. Bake for 25 to 30 minutes or until pastry is puffed and golden. Cool for 20 minutes.

5. Meanwhile, for sauce, in a small bowl combine the 2 tablespoons cold water and cornstarch; stir into cooking liquid in saucepan. If using, add vanilla bean. Cook and stir over medium heat until thickened and bubbly; cook and stir for 2 minutes more. Remove from heat. Remove vanilla bean, if using, or stir in vanilla. Serve pears with sauce. **Makes 4 servings.**

PER SERVING: 178 cal., 2 g fat (1 g sat. fat), 0 mg chol., 21 mg sodium, 40 g carb., 4 g fiber, 1 g pro.

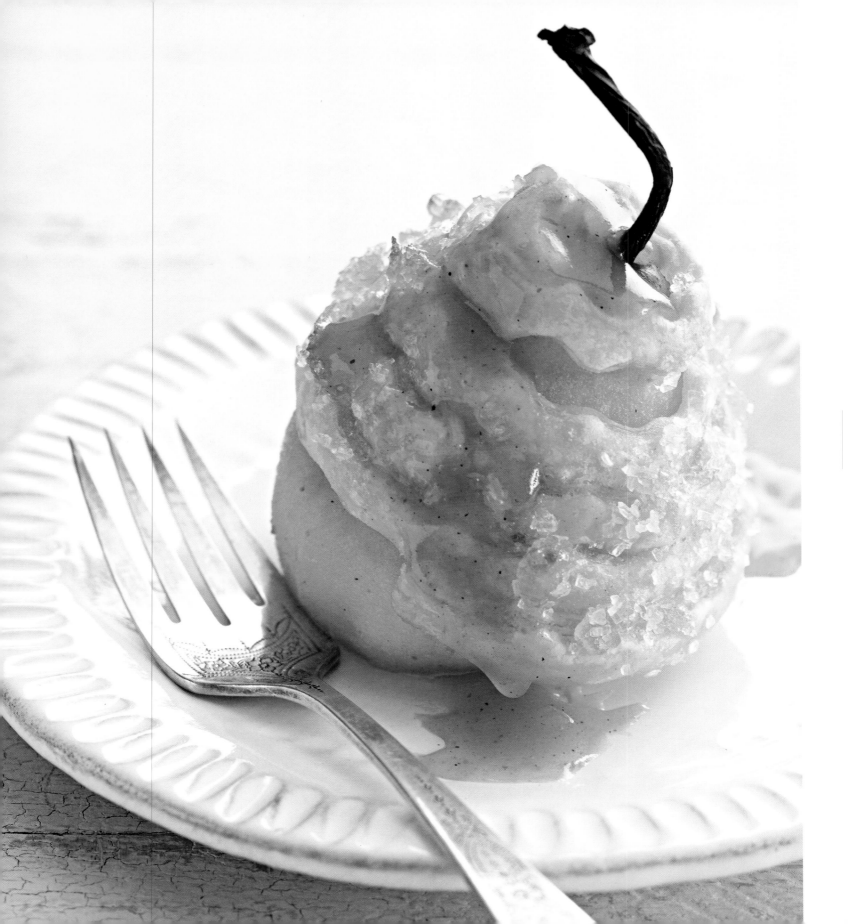

Look for the sturdy Italian (Savoiardi) ladyfingers for this tiramisu, if you can find them. They're crisper and harder than traditional sponge-like ladyfingers and hold up better in this chilled dessert.

maple-bourbon chocolate tiramisu with pecans

PREP: 35 minutes   **CHILL:** 4 hours

⅓ cup boiling water
2 tablespoons instant espresso coffee powder
⅓ cup light maple-flavor syrup
2 tablespoons bourbon (optional)
6 ounces reduced-fat cream cheese (Neufchâtel), softened
3 tablespoons fat-free milk
1 teaspoon vanilla
⅔ cup frozen light whipped dessert topping, thawed
2 3-ounce packages ladyfingers, split
1½ cups prepared fat-free sugar-free chocolate pudding*
⅓ cup chopped pecans, toasted (see tip, page 64)
Dark chocolate curls (optional)

1. For syrup mixture, in a small bowl combine the boiling water and espresso powder; stir to dissolve espresso powder. Stir in maple syrup and bourbon (if using). Set aside.

2. In a medium mixing bowl beat cream cheese with an electric mixer on low speed until smooth. Add milk and vanilla; beat until smooth. Fold in dessert topping. Set aside.

3. Arrange half of the ladyfinger halves in the bottom of a 2-quart rectangular baking dish. Brush with half of the syrup mixture. Top with chocolate pudding, spreading evenly. Top with remaining ladyfingers. Brush with remaining syrup mixture. Top with cream cheese mixture, spreading evenly. Cover and chill for 4 to 24 hours.

4. To serve, cut into 12 portions. Sprinkle each serving with pecans. If desired, garnish with chocolate curls.
Makes 12 servings.

PER SERVING: 154 cal., 7 g fat (3 g sat. fat), 42 mg chol., 180 mg sodium, 18 g carb., 1 g fiber, 5 g pro.

*tip: For easy pudding, prepare a 4-serving-size package fat-free sugar-free chocolate instant pudding mix according to package directions. Use 1½ cups in the tiramisu.

A slice of 9-inch, two-layer carrot cake with cream cheese frosting can contain as many as 850 calories. The calorie saving trick to this recipe is two-fold: A good portion of each serving is fresh pineapple layered between crumbles made from a lightened up carrot cake.

carrot cake parfaits

PREP: 30 minutes   **BAKE:** 20 minutes at 350°F   **COOL:** 10 minutes

1	cup all-purpose flour
1	teaspoon ground cinnamon
½	teaspoon baking soda
½	teaspoon ground nutmeg
½	cup unsweetened applesauce
¼	cup granulated sugar
¼	cup packed brown sugar
1	egg, lightly beaten
2	tablespoons vegetable oil
2	cups shredded carrots (4 medium)
1	8-ounce container frozen fat-free whipped dessert topping, thawed
2	tablespoons pureed baby food carrots
¼	teaspoon ground ginger
1	cup chopped fresh pineapple
¼	cup finely chopped walnuts

1. Preheat oven to 350°F. Grease a 9-inch round baking pan; set aside. In a small bowl combine flour, cinnamon, baking soda, and nutmeg; set aside.

2. In a medium bowl stir together applesauce, granulated sugar, brown sugar, egg, and oil. Stir in shredded carrots. Add flour mixture, stirring just until combined. Spread batter in the prepared pan.

3. Bake for 20 to 25 minutes or until a toothpick inserted near the center comes out clean. Cool in pan on a wire rack for 10 minutes. Remove from pan. Cool completely on wire rack. Coarsely crumble cooled cake (the crumbles will be dense and moist).

4. In a medium bowl fold together dessert topping, baby food carrots, and ginger just until combined.

5. To assemble desserts, divide half of the crumbled cake among ten 6-ounce parfait glasses or dessert dishes. Top with half of the dessert topping mixture. Top with pineapple, the remaining crumbled cake, and the remaining dessert topping mixture. Sprinkle with walnuts. **Makes 10 servings.**

PER SERVING: 198 cal., 5 g fat (1 g sat. fat), 21 mg chol., 101 mg sodium, 34 g carb., 2 g fiber, 3 g pro.

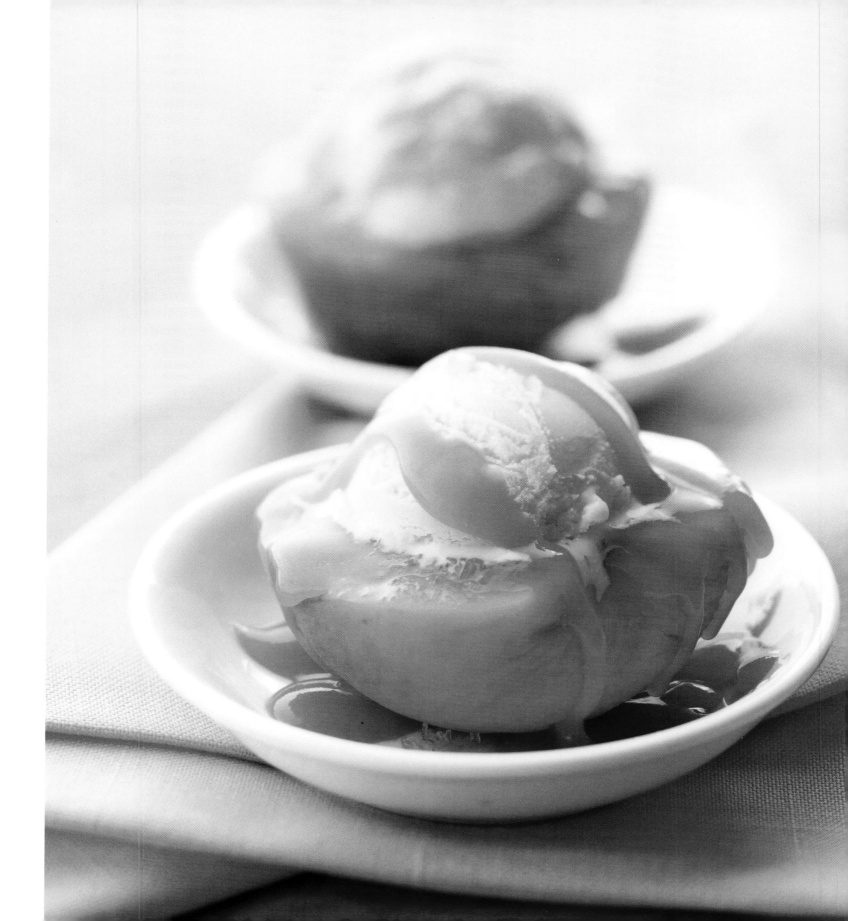

● **GLUTEN FREE**

Perfectly ripe peaches are the key to this simple dessert featuring a homemade caramel sauce and a scoop of frozen vanilla yogurt. Peaches are at their peak in July and August.

brown sugar peaches

START TO FINISH: 20 minutes

4	peaches, halved and pitted
¼	cup packed brown sugar
1½	teaspoons cornstarch
2	tablespoons water
3	tablespoons half-and-half
1	tablespoon light-color corn syrup
1	tablespoon butter
¼	teaspoon vanilla
2	cups light vanilla frozen yogurt
2	tablespoons coarse raw sugar or packed brown sugar (optional)

1. Fill a large Dutch oven with water to a depth of 1 inch. Bring water to boiling. Place a steamer basket in the Dutch oven. Place peaches in the steamer basket. Cover and steam about 5 minutes or until peaches are tender. Remove peaches from steamer basket and place in a large colander to drain.

2. Meanwhile, for caramel sauce, in a small heavy saucepan combine the ¼ cup brown sugar and the cornstarch. Stir in the water, half-and-half, and corn syrup. Cook and stir until thickened and bubbly (mixture will appear curdled before it thickens). Cook and stir for 2 minutes more. Remove saucepan from heat; stir in butter and vanilla.

3. Serve peaches topped with small scoops of frozen yogurt and drizzled with caramel sauce. If desired, sprinkle with coarse raw sugar. **Makes 8 servings.**

PER SERVING: 141 cal., 4 g fat (2 g sat. fat), 13 mg chol., 61 mg sodium, 26 g carb., 1 g fiber, 3 g pro.

The meringues can be made ahead. Once they're completely cooled, store in an airtight container at room temperature for up to one week. To serve, prepare the filling and serve as directed starting in Step 4.

chocolate-filled lemon meringues

PREP: 35 minutes   **STAND:** 30 minutes   **BAKE:** 25 minutes at 300°F   **STAND:** 1 hour

2   egg whites
⅔   cup sugar
1   teaspoon finely shredded lemon peel
¼   teaspoon cream of tartar
4   teaspoons sugar
1   tablespoon unsweetened cocoa powder
⅓   cup mascarpone cheese or reduced-fat cream cheese (Neufchâtel), softened (about 3 ounces)
½   teaspoon vanilla
2   to 3 tablespoons fat-free milk
1   cup fresh raspberries and/or blueberries
    Finely shredded lemon peel and/or unsweetened cocoa powder (optional)

1. In a large mixing bowl let egg whites stand at room temperature for 30 minutes. Meanwhile, cover a large baking sheet with parchment paper or foil. Draw twelve 2-inch circles 3 inches apart on the paper or foil; set aside.

2. Preheat oven to 300°F. For meringues, in a small bowl stir together the ⅔ cup sugar and the lemon peel; set aside. Add cream of tartar to egg whites. Beat with an electric mixer on medium speed until soft peaks form (tips curl). Add the sugar-lemon peel mixture, 1 tablespoon at a time, beating on high speed until stiff peaks form (tips stand straight). Spoon egg white mixture into the circles on the prepared baking sheet, building up sides slightly.

3. Bake for 25 minutes. Turn off oven. Let meringues dry in oven with door closed for 1 hour. Remove from oven; cool completely on baking sheet.

4. For filling, in a small bowl stir together the 4 teaspoons sugar and the cocoa powder. In another small bowl stir together the mascarpone cheese and vanilla. Stir in the cocoa mixture and enough of the milk to make of spreading consistency.

5. Spread filling into cooled meringues. Top with berries. If desired, garnish with additional lemon peel and/or unsweetened cocoa powder. **Makes 12 servings.**

PER SERVING: 91 cal., 3 g fat (2 g sat. fat), 9 mg chol., 15 mg sodium, 15 g carb., 1 g fiber, 2 g pro.

tip: Increase your intake of plant foods. They contain phytochemicals—naturally occurring substances believed to enhance your body's natural defenses. Heart healthy anthocyanins are an example; they're found in blue and red foods like blueberries, strawberries, and raspberries.

Crystallized ginger adds a touch of sweet heat to these lovely poached pears. Look for it in the baking aisle of your supermarket.

gingered pears

PREP: 15 minutes **COOK:** 7 minutes

4   **small pears, cored**
     (about 1½ pounds total)
2   **tablespoons sugar**
2   **tablespoons water**
1   **teaspoon finely shredded lemon**
     peel
2   **tablespoons lemon juice**
1   **tablespoon butter**
¼   **teaspoon ground ginger**
1   **tablespoon chopped crystallized**
     ginger

1. Fill a large Dutch oven with water to a depth of 1 inch. Bring water to boiling. Place a steamer basket in the Dutch oven. Place pears in the steamer basket. Cover and steam for 7 to 9 minutes or until fruit is tender. Remove fruit from steamer basket.

2. Meanwhile, for lemon sauce, in a small saucepan heat and stir sugar, the water, lemon peel, lemon juice, butter, and ground ginger over medium heat until butter is melted and sugar is dissolved.

3. Serve pears with lemon sauce and sprinkle with crystallized ginger. **Makes 4 servings.**

PER SERVING: 122 cal., 3 g fat (2 g sat. fat), 8 mg chol., 27 mg sodium, 26 g carb., 4 g fiber, 1 g pro.

Semifreddo (Italian for "half cold") is an elegant, impressive dessert that is not difficult at all to make. If you'd like, substitute seedless blackberries for the raspberries.

raspberry semifreddo with pistachios and raspberry swirl

PREP: 30 minutes **FREEZE:** 6 hours **STAND:** 10 minutes

1 **pound fresh or frozen red raspberries, thawed (3½ cups)**
¼ **cup sugar**
2 **tablespoons lime juice**
Pinch salt
3 **eggs**
1 **8-ounce container frozen light whipped dessert topping, thawed**
¼ **teaspoon almond extract**
½ **cup chopped pistachio nuts**
8 **ounces fresh red raspberries (1¾ cups)**
2 **tablespoons honey**
Chopped pistachio nuts (optional)
Fresh mint leaves (optional)

1. Line a 9×5x3-inch loaf pan with a double layer of plastic wrap, extending wrap 2 inches on all sides. Set aside.

2. In a food processor combine the 1 pound raspberries, 2 tablespoons of the sugar, lime juice, and salt. Cover and process until pureed and smooth; strain through a fine-mesh sieve; discard seeds. Set puree aside. In a medium heatproof mixing bowl combine eggs and the remaining 2 tablespoons sugar. Beat with an electric mixer on medium speed until combined. Place bowl over a saucepan filled with gently boiling water (the bowl should not touch the water). Cook, beating constantly on medium speed, until an instant-read thermometer inserted in center of the mixture registers 140°F and maintains that temperature for 3½ minutes (10 to 12 minutes total cooking time) or reaches 160°F. Remove from heat. Remove bowl from over the water; continue cooling until cooled to room temperature (about 5 minutes).

3. In a large bowl combine whipped topping and almond extract. Fold cooled egg mixture, the raspberry puree, and ½ cup pistachio nuts into whipped topping mixture, leaving some swirls. Pour into prepared pan; smooth the top. Cover with plastic wrap; freeze for 6 to 24 hours or until firm.

4. To serve, toss the 8 ounces fresh raspberries with honey. Remove semifreddo from freezer and let stand for 10 to 15 minutes to soften slightly. Remove semifreddo from pan by pulling up on the overhanging plastic wrap, then inverting onto a cutting board and peeling off plastic. Cut into ¾-inch-thick slices and transfer to serving plates. Top with some of the raspberries and serve immediately. If desired, sprinkle with additional chopped pistachios and fresh mint. **Makes 12 servings.**

PER SERVING: 147 cal., 6 g fat (3 g sat. fat), 47 mg chol., 48 mg sodium, 22 g carb., 4 g fiber, 3 g pro.

The tanginess of the yogurt and buttermilk in this frozen dessert is so refreshing. It's the perfect thing to serve when you want a treat that feels special but isn't the least bit heavy.

coconut-almond frozen greek yogurt with hot chocolate drizzle

PREP: 15 minutes   **FREEZE:** 3 hours

24   ounces plain fat-free Greek yogurt
½   cup low-fat buttermilk
⅓   cup honey
⅓   cup unsweetened shredded coconut, toasted
⅓   cup sliced almonds, toasted (see tip, page 64)
1   teaspoon coconut extract
4   ounces semisweet chocolate, chopped
6   tablespoons unsweetened almond milk
     Shredded coconut, toasted (see tip, page 64) (optional)

1. In a large bowl whisk together yogurt, buttermilk, honey, the ⅓ cup coconut, almonds, and coconut extract until well mixed.

2. Freeze yogurt mixture in a 1½-quart ice cream freezer according to manufacturer's directions. Transfer yogurt mixture to a freezer container. Cover and freeze for 3 to 4 hours or until firm enough to scoop.

3. Just prior to serving, in a medium saucepan combine chopped chocolate and almond milk. Cook and stir until chocolate is melted and mixture is completely smooth. Drizzle chocolate mixture over scoops of the frozen yogurt. If desired, sprinkle with additional toasted coconut. **Makes about 10 servings.**

PER SERVING: 153 cal., 6 g fat (3 g sat. fat), 1 mg chol., 44 mg sodium, 21 g carb., 1 g fiber, 7 g pro.

index

Metric Information

The charts on this page provide a guide for converting measurements from the U.S. customary system, which is used throughout this book, to the metric system.

Product Differences

Most of the ingredients called for in the recipes in this book are available in most countries. However, some are known by different names. Here are some common American ingredients and their possible counterparts:

- Sugar (white) is granulated, fine granulated, or castor sugar.
- Powdered sugar is icing sugar.
- All-purpose flour is enriched, bleached or unbleached white household flour. When self-rising flour is used in place of all-purpose flour in a recipe that calls for leavening, omit the leavening agent (baking soda or baking powder) and salt.
- Light-color corn syrup is golden syrup.
- Cornstarch is cornflour.
- Baking soda is bicarbonate of soda.
- Vanilla or vanilla extract is vanilla essence.
- Green, red, or yellow sweet peppers are capsicums or bell peppers.
- Golden raisins are sultanas.

Volume and Weight

The United States traditionally uses cup measures for liquid and solid ingredients. The chart below shows the approximate imperial and metric equivalents. If you are accustomed to weighing solid ingredients, the following approximate equivalents will be helpful.

- 1 cup butter, castor sugar, or rice = 8 ounces = ½ pound = 250 grams
- 1 cup flour = 4 ounces = ¼ pound = 125 grams
- 1 cup icing sugar = 5 ounces = 150 grams

Canadian and U.S. volume for a cup measure is 8 fluid ounces (237 ml), but the standard metric equivalent is 250 ml.

1 British imperial cup is 10 fluid ounces.

In Australia, 1 tablespoon equals 20 ml, and there are 4 teaspoons in the Australian tablespoon.

Spoon measures are used for smaller amounts of ingredients. Although the size of the tablespoon varies slightly in different countries, for practical purposes and for recipes in this book, a straight substitution is all that's necessary. Measurements made using cups or spoons always should be level unless stated otherwise.

Common Weight Range Replacements

Imperial / U.S.	Metric
½ ounce	15 g
1 ounce	25 g or 30 g
4 ounces (¼ pound)	115 g or 125 g
8 ounces (½ pound)	225 g or 250 g
16 ounces (1 pound)	450 g or 500 g
1¼ pounds	625 g
1½ pounds	750 g
2 pounds or 2¼ pounds	1,000 g or 1 Kg

Oven Temperature Equivalents

Fahrenheit Setting	Celsius Setting*	Gas Setting
300°F	150°C	Gas Mark 2 (very low)
325°F	160°C	Gas Mark 3 (low)
350°F	180°C	Gas Mark 4 (moderate)
375°F	190°C	Gas Mark 5 (moderate)
400°F	200°C	Gas Mark 6 (hot)
425°F	220°C	Gas Mark 7 (hot)
450°F	230°C	Gas Mark 8 (very hot)
475°F	240°C	Gas Mark 9 (very hot)
500°F	260°C	Gas Mark 10 (extremely hot)
Broil	Broil	Grill

*Electric and gas ovens may be calibrated using celsius. However, for an electric oven, increase celsius setting 10 to 20 degrees when cooking above 160°C. For convection or forced air ovens (gas or electric), lower the temperature setting 25°F/10°C when cooking at all heat levels.

Baking Pan Sizes

Imperial / U.S.	Metric
9×1½-inch round cake pan	22- or 23×4-cm (1.5 L)
9×1½-inch pie plate	22- or 23×4-cm (1 L)
8×8×2-inch square cake pan	20×5-cm (2 L)
9×9×2-inch square cake pan	22- or 23×4.5-cm (2.5 L)
11×7×1½-inch baking pan	28×17×4-cm (2 L)
2-quart rectangular baking pan	30×19×4.5-cm (3 L)
13×9×2-inch baking pan	34×22×4.5-cm (3.5 L)
15×10×1-inch jelly roll pan	40×25×2-cm
9×5×3-inch loaf pan	23×13×8-cm (2 L)
2-quart casserole	2 L

U.S. / Standard Metric Equivalents

⅛ teaspoon = 0.5 ml	
¼ teaspoon = 1 ml	
½ teaspoon = 2 ml	
1 teaspoon = 5 ml	
1 tablespoon = 15 ml	
2 tablespoons = 25 ml	
¼ cup = 2 fluid ounces = 50 ml	
⅓ cup = 3 fluid ounces = 75 ml	
½ cup = 4 fluid ounces = 125 ml	
⅔ cup = 5 fluid ounces = 150 ml	
¾ cup = 6 fluid ounces = 175 ml	
1 cup = 8 fluid ounces = 250 ml	
2 cups = 1 pint = 500 ml	
1 quart = 1 litre	

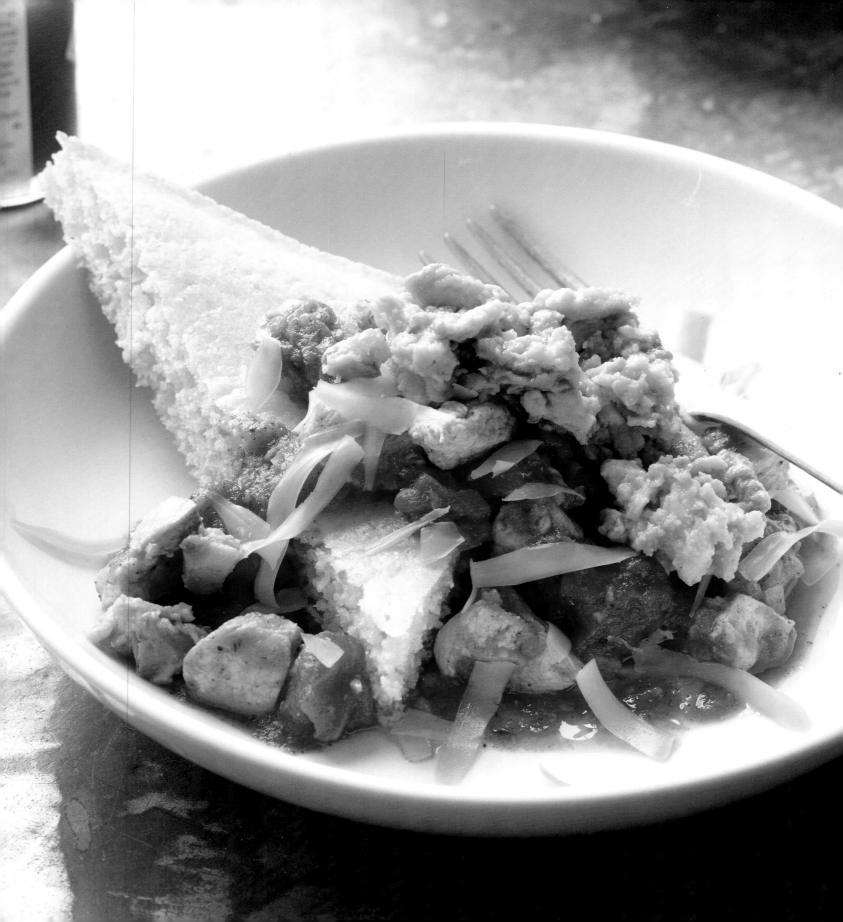

the nutrition breakdown

Each dish in this book is within a reasonable range of fat, calories, and fiber.

ENTRÉES

Calories: 425 or less
Fat: 15 grams or less
Protein: more than 10 grams
Fiber: 3 grams or more

SIDES AND SNACKS

Calories: 175 or less
Fat: 5 grams or less
Fiber: 1 gram or more

DESSERTS

Calories: 200 or less
Fat: 8 grams or less
Fiber: 1 gram or more

Look for icons indicating a recipe meets the following criteria:

● HIGH FIBER 5 or more grams per serving
● VEGETARIAN No ingredients contain meat or meat products
● GLUTEN FREE No ingredients contain gluten*

*****Gluten free:** These recipes can successfully be prepared with all gluten-free ingredients and may be suitable for people with celiac disease or other gluten sensitivities. Check the ingredient lists on all foods you use in these recipes to ensure they do not contain gluten.

get the skinny

Whatever your motivation for seeking out healthy food—for weight loss or simply to provide your body high-quality fuel for optimum health, the most common and commonsense advice from a variety of sources is this: Don't diet—change your lifestyle. That means learning how to trim calories from every dish and making nutrient-packed meals built around fruits and veggies, lean proteins, and whole grains.

That's what *Better Homes and Gardens® Skinny Dinners* is all about. It's filled with good-for-you recipes that make it easy to get a delicious, healthful dinner on the table any night of the week. The editors and dietitians behind *Skinny Dinners* know that if changing your lifestyle is not easy to achieve, you are more likely to abandon your weight-loss goals. Cooking and eating a new way has to fit into the busy, often hectic, lives we all lead. The calorie-smart recipes in *Skinny Dinners* trim time and hassle from the cooking process but they do not cut corners on great taste or nutrition—so you can feel confident that everyone in the family will love the food you make and will benefit from eating it.

A lively, interesting variety of dishes, including casseroles, stir-fries, main-dish salads, 5-ingredient recipes, and meals from the pantry ensures that you'll never tire of cooking and eating skinny. These nourishing and tasty recipes don't constitute a "diet," but simply a new way to eat and live—well, happy, and healthy!